Partial Truths and Our Common Future

A Perspectival Theory of Truth and Value

DONALD A. CROSBY

Cover image from iStock by Getty Images.

Published by State University of New York Press, Albany

For information, contact State University of New York Press, Albany, NY
www.sunypress.edu

Library of Congress Cataloging-in-Publication Data

Names: Crosby, Donald A., author.
Title: Partial truths and our common future : a perspectival theory of truth
    and value / Donald A. Crosby.
Description: Albany : State University of New York, 2018. | Series: SUNY
    series in American philosophy and cultural thought | Includes bibliographical
    references and index.
Identifiers: LCCN 2017053069 | ISBN 9781438471334 (hardcover : alk. paper) |
    ISBN 9781438471341 (pbk. : alk. paper) | ISBN 9781438471358 (ebook)
Subjects: LCSH: Truth.
Classification: LCC BD171 .C76 2018 | DDC 121—dc23
LC record available at https://lccn.loc.gov/2017053069

10 9 8 7 6 5 4 3 2 1

Partial Truths and
Our Common Future

SUNY series in American Philosophy and Cultural Thought

Randall E. Auxier and John R. Shook, editors

Contents

Preface

New York Times political columnist David Brooks speaks in one of his columns of people in political systems who "delegitimize compromise and deal-making. They're willing to trample the customs and rules that give legitimacy to legislative decision-making if it helps them gain power." He goes on to observe, "Ultimately, they don't recognize other people. They suffer from a form of political narcissism, in which they don't accept the legitimacy of other interests and opinions. They don't recognize restraints. They want total victories for themselves and their doctrine."[1]

Such people are committed, consciously or unconsciously, to the idea that there are such things as *absolute truths*, truths that are so all-encompassing and exclusive as to prevent related but different views from having legitimate claims to truths of their own. In other words, people with this outlook are oblivious *to the idea* of *partial truths*, truths that are not final or complete in one's own outlook or in any possible outlook, and that different truths, also partial, may well be contained in the cherished outlooks of other persons or groups. All of us are tempted by this idea at one time or another, but some are much more so than others.

This is not to say that the two or more different visions of truth have to be *equally* partial; it is only to say that no one of them has all of the truth. The notion of particular persons or groups being in possession of absolute, non-negotiable, non-debatable truths has been a bane of civilization and of orderly, just societies from the earliest time to the present. It has all too often virulently infected and corrupted religion, philosophy, science, morality, the arts, politics, economics and other human enterprises, pursuits, and relationships throughout history. And even the most brilliant and deeply researched historical accounts cannot avoid being partial and selective as different narrative forms are imposed on historical events and because these accounts must depend necessarily on artifacts, documents, and other kinds of evidence that happen to be available at a given time.

The antidote to the potentially inflammatory and destructive outlook of insisting on the absolute truths of one's own perspective is the thesis of this book. The thesis is that all claims to truth are partial, although they are not necessarily *equally* partial, and that recognition and respect for this idea can provide the requisite basis for instructive dialogue, peaceful settlement of disputes, meaningful compromise among differing views, and expanding ranges of progress in comity and understanding among those who take different positions on disputed issues.

I am well aware that my contention that all claims to truth, even those concerning seemingly small or insignificant matters, can only be partially true might seem preposterous. At the very least, it is open to debate. I defend it here with conviction and in considerable detail because I am convinced that a great deal in the realms of human knowledge and human affairs hangs on its recognition. It is a meta-claim, that is, a claim about claims to truth. But I am open to the possibility that I could be proven wrong about it or that it needs amendment in some basic way or ways. I submit it in the spirit of discussion and inquiry and invite responses to the reasons I marshal in its defense.

To recognize that all claims to truth are partial at best, for reasons to be developed throughout this book, and that this idea applies to one's own beliefs and those of one's own group as well as to the beliefs of other persons and groups, is to acknowledge the need to be receptive to what can be learned from others. Such an attitude does not require that one give up the claims to truth in one's own firmly held views. Calling attention to the measures of truth in one's views to the extent that one is sincerely convinced of the warrant and supporting evidence for these views is entirely appropriate.

But to acknowledge one's claims to truth as only partially true in some significant degree is also to be encouraged to seek out the views of others with recognition of possibly important and informative truths in their views and to hope to learn with them how to expand the different views in question so that each of them can gain a greater amount of truth than before. Such an approach to putative truths and response to disagreements about affirmations of truth is to move in the opposite direction from the kind of intolerant, close-minded, pernicious—and sadly all too prevalent—narcissism of which Brooks rightly complains. It is to move in the direction of more tolerant, comprehensive degrees of understanding and more harmonious, mutually beneficial relations with one's fellow human beings. Such at least is the central assertion of this book. I hope that readers will examine my arguments for it judiciously and weigh its wide-ranging implications with appropriate care.

In chapter 1 I discuss some central tensions and paradoxes of religious faith that bring to light the partiality of truths in its assertions, symbolizations, attitudes, and commitments. The objects or foci of such religious faith, whether they be theistic, monistic, naturalistic, or of some other character, are necessary blends of the knowable and the unknowable, the sayable and the unsayable, the immanent and the transcendent, the particular and the general, the local and the cosmic, the enduring and the changing, and the confident and the daunting.

To absolutize either side of these tensions and paradoxes and fail to acknowledge the truths of their other side is to slide, on the one hand, into a haughty, close-minded fanaticism that dismisses all claims to religious truth other than one's own or to descend, on the other hand, into a murky mysticism or bland relativism that has little or no conceptual content or firm conviction of its own and can provide no clear path of hope and salvation. To be receptive to what can be learned from other religious traditions and from proponents of other forms of religious faiths is humbly to acknowledge the partiality of truths in one's own form of faith and to seek through careful attentiveness and continuing dialogue to enlarge the amounts of truth in each type of faith. This point also applies to interactions of religious and secular types of faith. Such attentiveness and openness to dialogue are perspicuous *moral* duties in a world where people must learn to live together in an increasingly global community of diverse religious and secular outlooks.

But these responses constitute compelling *religious* duties as well, and they turn to a significant extent on frank and honest admission that all faiths, whether religious or secular, contain and can contain only partial truths. This does not mean for a moment that the different claims to truth and the various kinds of faith they express are unimportant because they are only partial. Nor does it entail that all religious claims must be regarded as equally cogent and true. Partial truths are real truths, and they should not be overlooked, underestimated, resisted, or impugned.

There is much to be learned from these partial truths as proponents of all faiths struggle together to broaden and enrich their responses to the awesome challenges and wonders of life in the world. Frank recognition of the inevitability of partial truths in all religious commitments can also call needed attention to elements of falsity, distortion, incompleteness, or inadequacy in these commitments. This recognition can encourage people to strive together for challenging and fulfilling ways of conceiving and practicing their particular faiths and for learning how to incorporate into their own perspectives aspects of deep-lying truths in the faith stances of other traditions, other communities, and other persons.

Chapter 2 addresses the issue of partial truths in science. The sciences, and especially the natural sciences, are sometimes thought to contain unassailable truths, arrived at on the basis of impeccably reliable methods of analyzing problems and verifying hypotheses. The results of scientific investigation are in this way viewed as entirely "objective" and as being so in a manner inaccessible to nonscientific modes of investigation. Scientific truth claims alone, in this outlook, qualify at present and have the sole prospect of qualifying in the future as whole truths and not just as partial ones. Science is sometimes said to be equipped in principle to describe the universe and all that is in it in a completely dependable manner, eliminating all error and shining a clear and unambiguous light on truth. I take issue with this view of science by arguing that the truths of science, like the truths in all other domains, are and cannot help but be partial.

This observation does not mean that scientific truths are unimportant. They have great significance for understanding the world and us humans as creatures of the world. But scientific truths need to be complemented with truths from other domains, and they sometimes stand in need of qualification, revision, or supplementation by truths from those domains. Scientific thought encompasses selective regions of human investigation and experience. It gains its usefulness and reliability by virtue of this selective focus and emphasis. But it needs to be kept in dialogue with other selective disciplines and areas of thought and action for the sake of more inclusive clarity of insight and practice.

Moreover, scientific thought rests on a number of key assumptions that are presupposed by science rather than proved or provable by it. Scientific claims can contain only partial truths because these claims rest on beliefs that have to be assumed in order for science to operate—beliefs that cannot themselves be scientifically adjudicated. What is true of science is true of all fields of thought. All of them have to take for granted certain usually tacit beliefs that make the outlooks and investigations of these fields possible. And there are no absolute foundations, no such thing as principles or beliefs—no matter how deeply embedded or ardently adhered to—that cannot in any manner be questioned or stand in need of possible revision.

One important task of philosophy, as I understand philosophy, is to bring such fundamental beliefs that underlie the various fields of thought clearly into view and to subject them to critical inquiry and examination. The history of philosophy makes the indispensable value and need for this ongoing process of investigation and criticism readily apparent. Even the most seemingly intractable or indefeasible intuitions that all life and practice presently find it necessary to rely upon can be properly subjected to at least some degree of reasonable questioning and doubt. This thesis applies as much to science as it does to all other aspects of human thought and endeavor. And of course it also applies to philosophy itself, showing its claims, no matter how deeply probing they may be, to be partial.

Certainty as a psychological stance should be distinguished from irrefutable truth as an epistemological characteristic. We humans have been certain about many things in the past that have turned out to be regarded as uncertain or false in the present. I argue throughout this book that epistemological certainty or absolute truth is unattainable, no matter how beguiling our psychological certitude at any time may be. Thus, there are no absolutely certain truths about the world. All alleged truths, scientific or otherwise, are partial. Limited degrees of probability and plausibility mark even the seemingly most dependable assertions or assumptions concerning ourselves and the world. Unassailable epistemological certainty or final truth is a seductive will-o'-the-wisp and not an attainable possibility.

To recognize this observation as inevitably the case for even the most rigorous and highly regarded sciences, we only have to give serious attention to the history of science. There have been two fundamental scientific revolutions to date, each of which has left many basic features of the older ways of thinking behind. One of these revolutions took place in the seventeenth century, and the other in the twentieth century. Each has radically altered the then regnant scientific view of the world. Neither was predicted prior to its occurrence. We have no way to be sure in the present that such a thing will not occur again in the future. There may be for our time, as for those earlier times, not yet imaginable ways of thinking scientifically and of arriving at radically different and perhaps in some ways more adequate scientific conclusions. Our presently assured scientific tenets, outlooks, and theories are partial truths that are subject to doubt and perhaps even radical revision, if for no other reason than that none of us knows what the future will bring in the form of unprecedented, unpredictable scientific interpretations of the world.

The relationship between truth and goodness is one of the topics I take up in chapter 3. I consider here the fact that truth is usually regarded as something good to search for or to be in possession of. But I also seek to show that neither truth nor goodness can be reduced to one another, despite such statements as "It is true that she ought not to lie in order to achieve her goal." There is a crucial difference between saying that something *is* the case and asserting that it *ought* to be the case. This being said, however, facts are not irrelevant to considerations of obligation but have a significant role to play in relation to them. And actions that accord with the sense of moral obligation can bring about significant changes in existing states of affairs. Moreover, moral theories can present true statements and observations and arguments in support of such statements that concern the nature of moral goodness and a responsible moral life.

Chapter 3 is in the main a critical comparison and contrast of six famous moral theories of the past and one of the present, showing that each of them contains important, not to be ignored truths about the character of moral discernment, moral obligation, and the moral life. But I also argue in this chapter that none of these theories—those of Aristotle, Thomas Hobbes, David Hume, Immanuel Kant, John Stuart Mill, or John Rawls—contains or gives full expression to all of the truths necessary for understanding morality, and that each one of them is needed as a corrective to the partial truths of the others. However, not even all six of these influential theories taken together are able to capture the extremely complex character of morality itself or to do justice to the perplexing kinds of moral dilemma that can confront us in the moral life.

The best that any single moral theory can do is to put into perceptive perspective certain essential aspects of morality and to present them and organize them in a systematic, coherent, and illuminating manner. What is needed, therefore, is a pluralistic approach to insightful moral theories. In this approach, there is no single *summum bonum* to be found that elucidates the whole field of moral choice and action, and no such thing as a completely adequate theoretical way of interpreting and apprehending the whole of morality. Different moral theories are incommensurable to some degree, but I point out ways in which they can also overlap with and critique one another in meaningful ways. At the very best, each of the moral theories I discuss contains partial truth about the whole range of moral thought and action. Nevertheless, it is far better to have partial truth than no truth at all.

Chapter 4 is devoted to investigation of partial truths in various aspects of the closely connected fields of economics and ecology. I show that the partial truths contained in certain current economic theories, if not qualified, corrected, and brought into balance with other ways of thinking, can have and presently are having, disastrous effects not only on human lives but also on the lives and environments of all of nature's creatures. I discuss a founding myth regarding the relations of human beings to the natural environment that has become deeply rooted in Western culture and that has tended to be taken for granted by certain kinds of prominent and widely influential economic outlooks.

This myth was given succinct expression in seventeenth-century philosopher John Locke's *Second Treatise of Government*, which exhibits how profoundly his economic outlook, which deals with property, money, and trade, is informed by regnant assumptions of his time regarding the place of human beings in or in relation to nature. Similar assumptions continue to influence the economic thinking of our own time, often in unrecognized ways. This founding myth needs to be brought sharply into focus and subjected to critical examination for many reasons, including its continuing powerful influence on current economic beliefs and practices.

I acknowledge significant partial truths in these beliefs and practices but also seek to show how critically important it is that the truths be brought into tension and balance with the truths of different perspectives, economic and otherwise. Among these different perspectives is our current evolutionary and ecological understanding of humans as integral parts of nature and of basic human attitudes and practices—including the economic ones—as having profound effects for good or ill on the entire earthly biosphere.

The etymology of the two terms *economics* and *ecology* suggests their close affinity. Both have to do with the "household" (*oikos*) of humans, in the first instance, and of the vast community of life forms on earth of which we are only a small part, in the second instance. Basic human economic attitudes and actions impact existing ecological conditions in countless ways. Conversely, the ecological conditions of planet earth can have salutary or disastrous effects on the economic wellbeing of humans throughout the world, as we are now becoming increasingly aware. A signal example of the latter consequence is the ominous threat of global climate change that portends many kinds of calamity for humans and nonhumans alike. The pending human calamities include tragic disruptions of the economic hope and stability of peoples and nations everywhere on earth, disruptions that are likely to initially affect the poorest and most needy peoples and nations most of all. Thus we can no more separate issues of human economics from those of earthly ecology than we can expect—with no predictable consequence—to separate living peoples' hearts from their lungs. The heart supplies essential blood to the lungs, and the lungs supply essential oxygen to the blood. In the same manner, economics and ecology are unfailingly interdependent and conjoined.

The economic theories I discuss in chapter 4 are five in number. They range from the celebration of unregulated free markets, to the notion that healthy economic systems must always exhibit steady growth, to the conviction that globalization will necessarily be of benefit to all, to the belief that government deficits should be adamantly avoided whenever possible, and to the allegation that unregulated capitalism is always good and that any sort of socialism or central governmental oversight, correction, or control is bad. I identify some important partial truths in each of these five positions but also demonstrate their defects when absolutized and not brought into dialogue with equally important different outlooks and theories. Most importantly, I point to the severe ecological consequences that can follow from these views not being tempered and qualified in appropriate ways and from other economic perspectives.

Chapter 4 concludes with a discussion of two menacing dangers relating to the inevitable partiality of all claims to truth. The first is the danger of treating a partial truth as an absolute truth and insisting on the absolute falsity of claims that differ from it. This strategy has caused a lot of unnecessary conflict and woe throughout human history and in the lives of human beings in their relations to one another. The second danger is overlooking or dismissing a claim to truth on the ground of its being only partial and not absolute. This approach closes the mind to much that can be learned and needs to be learned from contending claims to truth, no one of which, no matter how ingeniously envisioned or competently defended, can pass muster as being a final or complete truth about the world or about life in the world. Assessing degrees of truth is the relevant enterprise, and it should be contrasted with the temptation to dismiss a claim to truth on the ground of its partiality. To do so would be to ignore the thesis of this book, namely, that all declarations of truth are partial in varying degrees.

Chapter 5 brings into view partial truths contained in my own discipline of philosophy. I address sharp binary distinctions sometimes alleged by philosophers in five major subject areas and argue that these hard-and-fast distinctions do not hold. Instead, each side of the distinctions contains partial rather than absolute truth and needs to be brought into appropriate relations with the other side. The binary distinctions are those between fact and value, continuity and novelty, rationalism and empiricism, mind and body, and good and evil. Rather than being opposed to one another, each factor in these distinctions derives a significant part of its intelligibility, proper role, and function in its connections with the other factor in the relationship, meaning that the two factors cannot be rigidly separated from one another. They are nodes in a kind of continuum rather than being entirely distinct conceptions. Neither node is complete in itself. Thus neither can by itself be the whole truth of the matter. When brought into proper relation with one another, greater—although still inevitably partial—truth can be achieved.

I argue, for example, that there are no values without supposed facts or factual situations to be valued, and that there are no such things as facts except in contexts of experience, thought, and inquiry in which some things can be valued as relevant facts. Both facts and values reside in the relationships between subjects and aspects of the world, not in either to the exclusion of the other. In similar fashion, dynamic and temporal continuity make no sense unless novelty is given its proper role, and novelty requires a context of continuity for its occurrence and recognition as such. Human knowledge exists only because there is a necessary relationship between aspects of experience and the innate resources of the human mind. Hence both traditional empiricism and rationalism contain important elements of truth but are inadequate and radically incomplete when set at odds with one another.

Rigid mind-body dualism provides no explanation of how the two can relate with one another as they routinely do, and reduction of mind to body or body to mind leaves out much that needs to be taken fully into account and explained. Both are realities in their own rights, but any theory about their relationships also needs to keep their mutual dependency constantly at the center of its attention. Finally, good and evil are of necessity woven together in many different ways, and what is good and what is evil in particular circumstances is often a matter of different perspectives on the same phenomena rather than one of rigid opposition between them. I also argue that total goodness and total evil are not even clear as conceptions and that they cannot be intelligibly attributed to anything human, natural, or divine. This is not to say that they cannot be distinguished; it is only to say that they cannot be set in absolute opposition to one another.

There will be situations where one is more dominant, and perhaps markedly more dominant, than the other, but the two still cannot be completely untangled one from the other. In cases of wondrous goodness, some aspects of evil will still remain, and cases of notorious evil, some aspects of goodness will still be present. The axiological ambiguity of all such cases cannot be entirely eliminated. I remind the reader that this meta-claim, like others stated elsewhere in this book and in its central thesis could also turn out to be in need of qualification or abridgment in some way unknown to me. I present and argue for all such meta-claims in a bid for their careful consideration.

The image of a spectrum with two extremes, neither of which is ever quite reached, is an appropriate one here as elsewhere in this book. My insistence that all claims to truth (regarded as objects of the meta-claim or *truth about truths* that is this book's pervasive theme) are partial can also be expressed in the observation that they all lie somewhere on a spectrum of truth and falsity and never at its absolute opposite ends. They can approach more or less toward one or the other extreme, but they will never reach it. The degrees of truth in particular truth claims are still of great importance and should not be slighted. Partial truth is real truth, not bogus simply because it is partial. We should strive always to recognize and respect partial truths even as we endeavor to critique them, correct them, and make them less partial.

A question could be raised at this point about the fourth-century BCE philosopher Aristotle's three fundamental principles of logic, namely, those of identity, non-contradiction, and excluded middle.[2] If we transmute these principles into modern symbolic logic, which has to do with the relations of whole sentences or *propositions* to one another, rather than, as with Aristotle, the relations of *classes* of things to one another, we can note that a proposition "p" is assumed always to have the same or identical meaning through a train of reasoning; that "p" is completely opposed to "not-p," meaning that it would be contradictory and meaningless to assert them both together; and that there is no middle ground between the truth of "p" and its falsity. But these principles—useful and important as they are—should be recognized to be purely formal in their character and to be saying the same thing in three different ways. The three principles are not observations or claims about the world but stipulations about how a self-contained, non-referential, rules-of-the-game system of logical reasoning is set up to work.

What I endeavor to show throughout this book is that there are only partial, and not absolute, truths about the experienced or experiencable world actually available to us, and thus that a sort of middle ground or tensional relationship between the extremes of absolute truth and absolute falsity is the best we can ever achieve. But even the term *middle ground* is misleading, because, as I argue, the amount of truth or falsity in a particular empirical statement, belief, outlook, or theory can vary in significant degrees and does not always reside squarely in a supposed middle ground between the two extreme poles.

Chapter 6 has as its focus Immanuel Kant's metaphor of the crooked timber of humanity as it relates to his dream of ongoing social and political progress, and suggests how this metaphor can be interpreted to disclose two complementary partial truths. The partial truths are that humans have the *capacity* to bring about more just and peaceful societies as well as more sustainable ecological conditions in the future and that they can be expected to have the *will* to do so. Can humanity strive upward in a cooperative and visionary manner, or will it move downward, producing mutually distrustful and increasingly hateful and violent societies? And will it continue to destroy the earth's nonhuman creatures and the fragile ecosystems on which they—as well as we humans—ultimately depend for life and wellbeing? The claim that we humans are capable of moving in a positive and progressive direction is a partial truth because necessary evidence for its truth lies in what humans choose to do. Without these essential choices, claims about human capability ring hollow. I have confidence in our ability to choose rightly, as did Kant, but this confidence is a promissory note contingent on our choices and actions in the present and future, not something beyond reasonable question or debate.

With these ideas in mind, I devote a section of the chapter to some current straws in the wind that make serious doubt about the truths of the assertions concerning humanity's capability and strength of will dolefully compelling. But I devote a subsequent section of the chapter to a more hopeful note, citing current straws that give support to affirmation of our human capacity and resolve to work together for a more just, prosperous, and ecologically healthy world. The four straws of serious doubt I adduce concern unregulated capitalism, worldwide religious conflicts, the development of ever more destructive weapons of war, and the imminent threat of earth-wide ecological devastation.

I respond to each of these ominous trends with certain hopeful signals, trends, and options of the present as well as some of these made evident in the past that add credence to the proposition that we humans have both the capacity and the will to move toward the kind of societies and world of which Kant dreamed and toward which all right-minded people should aspire. There are partial truths on both sides of this issue, because continuing confirmation of either side depends on what takes place in the future—a future that cannot currently be known with the kind of relevant and supporting detail that would be required. Will humanity become ever more gnarled, deformed, and embroiled in destruction and evil as its history continues to unfold? Or will it find ways to grow straighter, more upright, and more progressive with the passage of time?

Only the future can tell. But enlightenment, effort, and commitment in the present are crucial determinants of how these questions will be answered by future events. This observation calls our attention to the realization that not all significant truths are already settled and fixed. Some of the most important of them can be made or unmade by the character of our continuing human choices, and these can either be ones of heedless omission and deplorable commission or ones of resolute focus and ardent commitment. Humanity is remarkably pliable and can twist itself downwardly toward increasing destructiveness and despair or straighten itself upwardly toward increasing creativity and hope.

Human progress is not inevitable, but neither is humanity's retrogression. There is partial conformation and truth on both sides of this issue, and that in itself is a sign of hope. The greater the truth of the one, the lesser truth of the other, and both are to a significant extent within our anticipation and control. As we strive for ways to work together for our common good and for the good of all of the earth and its creatures, we can write *diminuendo* alongside past notes of desperation and despair and inscribe *crescendo* by future notes of affirmation and hope. That we can actually do so is at present a partial truth, but I argue in this sixth chapter in support of our ability and resolve to make it more true and less false in the face of all odds.

The final chapter of this book, chapter 7, begins with some extended reflections on the statement "This is a cup." Is this not an example of an absolutely or indisputably true claim about something in the world, even though the claim is relatively trivial? I show in a number of ways that even this claim can be only partially, not absolutely, true and proceed to argue again that all claims, whether minor or momentous, must have this character. I do so by introducing the concept of perspectival realism, following the lead of philosopher of science Ronald N. Giere. I distinguish, as he does, perspectival realism from absolute objectivist realism, on the one hand, and subjectivist constructionism, on the other. The first of these alternative views argues that we can gain some kind of completely objectivistic, unmediated access to aspects of the world as wholly distinct from ourselves and our modes of knowledge, while the second one contends that all we are capable of doing is projecting our human categories and schemes of interpretation on the world, with no hope of accessing whatever it may be in and of itself.

The perspectival realist view that Giere and I defend contends that we can attain reliable truths about the world that are more than just our subjective projections upon it, but that these truths are always partial because they reflect the limitations of our sensations, languages, reasoning abilities, theories, instruments, and the like through which aspects of the world are made available to us. Truths about the world always lie, then, in the interactions between objects and subjects, and in neither one of these to the exclusion of the other. The truths are neither completely "in here" nor completely "out there," so to speak, but in the *relations* of these two locations with one another. Since this is the case according to perspectival realism, all truths are partial because necessarily limited by the perspectives by means of which they are brought into focus.

But perhaps God is capable of viewing the world exactly and completely as it is in and of itself, without need for any kind of perspectival mediation or limitation. I take issue with this alleged God's-eye conception of the world on the ground that if anything other than God can be said to exist, then God cannot completely or finally comprehend what it is like to be that thing without swallowing up that thing into God's own being. God can perhaps be said to enter with great empathy and imagination into the experiences of God's creatures, assuming that there are such, but God cannot envision the world in exactly the same ways they do, ways that mark their distinction from the outlook, character, and being of God.

God's perspective on the world can be claimed to be far more comprehensive, inclusive, and accurate than any other perspective, as it typically is for those of theistic persuasion, but it is nevertheless one perspective among others. Consequently, God's-eye truths about the world must be partial, although putatively far less so than the perspectives of any of God's creatures. If this line of reasoning goes through, as I think it does, then it is partiality and perspectivity of outlooks on and claims to truth all the way up and all the way down.

This is precisely the central and suffusive theme of this book. It is a theme of great epistemological significance, but I have also argued that its significance reaches beyond the field of knowledge into many other sorts of human inquiry, interaction, and practice, for example, those of economics, politics, religion, and morality. And it has profound bearing on the relationships of humans with the other creatures of earth and with the earthly environments and ecosystems which all of us—human and nonhuman—have in common and on which we crucially depend.

I also devote a brief section of chapter 7 to identification of commonly assumed and often implicitly or explicitly employed epistemic norms or standards that can guide us in assessing the relative degrees of truth and falsity in particular claims. Recognition and application of such norms safeguard against the seductions of epistemological relativism and of the kind of pure constructivism which regards truth as something made up from scratch or cut from whole cloth by individuals, societies, and cultures rather than having to be discovered and borne out by rigorous inquiry and by resolute appeals to ongoing experiences of the world. Successful inventions have to draw on truths, but truths themselves cannot be sheerly invented. This claim holds for all genuine truths, partial though all of them must, according to the arguments, of this book, be acknowledged to be in varying degrees. Partial truths are real truths and should not be scorned on account of their partiality. Instead, they should be welcomed for the measures of truth—slight or large—that they contain.

I greatly appreciate the encouragement, support, and suggestions for improvement of this book by two anonymous reviewers solicited by the State University of New York Press. Andrew Kenyon, the Press's Acquisitions Editor for Philosophy, and Senior Production Editor Diane Ganeles have provided courteous, helpful guidance and support along the way. Friend Monte Palmer and I have discussed some of the book's themes at luncheon meetings, and his support and suggestions have assisted me in thinking these themes through with his observations, questions, applications, and examples. My wife Pamela graciously read the developing manuscript with me over many months and made insightful suggestions concerning its style, clarity, cogency, and content. Some of the best support offered to an author comes in the form of critical responses to the author's earlier, vaguely conceived ventures of thought and analysis, and I am grateful to these persons in this regard. Their contributions have helped to reduce, but certainly not to obliterate, the partiality of truth in its central claims.

Chapter 1

RELIGION

Religion is at its best when it helps us to ask questions and holds us in a state of wonder—and arguably at its worst when it tries to answer them authoritatively and dogmatically.

—Karen Armstrong[1]

The first chapter of this book is on religion, because I think it is here that the major thesis of this book—that all stated truths are at best partial truths and need to be acknowledged as such—is most obvious or should readily be admitted to be so. Yet, in the field of religion, or perhaps even more so here, this thesis is commonly overlooked, impugned, or denied. The focus of all of the major religions of the world is on persons, presences, powers, attunements, or goals deemed to be radically *transcendent*—and thus to lie forever beyond full comprehension, description, depiction, or attainment. Wariness, tentativeness, and humility are the moods that must necessarily accompany an abiding sense of this radical transcendence.

Most important of all in religion is the haunting *wonder* of which religious scholar Karen Armstrong speaks in this chapter's epigraph. The religious sense of inexhaustible wonder, as she rightly points out, means that an attitude of certainty or close-mindedness with regard to fundamental religious claims is "misplaced, and strident dogmatism that dismisses the views of others inappropriate."[2] To put her point a different way, it is inevitably the case that all religious claims, no matter how hoary or well-thought-out and defended, are at best partial truths. What is the case in this regard for spokespersons of other religious traditions is also necessarily the case for one's own most cherished religious outlooks, convictions, and commitments—especially

1

to the extent that one's religious outlook is centered on some sort of radically transcendent religious ultimate.

I shall expand on and defend this idea through the rest of this chapter. I do so by discussing four paradoxes. The first is the paradox of the Dao and other religious ultimates that cannot be spoken. The second is the paradox implicit in faith in a God of all creation and all peoples. The third is a paradox of transcendence that relates to the radically *immanental* religious outlook I personally espouse, namely, Religion of Nature. And the fourth is the paradox lurking within what I call *existential certitude*.

The Dao and Other Religious Ultimates that Cannot Be Spoken

Here is how the *Daodejing*, the famous ancient Daoist text attributed to Laozi, begins:

> The way that can be followed
> Is not the eternal way;
> The name that can be named
> Is not the eternal name.
> That which is without name is of heaven and
> earth the beginning;
> That which is nameable is of the ten thousand
> things the mother.[3]

The transcendent, ineffable, unnameable character of the Dao or "Way" in Daoism is clearly stated in this well-known passage. But despite its insistence that the Dao, as the ultimate focus of Daoist religion, cannot be characterized or named, texts such as the *Daodejing*, the *Zhuangzi*, and others talk of the Dao at great length. What this initially puzzling phenomenon amounts to, in my judgment, and the way in which the paradox can be interpreted, is to understand that the Dao or Way that shines through and is made manifest in all things (e.g., the "ten thousand things" in the passage quoted) is not exhaustively or adequately made known in any or all of those things. To speak of the Dao exhibited in them is therefore to speak a partial truth. Similarly, to point to the unnamed and unnameable Dao is also to speak of a partial truth because the Dao is both concealed and revealed, hidden and manifested in the things of the palpable world of day-to-day experience.

The unnameable that is the source and sustainer of all things—the radically and inexhaustibly mysterious Way—is also nameable and knowable in the things that arise from it and are granted their being by it. Hence, one can write books about the nameable Dao, as Laozi, Zuangzi, and others do, even while constantly reminding the readers of those books that its nameability is only a partial truth, just as its total concealment must also be seen as a partial truth. Thus, each of these two partial truths contains important, never to be neglected information. Neither is to be overlooked or ignored. Neither should be rejected in favor of the other. The tension between them comes closer to being the adequate truth of the matter than either is by itself. But a tension or paradox is not a consistent statement of truth. It points beyond itself to a kind of truth for which no final, adequate, complete, or consistent statement is possible. It can be felt, sensed, intuited, or experienced, but it cannot be clearly spoken or rendered into completely intelligible language.

Later Islam developed two tendencies of thought when contemplating the names or attributes of Allah provided in the Qur'an and elsewhere in Islamic lore. These tendencies turned on the ideas of "difference" (mukhalafala) and "removing" (tanzih). Allah is radically different from anything in this world, so faithful Muslims should recognize and continually stress this difference. They can do so by removing from Allah's true nature any confusion with the natures of his creatures. The first tendency insists that names and phrases associated with Allah can still convey something of what Allah is like, and thus, when carefully qualified, can be usefully employed to bring to the mind of faithful Muslims important aspects of Allah's character and relations to his world. The second tendency is to advocate a kind of via negativa and to assert that what the names or traits associated with Allah in the Qur'an and tradition actually mean we cannot know and should not be so presumptuous as to inquire. How, then, should Muslims think and live? A common answer to this question is that Muslims should simply accept and affirm the teachings of the Qur'an and other traditional authorities as the basis of faith and not try to understand them more fully. They should place no trust in their intellects with respect to such matters.

In these two tendencies in Islam we can see the conflict between what is sayable and is thus thinkable about Allah and what, in the very nature of the case, can never be adequately understood. There is truth in both tendencies, we can assume, but neither can count as the whole truth. These two are partial truths; each must be held in tension with the other. Islamic faith, like the faith systems of all the major religions, must have conceivable, assertible content to be believed in and lived by. Without such content, there would be no religious path to set out upon or followed. But such faith must also constantly guard against taking this content too literally and thus foolishly regarding Qur'anic and other traditional language concerning Allah too anthropomorphically. To do so would mean thinking that the yawning gulf of difference between Allah and his creation can somehow be adequately bridged with puny human language or with conceptualizations derived from the world of Allah's creation.[4] It would mean commission of the grave sin of idolatry (*shirk*), that is, associating Allah with alleged other gods or things of the finite world.

The essence of idolatry or sacrilege in any high religion is to confuse the infinite *reach and reference* of powerful religious expressions with an alleged complete human apprehension and rendering of their infinite *meaning*. To do so is to mistake partial truths for whole truths, distorting and misconceiving the partial truths in the process. Such a mistake is akin to the error of a child who, fascinated by a shimmering soap bubble floating in the air, tries eagerly to capture and contain it, only to destroy it.

The radical transcendence attributed to the Dao and Allah is echoed in other religious traditions. It is seen in the stupendous revelation of Vishnu's awesome, inconceivable majesty, might, and glory in the *Bhagavad Gita*, as disclosed by the avatar Krishna to Arjuna. It is made clear in the distinction between the Brahman with qualities (*Saguna Brahman*) and the Brahman without qualities (*Nirguna Brahman*) in Advaita Vedanta Hinduism. It is forcefully disclosed to Job in the biblical Book of Job when Yahweh challenges him, a mere man, to even begin to comprehend the ways of the majestic, mysterious, all-encompassing creator and sustainer who has laid the foundations of the earth, brought forth its myriad creatures, and. stretched out the heavens above them.

At the same time, there is the avatar Krishna and his revelation of the mind-boggling reality of Vishnu. There is the Saguna realm of *maya* that manifests the presence of Brahman in all things. And there is Yahweh's gracious disclosure of himself to Job, in response to Job's plea for vindication of Yahweh's reality, justice, and sovereign reign over the earth and its creatures. In all three of these cases there is both hiddenness and revealedness. To opt for either to the exclusion of the other is to confuse, on the one hand, a partial truth with a whole truth and, on the other, to reject a partial truth on the ground that it is only partial. To go either way is to be guilty of a grave distortion and dangerous error—or so I shall continue to argue in this book.

The mistake is a distortion of truth because it fails to allow a partial truth to be accompanied by another partial truth that rightly calls it into question and saves it from being confused with a larger, more adequate truth. As I indicated above, the larger truth lies in the tension between the two partial truths, not in a choice between them. To neglect the partial truth of the radical transcendence of the ultimates in all the major religious traditions, including the ultimate of one's own faith, is to be tempted to make an absolute truth out of a partial one. If my religion is absolutely rather than partially true, it follows that other religions—to the extent that they disagree with it—must be absolutely false.

To ignore or deny the transcendence of a religious ultimate and the final inadequacy of all claims regarding it is to veer toward unquestioning authoritarianism, blind credulity, and haughty intolerance of religious traditions other than one's own. Human history is drenched with bloody gore flowing from this kind of one-sided, dogmatic, and potentially hateful religious perspective. To assume such a view is also to insulate oneself against what can be learned from other religious perspectives or other outlooks on the world and to deprive oneself or one's religious tradition of the kind of ongoing growth, adjustment, refreshment, and renewal needed in a rapidly changing and globally interacting world.

To reject the partial knowability and assertibility of a particular religious ultimate, on the other hand, and to insist without qualification on its complete transcendence and consequent unknowability is to deprive one's religious tradition and one's own religious outlook of meaningful conceptual content. It is to deny to the intellect any significant role in one's faith and to reduce faith itself to an unquestioning, uninquiring, uninformed sheer act of the will. It is to leave one defenseless in the face of conceptual challenge or criticism and incapable of dialogue with other points of view.

There can also be great danger to oneself and to others in unqualified insistence on the radical transcendence of the religious ultimate of one's own tradition, making matters of religious faith immune to questioning or critical reflection. Constructive, sane, engaged, compassionate religion requires continuing critical thought and open-minded interaction with those of different religious persuasions. Insisting on the absolute transcendence of one's own religious ultimate makes such interaction impossible. Absence of effective communication among people of different faiths can lead—and often has led in human history, as I noted above—to alienation, hostility, and violence. This point holds as much for interactions *within* historical religious traditions and institutions as it does for interactions of proponents of different religions with one another. Transcendence and knowability are not opposites. Neither are openness and conviction. These are two sides of the same coin of relevant, meaningful, and humane religious faith. Each side is an important partial truth.

A God of All Creation and of All Peoples

If one's religious faith centers—as does the faith of Jews, Christians, and Muslims—on a single God of all creation and of all peoples through the whole history of humankind, then the following questions present themselves. What can be believed concerning the outlooks of peoples who existed before these three religions arose? What can be believed regarding major religious traditions that differ today from these three monotheistic religions? And what can be believed, given that there are these three distinctive monotheistic traditions, each of which conceives of God and of God's putative revelations in significantly different ways? The universality of God seems to contradict the diverse cultures and traditions that do not focus on such a God or that do not focus on the same conceptions of such a God. Why would a supposedly universal God not ensure that all peoples of all times and all nations would conceive of him in the same or at least closely similar manner?

One way in which Jews, Christians, and Muslims have responded to this seeming conundrum is to argue that God has made Godself known in manifold compelling ways throughout history but that many peoples have rejected God and God's perspicuous natural and super-natural revelations of Godself. These peoples do not acknowledge and respond to God's claim on them, it is argued, because of their prideful close-mindedness and sin. Monotheists who make this accusation take for granted that their conception of God is the right one and the only right one. In other words, they assume without question that their conception of God is absolutely true and that all differing religious outlooks are, by this unquestioned standard, absolutely false. Defend-ers of the absolutely true view of God have the obligation to spread their view throughout the earth in the hope of saving the apostate others from sinful ignorance and perfidious pride.

A way to deal with the conundrum of differing ideas about God and his revelations in the three Abrahamic traditions is to argue that one's own monotheistic outlook and tradition is the culmination, fulfillment, and completion of the other ones. Thus, Christians have typically claimed that their religion is the culmination of Judaism, and Muslims have claimed that theirs is the completion of a history of divine revelation that incorporates and builds on but also goes beyond the revelations of Allah made known in Judaism and Christianity. In this way, or so it is believed, the finally true supplants the relatively true, and the possessors of final truth have the right and obligation to guide or even to rule over the proponents of mere relative truth. They also have the right, or so it can be believed, to persecute those who differ from them and reject the finality of their religious claims.

Thus, Jonah of the Hebrew Bible was sent by Yahweh to preach to the pagan peoples of Nineveh; Christians felt called to throw out the lifeline of Christianity and so-called Christian civilization in the Middle East, Asia, and other parts of the world; and Muslims set out on their path of righteous conquests both to the East and to the West of Arabia. In some cases, those judged to be unrepentant heretics or pagans were subjected to ostracism, fire, or sword in the name of the one true God. This practice was justified on the ground that it effectively warned others against pernicious beliefs and practices that threatened the integrity of divine revelation and the hope of their own salvation.

The same sort of reasoning can be applied to those who adhere to non-Abrahamic forms of religious faith. They may have ideas and insights pointing toward the true God in various ways, but they lack the benefit of a final revelation of God's awesome majesty and saving power. Judaism, Christianity, or Islam can claim to offer this final revelation in their own respective ways, a revelation that for each of them has been made known progressively throughout human history.

At the other extreme from the two absolutist or exclusivist approaches I have so far sketched in this section is radical relativism, that is, the notion that there is no way to adjudicate among different religious outlooks because none of them admits of any kind of convincing rational criticism or defense. In other words, or so it is held, religious beliefs are at bottom and by nature nonrational and purely emotional, conventional, or arbitrary in character. This statement can then be said to encompass all sorts of belief in a so-called universal God as well as the absence of such beliefs. Hence, there is no conundrum, just the pure, unresolvable fact of differing religious outlooks—monotheistic or otherwise—pitted against one another.

This is a third way in which the puzzle of universal monotheism and diverse forms of religion may be said to be resolved, namely, by simply dissolving the notion of any conundrum altogether. Religions differ from one another, including different forms of monotheistic faith, because matters of religious faith and conviction have, in the final analysis, little to do with rationality or rational criticism or defense. They are outcomes of acculturation or emotional predilection with little or no basis in critical thought, and with no need for grounding in such thought. Religious faith is reduced, in this view, to unquestioning obedience to external authority—the authority of one's own tradition, texts, teachers, tribe, and upbringing. The close resemblance of this idea to insistence on the intellectually impenetrable transcendence of a person's or tradition's religious ultimate can be clearly seen.

A fourth and in my judgment more promising way of dealing with the issue of how monotheistic faith can be reconciled with the fact of diverse religions in the world is to acknowledge a partial truth in historical and cultural relativism but to see it as nonetheless consistent with a type of monotheistic faith. It can be argued by monotheists that God is the God or all peoples, cultures, and times, but that God has allowed each of them to develop concepts of Godself as religious ultimate in a wide variety of ways that accord with the distinctiveness of their historically enshrined cultural beliefs and practices. It can be further argued that each of these ways, including different versions of monotheism itself, contains important truths to be pondered and lived by, but that all its statements of truth are partial. None can begin to exhaust the majesty and mystery of God or sound the depths of other, non-theistic types of religious ultimate such as Dao, Nirguna Brahman, or the Buddha Nature to which they can only feebly point. For monotheists, belief in God is the best approximation to religious truth, but they can also acknowledge that their claims about the nature of God are in the final analysis only approximations.

It does not follow from this fourth approach that all religious traditions, points of view, and claims are *equally* adequate and true. Nor must the clams of each and every one of them be deemed to be nonrational, arbitrary, and closed to inquiry. It does follow that each of them can and should be kept open to the possibility of containing partial truths and of acknowledging, each in its own manner, the presence of a graceful and compassionate God or some other sort of all-encompassing sacred power or saving goal present or available in the world. Staunch monotheists are allowed and even, I would say, *required* to have this fourth kind of outlook, one that can be viewed as consistent with faith in a magnificent God of all places and times.[5]

The theistic Sufi philosopher of the twelfth and thirteenth centuries, Muid ad-Din Ibn al-Arabi, issues a warning to this effect when he entreats,

> Do not attach yourself to any particular creed so exclusively that you disbelieve all the rest; otherwise you will lose much good, nay, you will fail to recognize the real truth of the matter. God, the omnipresent and omnipotent, is not limited by any one creed, for he says, "Wheresoever ye turn, there is the face of Allah."[6]

> Everyone praises what he believes; his god is his own creature, and in praising him he praises himself. Consequently, he blames the beliefs of others, which he would not do if he were just, but his dislike is based on ignorance.[7]

Each culturally and personally varying religious outlook, whether theistic or not, can with this attitude learn much and come to appreciate much from the others.

However, proponents of each religious perspective can also be appropriately and compassionately critical of some views of the others. I do not want to leave the impression that anything goes, that whatever others may hold to be religiously true is immune to critical reflection and articulation. We should not overlook the fact that the notion of partial truth implies that each partially true statement must also be partially false. The degree of truth and falsity in any given statement can vary—and sometimes widely—from statement to statement. A partial truth is not the same thing as a half-truth because there can be important degrees of truth on either side of the halfway mark. There is often no way of knowing what this degree is without careful consideration and examination—a care that may in many cases need to be patient and prolonged, continuously striving to become more knowledgeable and well informed about religious views different from one's own.

The scriptures of a religious tradition both arise out of tradition and are interpreted by emerging traditions. These in turn reflect the spiritual experiences and insights of great religious teachers and exemplars of the religious life. Special religious symbols come over time to mark these emerging religious traditions. Distinctive doctrines interpret the meanings of traditions, scriptures, and symbols. New symbolic expressions can be inspired, in turn, by these three. But none of them is able to give finally adequate expression to the religious ultimate itself, whatever that might be. To think otherwise is to be guilty of hubris, idolatry, or profanation of the sacred. All them are mere pointers to the religious ultimate in all of its majesty, mystery, and ineffability, and are not to be confused with it. A sufficiently high, exalted, awesome, and overpowering vision of the religious ultimate is or should always be a constant safeguard against the temptation to attribute non-partial or absolute truth to any and all texts, statements, analyses, or expressions of the nature of the ultimate and its relations to the world.

Transcendence and Immanence in Religion of Nature

The Religion of Nature I have elaborated and defended in a number of previous books is avowedly non-theistic. It has no conception of the supernatural, of God, or of anything outside of or beyond nature. For it, all that exists is natural. The natural constitutes the whole of reality.[8] In view of the fact that I take this position, it might be asked how I can support the idea that there is anything like a paradox of transcendence and immanence within the wholly naturalistic and seemingly wholly immanental religious outlook I support and propound. But I do support this idea and do so emphatically. Let me now try to show why.

In keeping with my contention that all truths are at best partial truths, I argue in this section that the immanence of nature, conceived as the focus of religious faith, is an extremely important but also a partial truth. It is made partial or paradoxical by important respects in which nature is also metaphysically and religiously transcendent. This is so without anything being conceived to lie beyond or outside of nature itself. The respects of transcendence I have in mind are three in number. Nature transcends itself over endless time; it exhibits ongoing active novelty as well as continuity; and it is shrouded in mystery and transcends complete human understanding.

1. Nature Transcends Itself Over Endless Time

As I view it, there are two fundamental aspects of nature: nature as it exists at any given time and nature as it continues to change over endless time. The terms *natura naturata* and *natura naturans* were used in the Middle Ages to indicate these two aspects. The first, "nature natured," refers to the present state of nature, nature as it exists here and now. The second, "nature naturing," refers to the dynamic, unceasing, transformative impulses or powers within nature that show it not to be something static and unchanging but to be continually undergoing change. Over eons of time these changes can radically transform the character of nature that existed in earlier periods—an idea that is brought vividly to mind by current scientific theories concerning the evolution of the present cosmos, the evolution of the solar system, the evolution of the planet earth, and the evolution of the earth's diverse forms of life. These evolutionary processes not only bring new things into being. They also leave older things behind. Creation and destruction are linked necessarily together.

The volatile interactions of creation and destruction have not only continued throughout the history of the present cosmos. We can surmise that they must also have been involved in the origin of this cosmos from earlier ones, and they will be involved in a destruction of the present cosmos that will give rise to subsequent ones. All change is therefore transformation of something already existing into something new. There is no *ex nihilo* or *de novo* origination of anything. Whatever *is*, including this present cosmos, comes from something that *was*. Out of sheer nothing, nothing can come (*ex nihilo, nihil fit*). One reason for this being the case, in my view, is that sheer nothingness is unintelligible. There is thus no absolute beginning of nature in any of its forms and no conceivable absolute ending of nature. Nature is everlasting, stretching from an everlasting past, through the present temporary state or face of nature, into an everlasting future.[9]

One way of stating these ideas is that *nature transcends or surpasses itself*. It does not stand still but exhibits endless processes of change. The *immanence* of nature consists in the fact that all of its everlasting transformations are natural. There is nothing supernatural or trans-natural about any of them, including the rise of a new cosmos out of the remnants of an older one or the coming into being of a future world from the collapse of a present one. All changes, whether minor or massive, are natural. They have no origin and need no explanation beyond nature. But the fact that these changes can, over large stretches of time, be radically transformative means that nature is continually *transcending* itself. Each and every "nature natured" is subject to a relentless, ever-surging and transforming "nature naturing."

The immanent and the transcendent are thus locked together. Either by itself is a partial truth. The ongoing tension between them constitutes a more adequate truth. The extent of this tension varies widely over the whole span of primordial, everlasting time. Being is both created and transformed by becoming, but at different rates and over different expanses of time.

2. Nature Exhibits Continuity As Well As Novelty

Our day-to-day experience of the passage of time shows that the past is transcended by the present, and the present is transcended by the future. This transcendence is only partial, not complete because something of the past continues on into the present, and something of the present continues on into the future. The respective degrees of continuity and novelty can vary greatly in particular cases, but there is never a total absence of the one in relation to the other. The necessary element of transcendence in the very notion of time as an immanental trait of nature can be a source of deep-lying responsibility and sustaining hope. It is also a warning of the transitoriness of things and of the urgency of present opportunity, obligation, and right action.

The reality of novelty means that the future is not closed but open and therefore that the present course of one's thinking, feeling, and acting—and the course of human history itself—is not inevitable or fixed. There is no place for anything like causal determinism, inexorable fate, or wholesale predestination in Religion of Nature. Real novelty in the universe makes way for real freedom in human actions and events and thus for the hope of real changes that can be brought about in oneself and in the world by human freedom. The effectiveness of this freedom, however, is also dependent on an appropriate sense of the transitoriness of time and the need for appropriate actions when the time is most suitable for such actions.

"There is no time like the present" is an appropriate aphorism for many of these free decisions and acts, while "haste is waste" may be more appropriate for some others. In either case, the opportunity and responsibility of striving to make a difference for the betterment of oneself, one's community or nation, and one's world beckon. And development of a keen sense of what is most timely and opportune is critical. Novelty transcends continuity, and this kind of transcendence, ever-operative within nature, has momentous religious significance. It is the sign not only of moral but also of profound religious responsibility and hope. The fact of such ongoing transcendence in nature is implicit in and figures prominently in the demand, assurance, and empowerment aspects of Religion of Nature.[10]

3. Nature Is Shrouded In Mystery and Transcends Human Understanding

Nature is in principle completely and finally knowable—a view sometimes assumed or proclaimed by natural scientists[11]—or nature is utterly strange and inscrutable—a view propounded by the character Antoine Roquentin in Jean Paul Sartre's existentialist novel *Nausea*[12]—neither of these claims states a whole truth. The terms *finally*, *completely*, and *utterly* need to be expunged from both. With this change, both are partial but deeply significant truths that need to be held together. They are such for Religion of Nature. Nature is partly knowable, but its intelligibility is also suspended over depths of impenetrable mystery.

Science and other modes of inquiry such as philosophy and religion may help to make numerous aspects of nature more intelligible, but all such inquiries are limited in their reach and comprehension. It is important to strive for knowledge and understanding as best as we can. But at the same time, there are dimensions and levels of intractable mystery that preclude complete knowledge of nature and its ways. This sense of impenetrable mystery in nature, even if regarded only as a partial truth, is an important ingredient in Religion of Nature. The bar to complete knowledge it insists upon is part of its recognition of the daunting massiveness, intricacy, changeability, and sublimity of nature stretching through endless time and of consequent limitations on what we finite, fallible creatures of nature are capable of rendering into clear and adequate statements concerning it.

For example, if novelty is real and operative throughout nature, as I claimed earlier, then the farther into its limitless future our projections and predictions extend, the less confidently determinable and knowable they become. When teaching philosophy to students in a university, I would sometimes ask them, "Do you think that there are any absolute truths?" After they had finished giving answers to this question, many of them quite confident and positive, I would cite some of the unquestioned "truths" of people in the past, putative truths such as the idea that there are four physical elements; that there are indivisible atoms; that all things come in binary oppositions such as male and female, hot and cold, dry and wet; that the earth is the center of the solar system and the solar system is identical with the universe as a whole; that Euclidian geometry is the only geometry; that Newtonian physics is the finally comprehensive and adequate physics; and so on.

We may smile condescendingly at such beliefs today. But who among us can be certain about what the future may bring in the way of presently cherished assumptions and unquestioned beliefs? Who can anticipate today the work of a Copernicus, Kepler, Newton, Darwin, Maxwell, Planck, or Einstein of tomorrow—work that may well produce radical new and different modes of thought about nature and its creatures? The further into the future we try to peer, the more murky the horizon and uncertain our vision becomes. Some if not many of our unquestioned "truths" of today may turn out to be just as quaint or even laughable at some time in the future as are many of those of the remote or even more recent past. So even if there were absolute truths, we would have no way of being completely confident of them or of asserting them without a smidgen of hesitation and doubt.

For Religion of Nature, the mysteries of nature and their transcendence of what is known or can be known about it is a necessary part of nature's religious ultimacy. It is task enough to try to understand the present cosmos. Who can rightly claim to understand all past or future ones? Who can claim to know what the world is like from the perspectives of nonhuman forms of life? Who can argue to have exhaustive or completely reliable knowledge of the memories, outlooks, experiences, and potentialities of any human creature, including one's own self? And yet, all of these perspectives are aspects of nature. There is no God's-eye view of them for any of us that can reduce them to a single, all-knowing, all-inclusive perspective. The different perspectives I have mentioned are in their very nature at least partly incommensurable.

Humble acknowledgment and appreciation of the pervasive mysteries of nature is an essential feature of the religious outlook of proponents of Religion of Nature. When we are properly attuned to them, the mysteries of nature can become almost overwhelming and overpowering. It is fitting that they be so if we want even to begin to comprehend the depths of nature and our place as humans within it. We may yearn to know and take delight in knowing, and it is natural for us to do so. But we should also delight in the fact that nature is wondrous enough, awesome enough, and elusive enough to evoke unceasing reverent meditation on its incomparable majesty and glory.

Any adequate response to nature, in my judgment as advocate for Religion of Nature, must begin with wonder, be suffused with wonder, and end with wonder. There are abundant miracles in nature, astounding miracles of everyday life and of the whole span of nature's history and histories before which we can only respond with wonder and awe when our sensibility and receptiveness to them are rightly awakened and cultivated.[13] And there is the wondrous mystery of the encompassing nature itself beyond and within us as creatures of nature that inspires and enables our fervent searches for truth. Nature's radical transcendence of our ability fully to comprehend it is only to be expected if all that nature is, has been, and will yet become is to be the focus of religious life and commitment.

Nondiscursive symbols of many different types are required for us even to begin to plumb or be properly attuned to nature's depths.

Literal assertions and theories, no matter what degrees of truth they may contain, cannot accomplish alone the task of access into or attunement with the wonders of nature. In fact, they frequently open up and make us aware of new dimensions of wonder and mystery hitherto unsuspected. The truths of propositions and the truths of evocative symbols are partial at best, each needing to be complemented by the other.[14] With nature as with the Dao, there is inevitably much that cannot sufficiently or finally be spoken, exhibited, or expressed.

The Paradox of Existential Certitude

What is existential truth? It is different from a truth of statements. It is the felt and experienced authenticity or certainty of a person's commitment to a religious ultimate. It is the sense of confident, sustaining, guiding rightness in that commitment. It is the truth of wholehearted engagement with that ultimate as the supreme source of meaning and value in the world and in one's life. It is a much more mysterious and deeply indwelling kind of truth than alleged truths of intellectual assent or assertion, although avowed beliefs are part of it. Here is the biblical Job's confession of existential truth in the midst of his grievous and inexplicable suffering:

> [A]s for me, I know that my Redeemer liveth,
> And that He will witness at last upon the dust;
> And when after my skin this is destroyed,
> Then without my flesh shall I see God;
> Whom I, even I, shall see for myself,
> And my eyes shall behold, and not another's.[15]

"Here I stand; I can do no other" was Martin Luther's expression of existential truth when he stood alone and in great personal danger before the Diet of Worms in the sixteenth century. His existential truth gave him courage and strength in the face of perilous opposition from the papacy and the Catholic Church of his day.

One part of the paradox implicit in existential truth is that it provides a sense of unshakable certainty and confidence that mere statements about it invariably fail to capture. One is existentially certain while at the same time being unable adequately to articulate and defend this certainty. Words are halting and failing in its presence. Existential truth defines who and what persons are in all of their aspects: dispositions, emotions, preferences, choices, actions, as well as intellectual beliefs. It is more like unshakable trust than mere intellectual affirmation. In fact, existential truth or certitude is another term for *faith*, whether that faith be religious or secular, when the nature of faith is properly understood and not assumed to be identical with mere belief. One can thus be certain about the meaning of life without being able fully to explain or prove it. This kind of truth transcends and is in tension with conceptual or propositional truth.

But of course one's existential truth at one time could turn out later to be perceived as false or misplaced. It is fallible, although in the spirit of passionate commitment it may not appear to be so. The sense of confidence, integrity, and integration it imparts to one's life at one time may no longer be operative or effective at a later time. So we can speak in this manner of existential truth as a kind of partial truth, as a precarious mixture of conviction and openness. This is another indication of the paradox of existential truth. Such truth is accompanied by a sense of vulnerability arising from having continually to confront the challenges and perplexities of life in the world, from ongoing self-searching and self-criticism, and from encounters with different kinds of existential truth operative in other human lives. One is sure and unsure at the same time.

There is a close connection between existential truth and what theologian Paul Tillich calls "the courage to be." This courage is made possible, he argues, because of the experienced power of "being-itself." The power of being-itself is what gives one the courage, in his view, to confront and effectively resist powers of negation such as fate and death, moral misjudgment and failure, and aimlessness and meaninglessness that threaten one's self-affirmation. How are we to understand the idea of being-itself? Tillich contends that we should see it as the manifestation of God in human life. But his conception of God is not that of a personal being. It is the sense of what gives support to all of life and all of the myriad beings and their intricate relationships that constitute the world. God is not a being but the ground of the existence and persistence in being of all things, as well as of their coming into and passing out of being.[16]

Tillich's thought is deeply influenced by that of the philosopher Martin Heidegger. The latter makes a fundamental distinction in his book *Being and Time* between *being* and *beings*, and constantly warns against the fatal mistake of confusing them with one another.[17] Rather than thinking of being-itself as some kind of abstract universal or arcane philosophical conception, we should regard it, Tillich insists, as the experience of undaunting persistence and courage in in the living of our lives in the face of all of the threats, uncertainties, and tragedies of life. This experience is, for the most part, simply given to us. We do not create it, although we can work to strengthen our awareness of it and our ability to draw on its resources.

One exceptionally telling way in which Tillich helps to understand the idea of being-itself is his pronouncement in the first volume of his *Systematic Theology* that "God does not exist. He is being-itself beyond essence and existence. Therefore to argue that God exists is to deny him."[18]

In other words, God for Tillich does not exist in the manner of all of the sorts of entity that can rightly be said to exist. To attribute to him existence of this sort is in fact to deny his reality. God or being-itself is what grounds and accounts for the existence of all things and, in the case of humans, for their courage to persist in being in the face of the negative potentialities and hazardous conditions of life that threaten their continuance in existence and confidence in existing. To assert that God exists in the manner of distinct, finite kinds of being is for Tillich a kind of atheism because it denies God's true character as the nonpersonal, nonparticular ground of all existing things. Human personality rests upon such a God, but God is not a personal being.

What does of this talk of being-itself have to do with the paradox of existential truth? The paradox of claiming that affirmation of the traditional God of personalistic *theism* is a type of *atheism* is similar in a way to the paradox of existential truth that cannot be denied and yet is capable of caving in to various kinds of adversity. It is so because there can be a kind of compelling existential truth in faith in God as a *symbolic* truth consisting in the unquestionable fact that many people are nurtured and sustained by what this symbolic truth can be taken to symbolize. It is true in this sense, but it is not a literal truth. It is in one way true and in another false.

The symbolism of God is true for Tillich to the extent that it points beyond itself to the power of being-itself or to the mysterious, suffusive courage to be of daily human life. But what gives inner strength to live and to affirm oneself as a living being, however it may be symbolized, can also be threatened by the trying struggles and haunting dangers of finite human existence. It is therefore at one and the same time certain but uncertain, confident but uneasy, a stubborn truth of life that is nevertheless always liable to becoming false and unreliable. Either side of the paradox can come to the fore in varying degrees at various times in a person's life.

For me, Tillich's power of being-itself is none other than the energizing and supporting power of *nature*, the mysterious natural forces, impulses, drives, and motivations of every living being to continue in its existence and to do so despite all obstacles, hazards, and uncertainties. This is nature, partially secreted in hidden depths, and yet also partially made known by the multiple beings and types of beings exemplifying and confirming nature's creative and sustaining powers. We fallible, finite human beings are upheld and sustained by nature in myriad ways—most of them usually taken for granted—from the steady beatings of our hearts and regular expansions and contractions of our lungs to our most cherished projects, plans, and relationships. The incalculable marvel is that we are generally able and willing confidently to persevere in the courses of our lives despite being continually aware of—and at times being brought squarely up against—obstacles, perils, and tragedies that threaten our lives from every side.

Not to be able or any longer willing to bear up under such threats or experiences is commonly mourned as a deficiency or sickness, not as the emblem of a normal human life. It is just this normality that is most striking and miraculous, and that is brought vividly to mind in the concept of existential truth. While the experience of existential truth indwells most people at most times, existential truth can also falter, decline, or collapse into despair. Self-affirmation can degenerate into self-abnegation or even self-destruction, and it is never entirely immune to this possibility. Finite existence, while grounded in the sustaining, enlivening, embolding powers of nature, can never be entirely safe or secure. It walks a tightrope, as Tillich observes, between the power of being and the menace of non-being, between confident assurance and unnerving anxiety. The former is existential truth, and the latter is by the same token existential falsity. Neither by itself is the final word for all peoples or all times. The unending tension between them comes closer to being the full truth of the matter for finite beings such as ourselves.

Religion as I view it involves at its heart the sense of an inexhaustible mystery, depth, and power by which we are sustained, challenged, perplexed, enlivened, and given a strange inner peace, joy, and hope. It is the sense of being at home and of being where we belong—an appropriate part of an immense, all-encompassing whole—and of yearning to become ever more fully responsive to the astounding fact that this is so. This sense lies far beyond complete or final description, analysis, or examination, but it includes everything that is or can be designated and understood.

For a religious naturalist like me, as I indicated earlier in this chapter, the appropriate name for the focus of this religious sense is *nature*, which I view in the two-sided character of *natura naturata* and *natura naturans*—the side of all that presently is, on the one hand, and the side of all that lies in the past and is yet to come, on the other. Nature as thus perceived is over endless time dynamic and ever-changing, a restless process of creations and destructions—even though its present face or character is relatively stable and enduring. Concerning nature in all its guises and manifestations, only partial truths are possible, although some truths are less partial than others.

The enthralling sense of the inviolable and daunting ultimacy of nature, like the sense of what is differently named and understood as ultimate in other religious perspectives, invites and demands serious, open-hearted cultivation and expansion throughout one's life. I am constantly and necessarily assisted in the course of my own religious thought and practice by countless other past and present interpreters of this deep-lying religious sense, including those of quite different religious persuasions than my own. What I am struggling to allude to and haltingly describe here can be simply but profoundly called *a sense and taste for the holy*, a holiness that for me resides entirely and sufficiently in nature itself. As awesomely and overwhelmingly holy, nature is nameable and unnameable, conceivable and inconceivable, describable and indescribable. Consequently, all claims to truth about it are partial at best.

Chapter 2

SCIENCE

... [T]he dismantling and reconstructing of everything that is[,] which is carried on by modern science represents simply a particular domain of expansion and mastery, which is limited just to the degree that the resistance of what exists to objectification cannot be overcome.

Consequently, it cannot be denied that science always has and always will come up against a claim of comprehension (*Begreifens*) in the face of which it must fail—and indeed which it should forego.

—Hans-Georg Gadamer[1]

In the previous chapter I argued that all the truths brought to expression in religious traditions, systems, theories, teachings, or particular religious lives are at best partial truths, truths open to debate, criticism, revision, doubt, or even possible rejection in various contexts or in varying degrees. Thus, I submit that there are no absolute truths—or ones that can even in principle be known as such—of religion in any of its forms, expressions, or manifestations. But to say that a truth is only partial is not to say that it should be rejected or dismissed on the ground of its partiality. It is also not to say that all religious truths are partial in equal degrees.

Nor, therefore, is it to admit to a radically relativist view of religious claims to truth or of instantiations of such truth in the lives of religious persons. It is not the case that anything goes in the realm of religion any more than it is the case that any one religion can claim to have all the truth. Partial truth is genuine truth and needs to be respected as such, even while being kept open to appropriate questioning and revising. In the domain of religion, partiality of truths is a necessary reminder of the prodigious extent to which any religiously adequate ultimate transcends the limits of finite human understanding, expression, and realization.

In this chapter, I defend a similar claim about the natural and social sciences. They too can contain, at best, only partial truths. This is bound to be so by their very nature as undeniably important and essential sources of truth among other important sources. The philosopher Hans-Georg Gadamer, in the epigraph to this chapter, insists that science occupies one significant domain of investigation and inquiry among others. This domain, he contends, is concerned or tries to be concerned with what are assumed to be strictly *objective* truths—at least to the extent that these are scientifically attainable—that is, truths that can be formulated and tested in ways that admit of high degrees of impersonal, unbiased, nonsubjective modes of verification and falsification. Such objective modes include mathematical or otherwise very precise formulations of theories, explorations of their deductive or at least highly probable relations and implications, the setting up of relevant experiments, and subjecting these experiments to rigorous and replicable empirical assessment. The scientific enterprise is devoted to making objective, public, and convincingly verifiable or falsifiable as many topics of investigation and claims to truth as possible.

Gadamer's book *Reason in the Age of Science* is devoted to showing that scientists are susceptible to the illusion that all reliable truths are of this kind and therefore that only claims of truth amenable to scientific adjudication and testing are genuine truths. In other words, scientists are in danger of a kind of unquestioning absolutism when it comes to the province of science in relation to other sorts of inquiry. For Gadamer there are extremely important areas of significant truth that lie beyond the bounds of science, and this fact needs to be kept constantly in mind.

For him, these areas have to do principally with the language of everyday human consciousness, a language that the technical languages of scientific investigation and conclusion cannot entirely encompass and for which they cannot substitute. I shall come to a similar conclusion in this chapter by developing various ways of understanding that scientific claims to truth are all partial, not absolute. Among other things, this means that we need to supplement the claims of science with claims from other domains because the claims in all domains—including the domain of science—are at best partial in the natures and scopes of their truth-values.

In this chapter, I develop a case for the partial truths of scientific affirmations under four main headings: an examination of the claim to scientific objectivity; some nonscientific or extra-scientific assumptions on which the sciences must rely; the need for ongoing dialogue between the sciences and other fields of thought; and the unknown and unknowable futures of present scientific theories.

The Claim to Scientific Objectivity

A well-established scientific claim or theory deserves to be regarded as more reliably and publicly testable than a claim such as "There was a UFO from another world last night because my neighbor said he saw it in the sky." But is any scientific claim completely objective, in the sense of being finally and indisputably true, and immune to further analysis or criticism? This would require, among other things, that we be capable of completely isolating the claim from dependency on any other beliefs or contexts. But clearly, no claim, whether scientific or not, can be said to be completely isolable from larger contexts of assumption, belief, discourse, and experience. Any specific scientific claim to truth is nested, for example, within a much larger context of the scientific enterprise as a whole, including its history, its methods, its dominant claims and theories, its regnant languages or other kinds of symbolism, and its present specialties and communities of inquiry and their principal commitments. Moreover, the scientific enterprise is nested within the even larger context of *nonscientific* human discourse, interaction, assumption, belief, and commitment, as Gadamer observes.

The scientific enterprise is contained within and depends for its credibility and meaning, in the final analysis, on the whole tangled web of human thought, action, valuation, and belief, including all that makes possible effective sharing and communication of these matters with one another. Without the resources of ordinary language, for example, much of the technical language of science could never have been devised. And without the skills in communication and shared investigation and problem-solving ordinary language provides, the sciences would never have gotten off the ground. This is to say nothing of the indispensability of the things that make ordinary life possible, including the everyday beliefs, practices, interactions, and life-skills of scientists themselves. Scientists are human beings in the first instance and scientists in the second one. There is no hard-and-fast line of demarcation between the fallibilities of ordinary human life, on the one hand, and the deliverances of scientists, on the other, that can somehow guarantee the complete objectivity and incorrigibility of the latter.

All scientific claims, no matter how broad or narrow, and no matter how strong the support for them may seem to be, are open to some amount of doubt. There are, to be sure, important degrees of objectivity or assurance of truth among scientific claims, and these should be welcomed and taken seriously into account. But no scientific claim can be completely or absolutely true. Each one of them is partially true at best, even though such claims can rightly be acknowledged as true in varying degrees. In other words, some are more reliably true than others, depending on such things as their relative plausibility, testability, scope, and character.

It is interesting to note in this connection that two of the most reliable and far-reaching theories in current physics are those of quantum theory and the general theory of relativity. Both theories are remarkably true in the sense of having been borne out by numerous experiments. But they contradict each other, meaning that each must be acknowledged to be a partial truth, not an absolute one. Will the contradiction or mismatch between the two theories someday be resolved? We do not know at present. And even if a "quantum gravity" theory such as string theory or loop quantum gravity were somehow shown experimentally to be a viable candidate for such a resolution, it would also constitute a partial truth, for reasons being discussed in this chapter. But it would perhaps be less partial than the truths expressed in the opposing quantum and relativity theories of today.[2]

Furthermore, science does not have a monopoly on what can be recognized as objectively true. Objective truth in the form of deep and abiding insight into human life and human affairs can be provided by a great poem, play, movie, or novel, for example. And it can be continually brought to the test of ongoing and shareable human experience. After experiencing and reflecting on such things, we can justly be regarded as having gained levels of plausible and reliable truth and understanding we did not have access to before. The same can be said when we are exposed to the presence, teachings, questions, or arguments of a wise and insightful religious leader, philosopher, politician, or ethicist. Such truths are not merely subjective, in contrast with a putative objectivity of meaning and truth in scientific claims. They have a compelling objectivity of their own kind, although it is not of the scientific kind. We can speak gratefully, therefore, of kinds and degrees of objectivity provided by the sciences, but it is a mistake to associate objective truth solely with the sciences.

Before we are tempted think of science as the sole source of objective truth, that is, truths that contrast absolutely with subjective beliefs, we should take careful note of the fact that without subjectivity there would be no such thing as science. Science is the outcome of conscious reflecting, questioning, and inquiring. It is born of subjectivity and continues to be evaluated and furthered by human subjects, either individually or collectively. A theory is true to the extent that it can be brought to the test of relevant criteria—methodological, logical, and empirical—and in this way be accepted, believed in, and acted upon as true. Accepting, believing, and acting are functions of human subjects. The line between subjectivity and objectivity is smudged. It can never be said to be completely clear-cut. Too much is at stake, and too much is involved. The distinction between the two is to some important extent artificial and misleading. This is one way of understanding the partiality of scientific claims to truth or of assumptions or arguments to the effect that the outcomes of responsible scientific inquiry can somehow be made indefeasible or entirely objective.

But perhaps the claim to the objectivity of scientific truth amounts to the notion that genuinely scientific claims are external, meaning that they rest on sensately observable facts rather than on the internality of conscious experiences. To make something scientific, therefore, we need to make it externally experienceable and observable—subject to the court of human consensus, that is, to the judgment of those equipped by experience, temperament, and training to recognize and endorse sensate evidence for a truth when they are brought up against it.

Behaviorist psychology, for example, bases its claims on what can be externally observed in modes of sensately manifest behavior, not on any kind of introspective analysis. For example, we cannot directly observe anxiety in a mouse, but we can assume its anxiety when it defecates under some kind of imposed stress. We can deduce that it has pain on the basis of its winces and cries. To make something like anxiety or pain objective, then, is to make evidence of it publicly accessible in such a manner so that all interested parties can witness it, interpret its meaning, and critically test assertions concerning it on the basis of one or more of the five senses. With this understanding of scientific objectivity, it is not necessary to worry about what a creature's inner life or firsthand experience is like. All we need concern ourselves with is how it behaves. All that can be or need be scientifically inquired into concerning it lies in this external sensate domain.

This understanding of objectivity is methodological and as such is commendable and useful in its own right as one important route to understanding. It holds true in some important contexts of inquiry. But when it is claimed to be the only reliable way adequately to understand anything, and when consciousness as such or subjective experiences altogether are swept into the dustbin of the untrustworthy, dismissible, and unknowable, then this claim should be brought up short and recognized to be itself unreliable and untrue. The objective and the subjective, more often than not, and in some important ways *always*, are bound tightly together. The test of the five senses comes down finally to what someone consciously sees, hears, tastes, touches, or smells, to say nothing of the conceptual meanings associated instinctively or habitually with such experiences. And what counts as verification or falsification of ideas, beliefs, or theories depends on how sensate experiences are set within the context of overarching theoretical expectations, interpretations, and significations—themselves of a conscious or unconscious sort.

The subjective cannot be converted without remainder into the objective in the sense of the latter term rightly prized and sought for by the sciences, and this qualifying observation needs constantly to be borne in mind. The completely objective or completely external, when thought to be entirely divorced from the subjective domain, would be completely meaningless. A claim to the objectivity of an assertion, theory, or network of theories in the sciences is at best a partial truth.

But is this meta-statement itself only partially true? It is, in the sense that it is open to ongoing dialogue and discussion and to reassessment in some way or ways currently unrecognized or not properly understood by me. I can be confident of it, as I clearly am, while still acknowledging its susceptibility to further interrogation and discussion. If, as I currently believe, all claims to truth are partial truths, then everything I claim in this book also comes under this heading. But there are degrees of partiality in truth claims of all sorts, and these degrees are significant and make important differences. A partial truth, even when recognized as such, contains elements or aspects of truth that need to be taken seriously. And on a spectrum stretching from "anything goes" relativism to "only one thing goes" absolutism, some claims are further along toward the asymptote or regulative ideal of absolute truth than are others.

Assumptions Lying Behind Scientific Reasoning

Scientific reasoning turns on critical assumptions that are presupposed by science rather than proved by science. The impressive successes of science can help to give credence to these assumptions, but without their presupposition science as we know it would not be possible. Moreover, some of these assumptions as well as others lie behind all human endeavors to attain knowledge and not just the endeavors of natural and social scientists. So the scope and critical importance of such assumptions is wide-ranging and apparent, and by no means restricted to scientific thought. In this section, I list and discuss some assumptions essential to the endeavors of scientists. What the list serves to show is that assertions of scientific truth are partial in the sense that they do not, need not, and could not make explicit all of the aspects of human belief and practice that are necessary for giving intelligibility, meaning, and plausibility to the scientific assertions themselves.

The latter do not stand alone but are surrounded, informed, and deeply influenced by a swarm of prior convictions. My broader thesis is that claims to truth in all domains, scientific or otherwise, are inexhaustibly interrelated with other things prejudged to be appropriate, relevant, or true, whether consciously so or not. We could never spell out in complete detail all of the assumptions, beliefs, experiences, memories, predilections, and the like that enter implicitly into any and every claim to truth. Each such claim is, by this token as well as others, partially true at best. There is no way it could be otherwise—in the sciences, other domains of inquiry, or the whole of human life.

A lot hangs on this realization. Among other things, it is a safeguard against arrogant close-mindedness and an invitation to mutually beneficial discussion, interaction, and cooperation among those with different convictions and points of view. If there is no such thing as absolute truth or at least of anything knowable as such, then it need not be assumed that one party in such engagements must be absolutely right and the other absolutely wrong when there is disagreement between them. Not only can there be searches for common ground; there can also be openness to possible truths in each of the opposing positions.

Here, then, are examples of crucial assumptions that are implicit in and entangled with scientific inquiries and claims to truth. The first one is the tacit belief that nature is intelligible, at least to a highly significant extent, and that we humans are capable of discovering and making explicit in a scientific manner important aspects of this intelligibility. A second assumption is confidence in appeal to one or more of the five senses as providing evidence for the verification or falsification of theories in the sciences. Implicit in this second assumption is belief that there is enough difference between theoretical predictions and empirical tests of those predictions to rightly regard the latter as confirmations of the truth of the former. In other words, it must be assumed that empirical tests are not themselves always so theory-laden or subject to theoretical skewing as to make them highly dubious and unreliable when regarded as evidence of the truth or falsity of the theories making appeal to them. A third assumption is that the distinction between correlation and causation is a meaningful and discernible one, so that it is possible, and routinely so, to avoid the *post hoc, ergo propter hoc* ("after which, therefore because of which") fallacy when providing causal explanations of phenomena.

A fourth assumption is that inductive reasoning is generally reliable, and a fifth one is that mathematical reasoning and deductive reasoning in general are fruitful sources of insight into and understanding of the workings of nature. Providing a causal explanation of why one has come to have a belief is different from being able to justify the belief, so a sixth assumption is that scientific investigators have the *freedom* to assess alternative beliefs and theories in light of reasons, and to choose the beliefs and theories that are judged to be the most reasonable. Confidence in the trustworthiness of researches and findings of colleagues in areas of scientific inquiry different from one's own is a seventh critical assumption, because no single scientist is capable of establishing all of the scientifically claimed truths indispensably relevant to the truthful outcomes of his or her own enquiries. An eighth assumption is acquiescence in the reigning scientific paradigm, at least in its most salient and pervasive aspects, whatever they might be at any given time. Thoroughgoing scientific revolutions are few and far between, and the reliability of "normal science" must generally be assumed.[3] A ninth assumption is conviction of the positive value and great importance of science itself, value and importance enough to justify committing one's life to scientific research and to warrant substantial university, government, business and other funding for its continuation.

Questions can be made and have been made concerning each of these assumptions in the history of thought, and especially philosophical thought. In chapter 1 I mentioned the outlook of the character Roquentin in Jean-Paul Sartre's novel *Nausea* as an example of radically denying the intelligibility of nature. In *The Specter of the Absurd* I mention Friedrich Nietzsche, Fritz Mauthner, Max Stirner, and Albert Camus as other examples of this outlook, which I call *cosmic nihilism*.[4] We might think we understand fundamental aspects of nature, but perhaps we really do not.

The reliability of the senses to give knowledge of a world external to or independent of the senses has been questioned and analyzed for a long time in the history of philosophy. David Hume's phenomenalism, George Berkeley's idealism, and Immanuel Kant's denial of the possibility of knowing the in-itself world are examples of ways in which the evidence of the five senses can be interpreted so as to question their relations to a world beyond themselves. See also in this connection the discussion of the anti-realist thought of twentieth-century philosopher Richard Rorty in chapter 5 of my book *The Philosophy of William James*. Truth for Rorty consists only in coherence within linguistic and conceptual systems, not in appeals to experiences believed to be in important degrees independent of those systems.[5]

The separability of theories from their alleged empirical confirmations or falsifications has been a topic of critical discussion in the philosophy of science. Even the instruments involved in testing scientific hypotheses have rightly been noted to be theory-laden.[6] Hume questioned the possibility of distinguishing between correlation and causation, arguing that the two, at bottom, amount to the same thing. And he argued that since, in his view, there is no necessary connection between causes and effects, inductive reasoning really has no rational basis. It is simply a matter of custom or habit, an unanalyzed assumption that the future will resemble the past.[7]

The relations of mathematics or deductive reasoning of any sort to the structures, laws, relations, and constituents of the world have long been a subject of dispute, with views ranging from the idea that the world is mathematical through and through; to the notion that it is amenable to mathematical analysis to a significant degree; to the view that mathematics is both synthetic (informative about the structures of experience) and analytic (its reasonings are certain or undeniable) but only within the domain of the world as we experience it, not in a world outside our experiences; to the idea that mathematics is purely formal or entirely analytic and has no intrinsic connections with the external world. The sixth assumption about human freedom in its essential relation to reasoning about and justifying claims to truth I noted above has been called into question—inconsistently in my view—by the thesis of causal determinism and its "compatibilist" variation[8] held by a sizeable number of scientists and philosophers.

Reported cases of lying, fudging, or cooking of empirical data by scientists—often in order to qualify for publication in reputable journals or for government, company, or other grants—raise questions about the trustworthiness of the findings of one's scientific colleagues. Such suspicion can also be aroused by cases of apparent unwarranted favoritism given to the ideas of some younger faculty at the expense of others by older mentors and colleagues, and by journal editors wary of unconventional but possibly valuable ways of thinking that might threaten or upset reputable holders of established views. Physicist, historian, and philosopher of science Thomas Kuhn and others have argued that current, deeply entrenched scientific paradigms hold most scientific thinkers in thrall, making all of their researches unconsciously theory-laden in high degree.[9]

Some people question the importance and value of science on grounds such as that it can lead to dangerously unpredictable genetic engineering of humans as well as animals; that it produces weapons of mass destruction; that its researches often involve cruelty to animals; that the machines and factories it helps to make possible are often threats to the ecosystems of earth; and that its AI researches could eventually lead to robots dominating human beings with their superior intelligence and have already led to robots taking over many jobs. Thus, the truth of a particular scientific claim, theory, prediction, or accomplishment could be acknowledged, while the truth of the assumption or claim on the part of scientists or others that such a thing will have positive, overriding, or undeniable value—especially clearly discernible practical value—in the long or short range could be called into question.

I will have more to say about relations between claims to truth and claims to value in chapters 3 and 5. These relations show the need for dialogue between science, on the one hand, and fields of thought devoted to the exploration of questions of value, on the other. There would be no science without the valuing of science, but its assumed value as a whole or in particular circumstances opens up a large area of questions that cannot be resolved scientifically.

Thus, not only do the assumptions I have listed play a powerful but generally unconscious role in scientific reasoning. They are also defeasible and open to critical questions of various sorts. I do not mean in any way to suggest by these observations that science is pervasively false, misleading, or worthless in its claims to truth. I only want to emphasize in this manner that its claims are at best partially true and not unassailably true.

The Need for Dialogue between
Science and Other Fields of Thought

As a way of showing that science needs to be in dialogue with other fields of thought, I make reference here to my own field of philosophy. The fact that many of the assumptions underlying scientific thought have been and continue to be discussed and debated by philosophers shows the importance of scientists being aware or becoming aware of such assumptions and the extent to which they influence scientific theorizing and empirical testing of theories.

Philosophers have helped to bring these assumptions into the clear light of day and in this way to expose them to critical analysis—not only by philosophers but by scientists as well. Their crucial even if often unacknowledged roles in scientific thinking, when recognized by scientists, can help to guard against scientists' viewing any scientific claim, theory, or practice as immune to doubt and as being absolutely or unqualifiedly true. Such awareness can open the way to the possibility of other ways of thinking or to possible innovations in thought that might lead to significant new levels or kinds of understanding. It can also help motivate scientists to take more directly and seriously into account problems and anomalies in current scientific thought that, when properly puzzled over in light of the assumptions underlying them, could lead to needed breakthroughs in current outlooks and beliefs.

Philosophy's ongoing dependence on developments in science is readily acknowledged by philosophers, historians of ideas, and others. I shall speak more fully of it in a moment. But it is also important that scientists be aware of ideas they take for granted, generate, or support that are susceptible to critical discussion. This is especially true at those points of the natural sciences that enter into areas of thought that can rightly be regarded as philosophical in their character and not scientific or not exclusively scientific. Examples of such points are identifications of minds with brains; computer-based theories of the workings of the brain; evolutionary explanations of such things as morality and religion; scientific assertions or assumptions of causal determinism and denials of chance or freedom of the will; scientific assertions of the unreality of the flow of time; the notion that meta-physics or conceptions of reality are the sole domain of science and have no place in philosophy; and the like.

When teaching the history of seventeenth and eighteenth philosophy, I devoted a fourth to a third of the course time to discussing the scientific revolution because it figures so fundamentally in the thinking of philosophers in those centuries. Prominent philosophers of the period such as John Locke, David Hume, Gottfried Leibniz, and Immanuel Kant—philosophers whose ideas are still influential today—were deeply affected and challenged by the scientific thought of their time, especially by that of the radical scientific innovator Isaac Newton.

In similar fashion, philosophers have continued to be influenced by developments in science from that time to this. Darwin's theory of evolution has had great impact on philosophy, as is shown by the rise of process philosophy, with its prioritization of becoming over being. Process philosophy has also been profoundly influenced by the quantum physics of the twentieth century and by scientific theories concerning the origin and evolution of the present universe, of the solar system, of the earth, and of the earth's innumerable life forms. Prominent examples of this fact are the philosophies of Charles Sanders Peirce, Samuel Alexander, Henri Bergson, Pierre Teilhard de Chardin, Charles Hartshorne, and Alfred North Whitehead. Philosophers of science such as Carl Hempel, Paul Feyerabend, and Karl Popper have explored the range, logic, and general character of scientific reasoning. The Logical Positivists of the twentieth century argued for ceding to scientific modes of reasoning the sole claim to cognitive meaning and reliable truths about the world. Examples of the influence of science on philosophy and of philosophy's continuing deliberate engagement and dialogue with science could be multiplied indefinitely. And I am, of course, a philosopher developing the thesis in this chapter that scientific truths are at best partial truths.

In the remainder of this section, I draw attention to an illuminating example of the partiality of scientific truths, an example that illustrates the need for continuing dialogue between science and philosophy on fundamental issues of mutual interest and concern. The example is the debate between the physicist Albert Einstein and the philosopher Henri Bergson on the nature of time. Einstein conceived of time as not only *measured* but *determined* by clock time. Since he also argued that rates of clock time (that is, rates of periodic change that would include such things as the vibrations of cesium atoms or regular metabolic rates of change in organisms) are altered depending on the proximity of material phenomena to the absolute speed of light, he concluded that time is relative.

Not only did Einstein identify time with the measurement of time, he was also convinced that time is ultimately an illusion. This notion was deeply influenced by his firm attachment to the theory of causal determinism and to the notion that the universe (and everything in it) is ultimately mathematical and therefore wholly deductive in its character. These two notions were undergirded by a deep-rooted and often readily acknowledged *religious* fascination with and commitment to the elegance and perfection of the universe he shared with the seventeenth-century religious philosopher Baruch Spinoza, whose ideas he deeply esteemed. So the debatable area of religious thought entered fundamentally into Einstein's outlook as well.[10]

Bergson vigorously debated Einstein on these ideas (of Einstein) about the nature of time. Bergson refused to identify the nature of time solely with the measurement of time, and he took forceful issue with Einstein's contention that the passage of time is purely subjective and illusory. For one thing, Bergson argued that Einstein's ideas about time failed to take into account the experienced fact that while the past is fixed, the future remains open. We can remember the past but not the future. We cannot change the past, but we can work in the present to bring about changes in the future. The passage of time takes up time and moves inexorably into the future. And as it does so, it brings about real change and change that in its very nature to some extent and in some cases to a large extent is unpredictable and unexpected—especially as we move further and further away from the past and into the future. Bergson did not dispute the *scientific usefulness* of Einstein's identification of time with clock time or even of his conceiving mathematically of time as a fourth dimension analogous in some ways to the three dimensions of space. But Bergson emphatically denied the *philosophical adequacy* of these ways of viewing time.

Was he right? Was Einstein right? I side with Bergson and thus conclude that Einstein's view was only partially true. I do so mainly on the ground that I cannot rightly conceive of time as an illusion. It is too much a fundamental, pervasive feature of everyday experience, including the experience of scientists such as Einstein, who come into being; mature; take time to devise, develop, test, and, if need be, alter their theories; grow old; and die. There is no Albert Einstein living today but not too long ago there was such a person. The main point I want to make here is that there is significant philosophical debatibility about Einstein's view of time and that it is not purely scientific but extends into or overlaps with the area of philosophy. Hence, a philosopher such as Bergson was entitled to consider and take issue with this view on philosophical grounds. I do not claim that Bergson's view of time is absolutely true, only that it captures an aspect of time that would need to be weighed in the balance as over against the view of it held by Einstein.[11] Each aspect is important, but neither is final or contains all that could be said or would need to be said about the topic as a whole. No theory, whether scientific or philosophical can completely unravel the pervasive and haunting mystery of time.

All truths are perspectival in the sense that each of them approaches its subject matter from a particular perspective or point of view. No truth encompasses all possible points of view on its subject. Each is partial and selectively abstract in its own manner. As philosopher Justus Buchler rightly insists, there are no *simples* into which everything or anything could finally be resolved. This is the case because each thing that might be supposed to be simple is necessarily tied to many other things and depends for its character on its complex relations to these many other things. Because the complexity of its relations is inexhaustible, analysis of any one thing is also inexhaustible and therefore incurably partial at every stage.[12]

Similarly, particular major disciplines such as science, philosophy, religion, art, morality, history, and the like are necessarily partial in their scope and partial in their outlooks, theories, and claims because the specific areas into which they inquire are necessarily linked in inexhaustible ways with areas of interest and investigation peculiar to the other disciplines. It is also important to note that each discipline buys its specificity and degrees of truth at the price of its need to bracket and overlook whatever does not fit readily into its own specific topics of concern. Concepts of matter under study in current physics, for example, are not concerned with the kind of full-blown conception of matter that would allow us to understand how material bodies such as our own can be conscious.[13] This means that each discipline has much to learn about the fullness and complexity of the world and diverse types of experience and interpretation of the world from the other partial disciplines and their own distinctive kinds of selectivity and abstraction.

Science and the Future

One kind of limited perspective that should always be kept in mind is the perspective of the present. This perspective can never contain or hope to contain all of the truth about anything because it is impossible accurately and fully to predict what the future might bring in the way of new ways of thinking and experiencing. The science of the present is therefore always to be recognized as containing only partial truths because of the inability of scientists in the present to know what science might look like in the future—especially in the more distant future. New discoveries, especially those of a more fundamental sort, will impact older ways of thinking and sometimes in unforeseeably radical ways. And scientific theories undreamed of today could bring about revolutions in scientific thought at some point in the future. Scientific theories are fated always to be only partial in their truth because scientists have no way of knowing in the present, and certainly not in fine detail, what the future will bring.

Who in the sixteenth century could have predicted the meticulous and groundbreaking work in physics of Isaac Newton in the seventeenth century? Who in the eighteenth century could have predicted the theory of natural selection as key to the evolution of the species promulgated by Charles Darwin and Alfred Russel Wallace in the nineteenth century? Who could have predicted, even toward the end of the nineteenth century, a Max Planck or Albert Einstein, and their ingenious contributions to the revolution in physics in the twentieth century? Such notions as the divisibility of the atom into different subatomic components; the existence of hundreds of billions of galaxies; the continuing expansion of the universe;[14] the four subatomic forces; the Big Bang; black holes; dark matter and dark energy; gravitational lensing; quarks; the creation of subatomic chain reactions; and the model of the DNA molecule basic to genetics had to await the theories and discoveries of the twentieth century and could not have been predicted in fine detail in earlier centuries.

We do not even have to believe that science is subject to radically discontinuous changes of paradigm over time to understand that the future of science cannot be known with anything like complete precision by the scientists of today. The scientific claims, theories, and findings of today may be subject to radical revision by scientists working in the future. This was true of the science of the past, and it is possibly true of the science of the present as it faces into the future. Scientific claims to truth in the present are necessarily partial in that they are subject to limited predictability about what will be believed to be true in the future.

Just as we may chuckle today at many beliefs presumed to be undeniably true by earnest, well-informed (for their time) thinkers in the distant past, so beliefs we might regard as indisputably factual or true in the sciences of today are subject to possibly condescending or even derisive responses by scientists (and others) of the future. No scientific claim at any given time should be regarded as absolutely true because absolute knowledge of the future is impossible.

Firmly held truths of the past have often been overturned, as we are well aware. Some, most, or perhaps even all of the core putative scientific truths of the present may continue to be maintained as true in the future, but there is no way we can be certain that they will.

As the nineteenth-century German philosopher Friedrich Schelling shrewdly pointed out,

> It is no less the case with true science than it is with history that there are no authentic propositions, that is, that is assertions that would have a value or an unlimited and universal validity in and of themselves or apart from the movement through which they are produced. Movement is what is essential to knowledge. . . . Absolute propositions, that is, those that are once and for all valid, conflict with the nature of true knowledge which involves progression. . . . For where there is no succession, there is no science.[15]

There is not only progression or change in outlooks to be expected in the future; there may also be changes in future understandings of aspects of the past—new ways of comprehending and making use of resources from the past hitherto unrecognized.

Claims to knowledge stubbornly fixed and dogmatically insisted on in the present are arbitrarily cut off from and oblivious to what an unpredictable future may hold. They are oblivious to what philosopher Jason M. Wirth, in his masterful book on Schelling, refers to as "the unprethinkable creativity of time."[16] Such claims to absoluteness of truth are therefore ill-conceived. As Schelling observes in the passage quoted earlier, putative scientific beliefs that are impervious to ongoing motion or change are actually unscientific in their refusal to acknowledge that the changes of the past, some of them radical and unexpected, portend unavoidable changes of scientific thinking and believing for the future.

My discussion throughout this chapter has focused mainly on the natural sciences, but most of it bears critically on the social sciences as well—at least as much if not more so. We should note that in the latter, debatable assumptions concerning human nature and human predilections, tendencies, and potentialities often enter prominently—even if not always explicitly—into the discussion. Is there such a thing as human nature? To what extent is human nature—if there is such a thing—malleable by historical and cultural situations and changes? Are human beings genuinely free? Are they basically egoistic or are they capable of, or naturally inclined toward, altruism?

Are humans predominately communal or individualistic in their out-look and character? Are there laws of human history? Is there such a thing as inevitable historical progress? Do humans stand outside of or over against nature, or are they integral parts of nature? Answers to such questions, whether assumed or announced, can deeply affect social sciences of all sorts, whether they be anthropological, political, economic, historical, psychological, or the like. All such answers are partially true at best, never absolutely so. At least we can never *know* them beyond question or doubt to be absolutely and everlastingly true.

What I am claiming in this regard about the natural and social sciences is not meant in any way to disparage them or to detract from the importance of their current theories and programs of research. It is only to emphasize that scientists, like the rest of us, are fallible beings and that even the most vaunted and impressive scientific claims of today are at best partially true, not absolutely or unquestionably so. In its own sphere and with its own specific methods of investigation and confirmation, science in its various forms has a vital, irreplaceable role to play in human life and human civilization. Its truths, like all human claims to truth, are partial and subject to change—perhaps in ways unknowable and unimaginable to us in the present. But partial truths, especially those that are highly credible (even if not absolute) in their respective domains, deserve our acknowledgment and respect.

We can be unabashedly grateful for the truths of today's science, partial though they inevitably must be. But we must also be on guard against the idea in some quarters that the only truly important and binding kinds of truth are scientific ones. As Gadamer reminds us, scientific truth is one kind of truth, not the only one or in all respects and areas the most dependable or significant one. Each of the major areas of thought and investigation, including that of science, has it appropriate boundaries and limitations. None can rightly claim to be all inclusive or adequate by itself to comprehend the multifaceted complexity of the world or the inexhaustible fullness of human life and experience. Continuing interdisciplinary dialogue and research among scientists and nonscientists can be a crucial safeguard against this illusion.

Chapter 3

MORALITY

> Philosophical doctrines of Morality are not designed to *replace* the rules of right conduct, but rather to show their significance by relating them to a broader theoretical context. Generalization about goals is hazardous, but most moral philosophers have tried to simplify, by one means or another, the task of the person who wants to know what it would be right to do.
>
> —Mary Mothersill[1]

It is doubtful in the extreme that most or even many people consciously guide their moral lives and make their everyday moral decisions on the basis of a particular moral theory developed by a philosopher. But philosophical theories are important because they encourage us to think deeply and critically about morality as a central aspect of human life, especially the lives of human beings in society. Questions of morality have important bearings on the quality of individual human lives, as I shall note further along in this chapter. But they relate most importantly to ways in which humans live in their relations to one another, to their local communities, and to the institutions and structures of society. We are also becoming increasingly aware these days of the relations of essential moral principles and moral actions to the community of all living beings on earth of which human beings are an integral and dependent part.

An important task of any theoretical interpretation or explanation is its relative ability to organize diverse phenomena of a given sort in such a manner as to call attention to genuine commonalities and patterns of interrelationship among the phenomena and in that way bring them into unifying, clarifying, and simplifying focus or perspective. But the theory in question, if it is adequately to perform its function, must also be able to do as much justice as possible to the distinctive integrities of those diverse phenomena and their differences from one another so as to avoid the errors of vague abstraction, unwarranted reduction, and misleading oversimplification.

As the philosopher Mary Mothersill suggests in this chapter's epigraph, each of the various moral theories developed by philosophers can have the significant value of relating the various aspects of morality—its motivations, assumptions, principles, rules, and obligations—to "a broader theoretical context." Such a context can not only help to unify, simplify, and make more intelligible the complex issues involved in moral choices and moral outlooks; it can also help to clarify the general character of morality itself as a fundamental dimension of human experience and culture. Philosophical moral theories do not construct the moral good from scratch, but they can help us to better understand it.

While I applaud the work of philosophers who have devoted or are now devoting themselves to developing moral theories and think that they do us all a great service in undertaking such a task, in this chapter I also want to defend the thesis that any and all such theories can only offer partial truths at best and that no one of them can qualify as providing absolute truths about morality. I shall go further to argue that each of the theories I briefly indicate highlights an aspect of morality that needs to be emphasized but that we need to regard the particular perspectives of these theories as complementary facets or avenues of insight into moral phenomena that are best viewed in a number of different way rather than in some allegedly singular, all-inclusive manner. In other words, I argue that no one theory captures all of the truth or awareness needed in an adequate way of looking at morality and that we need the perspectives of different historically influential theories, each of which is likely to have its own partial but informative measure of truth. Moreover, the value of the theories will vary, I contend, depending on particular contexts of moral choice and moral action in which each one of them may prove to be most useful.

Such a thesis is broad-ranging indeed, and I can provide in this chapter only a sketch of it. But I hope that my defense of the thesis will help to make the case that in the area of morality as in all other fundamental areas of thought, experience, and concern we can expect only partial truth, however well-conceived and persuasive any particular moral theory may appear to be. The absence of whole truth should not deter us from recognizing and appropriating the degrees of truth each moral theory may contain. And the conceptual tensions among different theories can often tell us a lot about moral truths not explicitly set forth in any particular moral theory. Thus, such theories can often be viewed as illuminatingly complementary rather than simply as being at odds with or contradicting one another. Important moral theories, despite their differences, can provide essential, insightful, and useful perspectives on the moral life as a whole.

My strategy in what follows is to refer to six influential moral theories with an eye to bringing into focus what I take to be the most important moral truths in each one of them and to compare and contrast these moral truths with one another. The exemplary moral theories I examine with this strategy in mind are those of Aristotle, Thomas Hobbes, David Hume, Immanuel Kant, John Stuart Mill, and John Rawls. Each of these theories highlights aspects of moral experience, thought, and obligation that need to be brought vividly and persuasively into view.

I obviously cannot in a brief chapter go into detail about these six theories, but I do intend to provide enough detail to show how each of them is incomplete and needs the perspectives of the others for its greater adequacy. But even this greater adequacy can give us only partial truth about the complex and elusive character of moral thought and moral action. Finally, I shall stress the idea that one of the theories I shall discuss may be more appropriate in one context and another in a different context. So we need to look at the six theories' relative situational suitability as well as their more general competency for illuminating various perplexities, challenges, and opportunities of moral life. Why do I choose these particular theories? I do so in order to suggest something of the range and diversity of theorizing about the nature and requirements of morality, at least in the West, as it stretches from the time of Aristotle in the fourth century BCE to that of Rawls in the twentieth century CE.

But before beginning this discussion, I want to take up a topic alluded to in chapter 2, namely, the relation of truth to goodness. This book is about truth and the partiality of claims to truth or manifestations of truth. What does truth have to do with the moral goodness that is the subject matter of moral theories and the focus of the present chapter? My response to this question can help to pave the way for the discussion of moral theories that is to follow.

Truth and Goodness

We can say something like "It is true that we should honor our parents" or "It is true that we have an obligation to care for one another." But the general concept of goodness is not explicated in such sentences. Rather, it is assumed. In fact, in all such statements it tends to be taken for granted that goodness is its own warrant, that is, that some particular thing should be done because it is good that it be done. But what, precisely, does "good" (or more specifically, "moral good") in these assertions mean?

I do not want to make the mistake of conflating questions of goodness with questions of truth, or vice versa. But at the same time, I want to call attention to the common assumption that truth is one extremely important good among others, and that the search for it and practice of it (that is, truthfulness of action and character) can be properly conceived as moral goods. Also, in the moral domain we want theories about moral goodness to be as accurate, inclusive, coherent, persuasive, and so on, as possible—and in those senses to be recognized as true. We can thus make relatively true or relatively false statements about moral goodness, but these all rely on an intuition or understanding, however vague, of what it is we are talking about. We can make a list of the sorts of things the concept of moral goodness should encompass, but such a list is not a theory. It is more like a catalogue of things such a theory should bring into unitary perspective and in that way help us to understand.

Thus, we are not primarily interested in noting important moral goods seriatim but in understanding what it is that they all are precepts and examples of, namely, moral goodness. The listing of such examples might be the starting point of a moral theory, but it would not be its end point. We have not explained moral goodness when we give examples of it; we have presupposed an intuition, inkling, or notion of it in doing so. Fleshing out the underlying idea of what entitles these examples to be seen as examples of moral goodness— that is, explicating the nature of moral goodness itself, is the task of a moral theory. A theory can be said to be "true" when it succeeds, to at least some significant degree, in doing so. But it would perhaps be less misleading and more adequate to speak of it as insightful, illuminating, or persuasive, so as to avoid a confusing conflation of truth with goodness.

Just what is this "moral goodness," then? It is the task of each moral theory to set forth an answer to this question. All such answers are and will inevitably be—I emphasize yet again—partial at best. And they will seek to elucidate something that is already intuited or divined, something that awaits the clarifying and unifying perspective of the theory. Let me turn, then, to the first two of the moral theorists I want jointly to discuss: those of Aristotle and Mill.

Aristotle and Mill

It might seem strange at first to group the moral theory of Aristotle of the fourth century BCE with that of John Stuart Mill of the nineteenth century CE, but I shall argue that they share some beliefs in common that warrant our grouping them together.[2] For one thing, Aristotle pointed out that moral theories are necessarily inexact and cannot offer the kind of precision of definition and argumentation that can apply in some other domains of human thought and experience. They are inexact because they are necessarily responsible to changing situational experiences and demands that cannot be brought within the scope of deductive reasoning. Mill at least tacitly agrees with this assessment in basing his moral theory primarily on experience, which is always probabilistic or inductive in its necessary dependence on the degree to which future consequences can be predicted. Second, human desires have a fundamental role to play in the moral theories of the two thinkers. Aristotle sees morality as requiring the subordination of desire to reason, but he also respects desire as a motivating factor behind moral choice and action. Mill asks us to consider what all desires amount to in the final analysis and concludes that they amount to the universal human desire for happiness.

In the third place, Aristotle's conception of *eudaimonia*, which is the main goal of moral life and which is frequently translated as "happiness,"[3] can be said to be closely associated with Mill's contention that the final arbiter or *summum bonum* of moral choice and action is the general human happiness. Fourth, Mill's distinction between two types of happiness, the pleasures of the flesh and those of the intellect is similar to Aristotle's distinction between the moral and intellectual forms of *eudaimonia*.[4] For both thinkers, it is in our nature as humans that the intellectual types should take moral precedence over the physical ones. For Aristotle, as I noted above, desire must be subordinated to both practical and contemplative reason, so as to harness the motivating power of desire for the guidance of reason. Delight in knowing, for example, can be a significant factor in our search for knowledge and understanding of all types, including the knowledge and understanding essential to the moral life. And for Mill, the morality of an action lies in the thoughtful and rationally appraised intention to enhance or preserve the general happiness. Thus, neither of the two moral theories is purely rationalistic or purely empirical. Both contain crucial and closely related aspects of rationality and empiricality.

For Mill, the universally experienced and profoundly important twin human feelings of or urges toward self-preservation and sympathy for others figure fundamentally in the appropriate self-regard and other-regard of right moral intention and action. These two kinds of moral regard can sometimes come into conflict with one another, and when they do, it makes rational sense as well as being in accord with the dictates of feeling, Mill contends, to think that sympathetic concern for the general happiness should take precedence over consideration of one person's individual happiness—even if that person is oneself. There is no convincing moral reason to consider oneself, as one human being among others, to be more deserving of moral considerability than any other person.

Hence, sixth, both theories are social rather than individualistic, or altruistic rather than egoistic, in their respective orientations. This is to say, they assume that humans are social beings in their fundamental nature rather than conceiving them primarily as separate individuals who come together in society for egoistic or prudential reasons. In neither case does the self-interest of the individual person trump or take precedence over the interests of others. For Aristotle, humans are social animals by nature, and for Mill, the goal of the moral life is seeking the happiness of as many persons as possible as the intended consequence of moral decisions and actions.

What, in the seventh place, is the role of specific moral precepts, principles, laws, or directives in these two moral theories? In both cases, these are subordinate to something more fundamental. In Aristotle's case, it is the development of thoroughgoing moral habituation and exemplary personal character. The morally upright person, for him, is equipped by carefully nurtured excellences or virtues of character to perceive and make the right moral choices in the right situations and at the right times. Moral rules are subordinated to moral character. In Mill's case, so-called "secondary goods," while they can be useful guidelines for the moral life, are subject to the goal of happiness as the ultimate umpire of moral action. Such an umpire is required, Mill reasons, given the facts that sometimes there is no rule appropriate for a particular moral situation, that such roles can sometimes conflict with one another, and that most if not all moral rules admit of exceptions in particular situations.

I believe that Aristotle's most distinctive contribution to our understanding of the moral life is his emphasis on the fundamental importance of each person's developing a moral character that is capable of discerning and acting on the prospects for moral goodness present in particular situations. His principal stress is on moral persons and not just on moral actions. And I am convinced that Mill's most distinctive contribution to moral theory is his emphasis on the kinds of decisions and actions that are focused on the happiness and wellbeing, as well as alleviation of suffering and want, of as many persons as possible in particular situations. Mill's focus on happiness—broadly conceived—is similar to Aristotle's goal of *eudaimonia*, and Aristotle's focus on character is implicit in Mill's recognition of the need for a developed ability rationally and effectively to appraise and intend the consequence of the greatest happiness for the greatest number by one's actions in specific situations.

What I regard as the major emphasis of the one moral theory is balanced by the major emphasis of the other. Neither is complete by itself. Each is a partial truth in its depiction of the fundamental nature of morality. What may be implicit in the one theory is accentuated in the other, and vice versa. Each theory as a whole is an insightful, useful, and not to be neglected—even if finally limited—perspective on the moral life. Later in this chapter I will make further critical comments about the moral theories of Aristotle and Mill. But now I turn to two other moral theories, those of Thomas Hobbes and David Hume.

Hobbes and Hume

Thomas Hobbes's moral theory was developed in a time of grave social and political crisis in the Britain of the seventeenth century. Its principal focus is on the need for protection and security of individuals from threats from other individuals. Hobbes is an ethical egoist who grounds ethical theory in a presumed state of nature where individuals are not organized into governments or societies and where they exist in isolation from and at the mercy of, one another. He reasons that such individuals will band together in society with appropriate systems of governance for mutual self-protection. And these individuals will devise moral principles, rules, and laws as part of this system. They will do so entirely for self-centered reasons. Hobbes combines psychological and moral egoism with a theory of social contract where morality consists in the necessary means for individual survival and protection. Without such a contract, he reasons, human life would be unbearably precarious and insufferable. His theory is entirely prudential in its character. Morality is the means to the protection of individuals from one another, and such protection is the supreme moral good.

Hobbes is right in thinking that morality has this kind of role, among others. But he is wrong, in my judgment, in *confining* it to such a role. He is wrong partly in thinking that there ever was such a thing as a historical social contract of the kind he describes. In contrast, Aristotle and Mill are right in thinking of humans as social beings with social instincts and predilections. As such, humans never have existed in isolation from one another. They have always been in societies of one sort or another, as all of the historical evidence seems to show. And with their social existence have gone moral principles, rules, and laws conducive to their collective wellbeing. Aristotle and Mill are right in seeing morality as having more than a protective role for (wrongly) assumed atomistic individuals and in denying out of hand Hobbes's psychological and moral egoism. Morality has the positive role of enhancing and expanding human life, not just that of avoiding a war of all against all.

Still, Hobbes's theory can be appreciated for the emphasis it places on individual wellbeing and for seeing each and every individual as entitled to moral regard for his or her protection and safety. This is its most salient merit. In this way he warns against a moral theory's putting so much emphasis on the need for altruistic other-regard or smooth and efficient social functioning as to forget the moral importance of the individual and the cultivation of appropriate self-regard. In this respect his theory is consistent with that of Aristotle and Mill. It should also be noted that Hobbes gives importance to rationally directed experience and desire in a manner similar to Aristotle and

Mill, although in his case it is solely the urgent desire for individual safety.[5]

David Hume's moral theory draws a sharp distinction between reason and questions of truth and falsity, on the one hand, and moral sentiment, taste, or feeling, on the other. Reason is needed to analyze all of the relevant aspects of a moral situation, and to do so in ways that are responsible for accuracy and truth in doing so. But once this is properly done, it is sentiment alone that tells us what the morally right thing to do is in that situation. In Hume's view, we are equipped by nature to discern the moral good by a kind of direct moral intuition or taste, just as we are equipped to recognize beauty when it is present, to detect a particular color or sound, or to know the difference in taste between a peach and a plum. Hume's view of morality is similar to that of evolutionary theorists today who argue that sociality and the sense of moral responsibility are a fundamental part of our evolved nature, a kind of strongly felt inbred instinct, preference, or predilection that enables us to exist as the social beings we are as a species. Without it, we simply could not function or survive.

Although sympathy is not itself a sentiment or passion, according to Hume, it is an outlook rendered inevitable by the principle of association he develops in other contexts. We naturally associate the aspirations and anxieties, delights and pains, needs and desires of others with those we ourselves experience. We do not just project our feelings onto the feelings of others; we feel them by association even as we feel our own. Sympathy makes possible the natural other-directedness that is for Hume, in contrast with Hobbes, so fundamental to morality.

In contrast with Mill, Hume does not view desire, and especially the desire for happiness, as the end of morality. Instead, it is a motivating cause moving us toward the moral ends discerned severally and situationally by the moral sentiments. And for Hume it not true that all human desires reduce to the desire for happiness. Their whole range is quite diverse. His moral theory is therefore not hedonistic. Hume also differs from Mill in viewing the moral demand of social *utility* as having nothing to do with reason as a morally commanding principle but as being recognized as such solely on the basis of feeling.

When we inquire into the theories of Aristotle, Mill, and Hobbes, we are struck much more with the interpenetrations of reason and desire, or reason and experience, than with their separations from one another. But Hume is insistent throughout on setting the two in as sharp a contrast as possible and on giving to the passions the sole authority in discriminating between moral goodness and moral evil. In the final analysis, Hume's views on morality have less the character of a rationally ordered and defended theory than of a descriptive account of the faculty of sentiment that enables humans naturally to discern the moral good in particular situations. The sense of moral goodness is not derived from reason or in any way dependent on reason. It is entirely autonomous, self-sufficient, and self-contained. This radical dualism of reason and feeling is, in my view, indefensible. Reason and feeling cannot be so cleanly separated from one another.

Hume makes the opposite mistake from Kant, to be taken up next in my discussion, but it is a mistake that also assumes too radically a separation of reason and feeling in the domain of morals. Whereas Hume gives the entire palm to feeling in this separation, Kant gives it to reason and even views feelings as impediments to the sense of moral duty rather than having a claim to be a contributing, even if subordinate, source of such duty. What we can safely say about Hume's intriguing reflections on morality is that he highlights the important role of feelings in moral thought, that he avoids the egoism and false monadic individualism of Hobbes, and that he views humans as social beings and their moral outlooks as determined by their nature as a species and not simply by virtue of some supposed artificial social contract rigged up for their mutual protection.

The most lasting and important thing about Hume's moral philosophy, in my judgment, is that it calls forceful attention to the role of feeling, showing it to be a critical and indispensable source of knowledge and awareness—in this case, knowledge and awareness of the moral good awaiting discernment and enactment in particular situations. His radical separation of feeling from reason, however, and his assigning to them two completely separate roles in the moral domain, are questionable steps that Aristotle, Mill, and Hobbes had the good sense to avoid. Where feeling leaves off and reason begins, and vice versa, is not nearly so easy to determine as Hume supposes. Discernments of moral goodness may not usually, if ever, have the form of strict logical deductions, but they also do not usually, contrary to Hume, have the form of sheer feeling unaccompanied and uninformed by prior or present rational reflection. Hume sees reason as the docile servant of the passions when it comes to moral judgments, that is, as having only an instrumental or enabling role for the realization of moral goods detected entirely by feeling. It is with this notion, so critical to Hume's ethical theory, that I must take issue.

Just as we can feel our way into a complicated argument by a hunch or vague impulse, so we can and should reason our way—at least in part—into a conclusion or policy relating to moral choice and action. Instead of one being the servant of the other, it makes more sense to me to conceive of feeling and reason as partners or coworkers for moral thinking and acting. In certain situations, for example, feelings of jealousy, revenge, or tribal loyalty may seem to indicate powerfully the right path of action, but is not at least a modicum of reason needed to question and appraise such feelings, not just instrumentally but inherently as well?

An additional problem with Hume's appeal to moral feelings relates to his assumption that such feelings are bestowed on all humans alike by nature. But when we ponder the relation of biology and acculturation, can we be so sure that feelings induced by the latter can be entirely distinguished from feelings induced or implanted by the former? Philip Clayton and Justin Heinzekehr emphasize "how greatly cultures vary and how deeply cultural systems affect the way a given society is organized and experienced."[6] This dictum surely applies to Hume and his own society in the eighteenth century, and it casts into doubt his assumption of the universality of moral feelings. At the very least, reason would be required to inquire into this matter, that is, to separate the "natural" moral feelings from the encultured ones, meaning that the so-called natural ones would not just shine out in their pristine purity, as Hume seems to suppose. Such criticisms of Hume's moral theory, along with the contrasting merits of theories different from his I have sought to bring into view, show that his moral theory exhibits partial truths at best—truths that can be applauded and incorporated into our understanding of moral goodness and moral life but not rightly claimed to be all-encompassing or final.[7]

Kant and Rawls

Immanuel Kant, writing in Hume's century, sets out to found morality on the basis of pure practical reason—a reason that mirrors or emulates the pure critical (or theoretical) reason of his *Critique of Pure Reason*. The latter was designed to bring into view the synthetic a priori foundations of the natural sciences of physics and mathematics, while the former seeks to elucidate the synthetic a priori ground or basis of morality. Kant wants to ground morality entirely on formal principles of a purely rational character and to insist that morality cannot be rightly based on any kind of sentiment or feeling. To do the latter to any extent would be to betray the absolute principles essential to moral duty and to safeguarding moral decision and action against any kind of compromise, exception, or rationalization that might result from empirical vagaries of preference, desire, or inclination. His moral theory is neither a blend of reason and feeling, nor is it based solely or finally on feeling. It is rationalistic through and through. Just as pure reason for Kant gives us access to the universal and necessary laws of physical nature, so it gives essential insight, when properly employed, into the universal and necessary laws of morality.

These laws, according to Kant, can all be derived from his three formulations of the categorical imperative, as set out in his *Ground-work of the Metaphysics of Morals*.[8] This imperative is "categorical" in the sense of not being hypothetical. It is not a mere means to some end such as utility, happiness, or the satisfaction of desire, but is an entirely rational, self-contained end in itself. The first formulation of the categorical imperative enjoins us to test any putative moral maxim against the standard of whether the moral agent can reasonably will it to be a universal law. It cannot be a universal law if it contains within itself seeds of its own contradiction or if it would, when put into practice, exhibit a kind of self-stultification. For example, lying is a departure from truth, and if lying were to become a universal law its contrast with truth would no longer be intelligible and its very meaning, as lying, would be destroyed. The obligation always to tell the truth, in contrast, allows lying to be a meaningful conception by its necessary distinction from or opposition to telling the truth. Truth is the positive principle; lying is its privation or negation. According to Kant, reason can figure this and similar relationships out entirely on its own with no need for appeals to experience.

The second formulation of the categorical imperative warns that we should never treat another rational being—that is, any other human being—merely as a means to some other end but should always regard another human being as an inviolable end in himself or herself. Human beings are in their nature autonomous, meaning that they are not subject to moral laws that do not stem from themselves. They are both legislators of such laws and the ones legislated by such laws as autonomous rational agents. For Kant, this means that each and every human being deserves unconditional moral respect as the final end or *raison d'etre* of the moral life. Morality exists for humans, not humans for morality. The third formulation of the categorical imperative urges us to strive ceaselessly for the kind of society in which the laws of morality can be recognized, affirmed, and practiced as universal and in which each and every member of that society is cherished as an inviolable end in and of himself or herself. Such a society, which Kant calls a *kingdom of ends*, would be for him a truly just society.

Kant's moral theory has a number of merits. One of these is its exhibition of the essential role of reason in determining moral principles. His moral theory is a useful counter to Hume's entire focus on feeling in this regard. Another merit is his insistence on the inviolable value and importance of each human life. A third merit is Kant's emphasis on the unconditional call of moral duty—a duty that should brook no compromise and allow for no softening of moral demand in the face of temptations to minimize, abridge, or evade one's moral responsibilities. A final merit is Kant's vision of a kingdom of ends, where all persons have equal and uncontested value and importance, where none are treated merely as means to the ends of others. Of these four merits, the most salient and distinctive, in my view, is the deontological or duty-oriented character of Kant's moral theory. He highlights the strenuous demands of moral duty and its radical resistance to considerations of compromise or mere prudence in a manner unmatched or unexcelled by other moral theorists.

These four merits having been acknowledged, however, there are weaknesses in Kant's moral theory that also need to be noted. These weaknesses show his theory to be only partially adequate or true as an account of the nature of morality and as needing the corrective balance of the other theories so far considered. One weakness of his theory, in my judgment, is its failure to recognize and take into account the tension between the first and second formulations of the categorical imperative. The first focuses on universality and necessity, while the second has to deal with particularity and contingency—a particularity and contingency that resist to some significant extent any kind of purely formal or rational analysis. Each human being is not only autonomous in Kant's sense of that term but also unique. And an adequate moral regard for each person must motivate us strive to take the uniqueness of persons as fully into consideration as possible.

If I am not to treat a person merely as a means to my ends, I must respect the distinctiveness of that person and seek as adequately as I can to discern and respect what is of most value and importance in that person's own life and vision of life. Similarly, a just society should allow for and even cherish as much contingency and difference among persons as is present and possible, just so long as these persons do not radically interfere with one another's freedom or wellbeing in living their lives. The tension between universality and contingency requires appeals to experience and not just reason. And it requires Aristotle's, Mill's, and Hume's kind of situational discernment, not just formal rules. The real differences among individual persons must be acknowledged if we are to treat them adequately as ends. These differences cannot be melted into some kind of universality or uniformity in the way that Kant's moral theory seems to require.

The emphasis on universality in Kant's theory accords in one way with the golden rule. I should do to and for others what I would hope they would do to and for me. Or, in another formulation, I should love others as I love myself. But if I am to do so, I must recognize that not everyone is like me. People have different needs, inclinations, desires, aspirations, capacities, ideals, and roles in social systems, and these differences must be taken into account if we are to treat one another morally and live peacefully and constructively together in society. Among the contingencies that need to be taken into account is the fact that I feel, and consider myself rightfully to feel, a greater sense of responsibility to my own children than I do to the children in a far off place such as Timbuktu or the island of Lesbos. My being my children's parent imposes this greater and more immediate sense of responsibility. This feeling should not be disregarded in the interest of some kind of formal universality that would require that I regard or treat all persons in exactly the same manner. Universality and contingency—rationality and empiricality—should be held in tension with one another. The fact of irreducible differences among persons and their particular circumstances requires that this be so.

Kant's emphasis on universality also tends to glide too easily over the experienced conflicts of goods that can sometimes if not often affect particular moral situations. The prohibition against lying, for example, might in some situation conflict with the need to protect a human life from injury or death. Or there might be situations where the dignity and autonomy of one person must be overridden in order for me to respect that of others affected by my action or inaction. In the second case, I am required morally to disobey in a particular situation the second formulation of the categorical imperative. Universality must be sacrificed for the sake of an urgent contingency. More generally, the particularity of persons and situations must be factored into moral decisions and actions.

It might be objected that this observation does not expose a weakness in Kant's moral deliberations. It only points to the problem of how to interpret its applications. But the point I am seeking to make is that problems of interpretation and application are integral features of moral thinking, deciding, and living and that Aristotle is right to insist on the development of the kind of moral character that can do more than follow a set of moral rules. A morally developed character is able to discern what needs to be done in particular moral situations and with regard to particular persons, with a kind of insight and wisdom that cannot be reduced to rules or formal imperatives. It is not just the devil that lies in the details. It is the angel as well.

Mill is also aware of this need with his emphasis on situational sympathy and awareness, but he can be faulted for thinking that all of ethics can be brought down to a universal desire for happiness. He may be abstractly right in thinking this to be so, but happiness is so vague and general a conception that it fails to give due cognizance to the many different ways in which individual human beings can and do interpret and seek for what amounts to happiness for them. Mill's *summum bonum* of general happiness, then, is in some ways as murky a guideline by itself for the detailed pursuits and avoidances of the moral life as is Kant's categorical imperative. The formal or purely rational approach and the empirical approach have their respective merits and demerits and must somehow be brought together in a more adequate and truly unitary moral theory. But in the case of all such theories, I contend that the best we can hope for is greater adequacy, not complete adequacy, a greater amount of truth, not all truth.

For example, Aristotle's admirable ethical theory correctly emphasizes the situational character of ethical decision and action, but it can be faulted for its familiar idea that virtues or excellences of character will always or universally have the form of an obvious mean between two extremes. What in one situation might look like either cowardice or foolhardiness (the putative extremes) for instance, might in another be rightly regarded as courage (the putative mean between the two extremes), which implies that the neat distinction between means and extremes will sometimes be fuzzy or ill-defined in the context of different circumstances. A conscientious objector, for example, can be seen by many as cowardly but may in fact be courageous in his or her willingness—while admittedly avoiding fighting in a particular war—to face the censure and opprobrium of self-styled patriots or fellow citizens. A soldier who passionately rushes a machine gun emplacement on the slim chance of saving his or her companions from death might by some or most people be seen as foolhardy when in fact the soldier could be rightly seen as acting courageously.

Means and extremes are matters of situational judgment, and analysis of the morality of an action in terms of means and extremes may not always work. The search for the mean between extremes might not in all or even most cases be the best approach to moral quandaries or assessments of moral character, as is suggested in the two examples above. What is a helpful general overview or guideline should not be converted into an absolute principle. Universality and fixity have a dialogical relation with contingency and variability, and this relation cannot be resolved in a purely logical or abstract manner. As Aristotle elsewhere rightly insists, contextual discernment and judgment are required. His analysis of the virtues as always pointing to a presumed particular mean between extremes is somewhat at odds with this insistence. All that I have said so far in the way of criticism of the six moral theories under consideration here carries the implication that the moral life is too intricate, complex, and variable to be brought within the confines of a single theory.

Rawls's social contract is meant to be hypothetical, not historical, in contrast with Hobbes, and it is not based on egoism. He also resists the conception of a rationalistic theory centered on Kant's notion of synthetic a prior truths. Rawls's theory is rationalistic, but not in Kant's "pure" or "transcendental" sense of that term. He also assents to the idea that all moral theories must rest, in the final analysis, on intuitions or sentiments to be exposed to critical judgment but not finally derived from logical reasoning or definition. Here he touches base with Hume and an aspect of Mill's thought, although he does not react favorably to Mill's utilitarianism. In stressing in his own manner the critical importance of reasoning in moral theory, however, he joins forces most obviously and firmly with Kant. He does so also by insisting on the deontological, not consequential, character of his justice theory.

Rawls readily admits that his is not a comprehensive moral theory but only a theory of social justice as an essential part of such a theory, and he also acknowledges that his elaborately worked out theory is at best a significant approximation to an adequate theory of justice. It can, he thinks, move us closer to the philosophical ideal of convincingness, adequacy, and completeness even though it does not finally achieve it. He frankly states that all moral theories, including his own, "are presumably mistaken in places."[9] With these admissions he indicates his agreement with the principal thesis of the present chapter and, more generally, with the thesis of this book as a whole.

The ideal of *fairness* lies at the heart of Rawls's theory of justice and is, I think, his most important contribution to moral theory. He characterizes and delineates this ideal in terms of two basic principles of justice. The first principle is that each person in a just society is entitled to as full an amount of liberty as is compatible with the liberty of others in that society. The second one is that the social and economic resources of a just society are arranged in such a manner that they are to everyone's advantage and open as opportunities to all. Equal liberty and equal opportunity are mandatory in a just society, a society in which fairness prevails. Rawls argues that these two principles are to be viewed in serial order, with the initial and most foundational importance accorded to the first one of them.

Rawls adds the additional qualification that the inevitable social and economic inequalities of a just society must be arranged so that they offer the greatest possible benefit to the least advantaged in the society. This qualification is a striking part of his moral theory that he insists follows from its focus on universal fairness. Implicit in these ideas is Kant's insistence on the inviolable freedom of each human being, his profound respect for the inalienable dignity of each person as an end, and his insistence on the unconditional responsibility of each person to be centrally concerned for the wellbeing of all other persons.

Now the problem is how to envision and establish such a society, and here is where Rawls's version of the social contract comes in. He sets up the hypothesis of an original position where there is a veil of ignorance. The veil hides from each person involved in the agreed upon contract such things as what will turn out to be his or her own place or position in the just society, the extent to which he or she will benefit from the distribution of the society's assets, his or her particular degree of intelligence, ability, and strength, or even other persons' conceptions of the moral good. The veil eliminates any ability to calculate or ensure one's own particular advantage or benefit in envisaging the character of a just society and is thus in this sense radically non-egoistic at the outset. The focus is not on individuals or the contingencies of individual differences. It is on the idea of what would constitute a just society as a whole, as most generally, universally, and unrestrictedly defined by the two principles of justice and their basis in the idea of fairness for all. Since one does not know what one's fate will be in such a society, one would endorse that conception of society that will work best for all with regard to justice. In other words, rational persons would want a society in which there is the best chance for everyone to benefit as fully as possible, since they do not know what their particular place in the society will be. The factual differences among particular individuals and particular situations are in this way eliminated from consideration in the original position with its veil of ignorance, and reason is allowed to deduce from the two principles alone what a just society would look like. In agreeing to such a society, each would legislate fairly for all.

The original position and its veil of ignorance substitute for Kant's categorical imperative with its basis in supposedly synthetic a priori principles and does not require the elaborately detailed, often contentious, and in many ways cumbersome and idiosyncratic apparatus of Kant's epistemological commitments. Rawls warmly acknowledges his debt to the inspiration of Kant's moral thought, but his theory of justice is a simplified and more readily accessible—and yet to all appearances equally rational—approach to Kant's principal moral conceptions. It is an excellent example of how a later moral theory can be built on and can advance in salient respects beyond an earlier one.

But there is a sense in which Rawls's theory is too broad and too rationalistic in its character. It tends to sweep relevant contingent differences of persons and circumstances under the rug of vague abstractions or fanciful conjectures. These differences would have to be given serious attention in any actual just society. What is fair in one case might turn out not to be fair in another. People's needs, emotions, preferences, beliefs, dependencies, and relationships can change radically over time. Fair treatment of one individual or group might need to be compromised or sacrificed—at least for a time—in order to attain or maintain fairness for another. Situations change, and sometimes in unpredictable ways. Moreover, despite the fact that Rawls rejects utilitarian consequentialism in favor of a deontological veil of ignorance, it could be argued that his theory of justice is built finally on the shared hope of the best consequences for all concerned. And there is a kind of unargued and simply assumed intuitionism, a mostly unexamined and deep-lying experiential source of value commitments, lurking in his two principles of justice. The tension between what can be rationally deduced and what has to be experienced, assumed, or posited is not entirely explicated or resolved.

Every just society is a work in progress, not a finished product. And the same is true of every moral theory, no matter how ingenious, compelling, or refined it may be. Rawls's theory certainly has these latter qualities in admirable degree. But as I noted earlier, it is to Rawls's credit that he does not hesitate to acknowledge the limitations of his own theory even as he proceeds to borrow from, focus critical attention on, and endeavor to advance beyond the earlier moral theories he brings into consideration. He even goes so far as to assert that no moral theory will ever attain the goal of complete or final truth about moral value or the prospects and demands of the moral life. This is a probabilistic prediction, not an absolute truth, but the evidence for it is persuasive when we consider all that a moral theory needs sufficiently and convincingly to describe, include, interpret, organize, propose, and explain. At the same time, we need to remind ourselves that every thoughtful, carefully devised moral theory has something, if not much, to teach us. Partial truths are real truths and should not be rejected on account of their partiality.

Obligations to Nature and All the Creatures of Nature

A crucial respect in which all of the moral theories thus far considered in this chapter are deficient is their neglect of moral obligations to nature and to all the creatures of nature. Rawls notes this missing feature in his own theory.[10] In our time of greatly augmented ecological awareness and ecological crisis, the idea of justice needs to be extended beyond human beings to the earth as a whole and to all of its creaturely inhabitants. It needs to give careful and concerted attention to the moral relations and obligations of humans to myriad other life forms, to their environments, and to the earth as a whole. Perhaps a kind of veil of ignorance could be devised where we humans are required to consider having to take on the possible status of one of these nonhuman creatures and its critical dependence on the resources of its natural environment. Would we not then want to opt for a planetary ethic and not just a human-centered one? Can we any longer continue to think of our human society as the only kind of society worth pondering morally and fail in that way to acknowledge and take seriously into account the wide earthly society of which we are a necessary part? I think that the answer to the first question must be affirmative and to the second one negative, as we continue to search for more adequate and inclusive moral theories than the ones we have focused on here.

Considerations of human justice and ecological justice are going to become more intimately entwined as the environmental crisis—with such daunting aspects as global climate changes; endangerments of species; pollution of land, air, and water; hazards to and restrictions on vitally needed water and food supplies; and the prospect of widespread migrations, human and animal alike—continues to grow more acute and increasingly to threaten in palpable ways the livelihood and wellbeing of large portions of earth's creatures. This extensive area of moral regard and responsibility can no longer be neglected. As ecological writer Terry Tempest Williams reminds us, "We are not the only species that lives and dreams on the planet. There is something enduring that circulates in the heart of nature that deserves our respect and attention."[11] By "respect and attention" she means more than human use or aesthetic appreciation. She certainly means to include moral response and responsibility as well. Thus, moral theories of the capacious, whole-earth regarding character of environmental ethicist J. Baird Callicott's aptly titled book *Thinking Like a Planet* are desperately needed.[12] Much work lies ahead for ongoing moral theorizing and moral vision.

The previous expressions of truth in this domain, including the six moral theories I have discussed here, are resourceful, thought-provoking milestones. Each can be fruitfully drawn upon for addressing particular circumstances. But none of them is entirely adequate as it stands. Each leaves important issues unaddressed or unresolved. Moreover, the tensions and differences among them are in many ways as informative as are their overlaps and similarities. The elements of insight and truth in each theory are important and not to be lost sight of, even though they are partial. No matter how resounding the ring of truth with which one or more of them may strike us at first, each theory must finally be recognized to be in some important ways incomplete and unsatisfying. The moral theorizing and reflection of the past require the unending critical correction, enrichment, and expansion of the future. New ways of thinking may be demanded that are presently unimagined. Partiality of understanding is not something to be regretted or deplored. It is a welcome invitation to more adequate comprehension and truth.

Chapter 4

ECONOMICS AND ECOLOGY

We started treating the atmosphere as our waste dump when we
began using coal on a commercial scale in the late 1700s and
engaged in similarly reckless ecological practices well before that.

Moreover, humans have behaved in this short-sighted way
not only under capitalistic systems, but under systems that called
themselves socialist as well (whether they were or not remains
a subject of debate). Indeed, the roots of the climate crisis date
back to core civilizational myths on which post-Enlightenment
Western culture is founded—myths about humanity's duty to
dominate a natural world that is believed to be at once limitless
and entirely controllable.

—Naomi Kline[1]

In this chapter I discuss partial truths associated with current economic assumptions, policies, and practices (some more partial or
lacking in truth than others) and highlight their critical relations
to glaring ecological problems of our time. Most basically, I contend
that economic issues and ecological ones are inseparable and that
this inseparability needs to be kept constantly in mind if we hope
to avoid ecological disaster with its dire social consequences. In this
arena, partial truths, when converted into absolute ones, can be
calamitous. Columnist, editor, and book author Naomi Kline, in this
chapter's epigraph, speaks to the same effect when she points out that
the roots of our present economic crisis transcend the distinctions
between capitalism and socialism and reach back into the early days
of the Industrial Revolution when we began extracting coal to fuel
the machines, appliances, and industries of that revolution. But as she

also observes, those roots go back much further, into the founding myth or unquestioned conviction that humankind is entitled and even obligated to dominate the earth—an earth whose resources were long thought to be limitless and to exist primarily for human exploitation and control. I start the discussion of this chapter by pointing out and examining the partial truth in this founding myth.

Earth as Warehouse of Resources for Human Use

As stated above, there are three aspects to the founding myth I now bring under discussion, namely, that humans are entitled and even obligated to dominate the earth, that the earth's resources are limitless, and that these resources exist primarily for human exploitation and control. There is some truth in each of these assertions, but a considerable amount of falsity as well. Each statement is in need of considerable qualification and restatement. Each is at best a partial truth. Yet each statement has seeped deeply into the consciousness or subconsciousness of people in the Western world and long lain there without question or qualification.

We can find evidence of this last claim in many aspects of Western culture, but one illuminating piece of evidence is a book written in the seventeenth century that had considerable influence on the thought, attitudes, practices, and institutions of the Western world in the early modern era and that has continued to do so to the present—often more subliminally than consciously. The book to which I refer is the philosopher John Locke's *Second Treatise of Government.* And I have in mind particularly the fifth chapter of that treatise that is entitled "On Property."

This chapter of Locke's book is a succinct statement of his economic philosophy, dealing with the nature of property, the role of money, and the importance of trade. But behind the economic philosophy is a view of humans and of their relations to their natural environments that brings vividly into focus the founding myth alluded to by Naomi Kline. Locke has no doubt that humans are entitled and obligated to dominate and control the resources of the earth. He states that "God, who has given the world to men in common, has also given them reason to make use of it to the best advantage of life and convenience. The earth and all that is therein is given to men for the support and comfort of their being."[2] He insists that it is human appropriation and use of the earth's resources that gives them value. It is only when humans claim some aspect of the earth as property by devoting their labor to putting it to use in some fit manner that a particular part of the earth's resources comes to possess value.

Apart from such human exploitation and use, the earth is "waste," and "the benefit of it" amounts "to little more than nothing."[3] "It is [human] labor," Locke contends, "which puts the greatest part of the value upon land, without which it would scarcely be worth anything. . . ."[4] The earth lies ready by God-given right, then, for human plowing, fishing, hunting, mining, smelting, manufacturing, collecting, and the like, just so long as humans put it to use by their labor. Land or some other kind of earthly resource has little or no value in its own right. It has value only when humans make use of it in order to satisfy their own needs and desires. Its value, in other words, is instrumental, not intrinsic. The earth and all that is in it or on it, such as arable land, minerals, or animals is little more than a pliant means to human wellbeing.

As part of his analysis of the concept of property, Locke argues that no one is entitled to take from the earth's resources more than he or she can make good use of. What is beyond the possibility of appropriate personal use should be shared with others. This principle applies especially to resources that will spoil if not put promptly to proper use, such as agricultural products. Money evolved, Locke reasons, because it does not spoil and is useful for compensating one who grows or acquires more perishable goods than he or she can use and seeks to share them with others before they rot and are no longer of use. But at the same time the property owner naturally wants to be compensated for the labor he or she has put into the land in order to produce a crop. Trade for one's excess productions warrants monetary reward for what is traded and thus preserves the principle of compensation for products of the property that is a person's rightful possession because that person's labor has been devoted to its development and maintenance.

Locke also discusses common or "unenclosed" property that is owned by a group of others, say, in a village or town. A single individual should not be allowed, he argues, to use this property in ways that infringe on the rights of others to its use. It is there to be shared, enjoyed, and used by all who have title to it. They have a right to it in common by virtue of their joint development and maintenance of it.

Moreover, Locke assumes that the resources of the earth are limitless. He exclaims that "there is land enough in the world to suffice double the inhabitants. . . ."[5] He was living in a time when the lands of the Americas had recently been discovered and when the population of those lands was relatively sparse. He frequently makes reference in this chapter to that fact, a fact that made the extent of the earth seem to him boundless. The population of Europe, apart from Russia and the Ottoman Empire was in Locke's time less than eighty million. And the population of the world then was something on the order of less than six-hundred million.

Little did Locke dream that it would be more than seven *billion* in the world of today and that it continues to grow at an accelerating pace—a pace of human population growth that is beginning seriously to strain the carrying capacity of the earth and that is endangering large numbers of its species. Locke also had no understanding of the vast amount of pollution that would be introduced into air, land, and water by the industrial revolution that originated in the century following his own and that has grown apace to our own time. Nor did he know anything about anthropogenic global climate change. And he did not have the benefit of the theory of evolution or of the ecological science that has become prominent and deeply significant in recent times.

Finally, Locke assumes that the natural world is entirely amenable to human exploitation and control. He seems to have had little sense of the recalcitrance or kickback capacity of nature in its relations to human beings. In our own time we are all too aware of ways in which we are crucially dependent on aspects of nature of which we are integral parts. Nature is not mere raw material for our use and control. It has integrity, power, and unpredictability that far exceed our efforts to harness it and bring it under our complete control. We humans are interdependent parts of a massive ecological system, and we are neither entitled to dominate it nor are we capable of bringing it to heel to suit only our own presumptuous and myopic human needs, desires, and purposes.

What is most notable in Locke's vision of humans and their relations to the earth is his seeming utter obliviousness to the intrinsic value and sacredness of the earth and its creatures, a value and sacredness that are independent of humans and would continue to exist were humans to be eradicated from the face of the earth. There is no sign of anything like an ecological ethic or a planetary ethic in Locke's outlook. The resources of the earth are simply there to be owned, exploited, developed, and traded by human beings. That is the end of the matter. In this attitude lie the seeds of our present ecological crisis and its accompanying human arrogance and indifference toward the wellbeing of the earth and its nonhuman creatures.

Locke's analysis also needs to be questioned and qualified when individuals acquire such abundant amounts of property, whether through inheritance, luck, capital growth, or trade, that they possess much more property, wealth, or capital than they can personally make just use of and yet are unwilling to share that wealth, whether through taxes or by other means, with others who are far less wealthy and in great need. And his analysis should be qualified in light of the fact that personal property is often subjected to development and maintenance by cheaply exploited labor of persons far less fortunate than the property's owner or co-investors in that property. A consequence of these factors can be radical and unnecessary disparity between the economic status of the extremely rich and the desperately poor, or even between the rich and a middle class whose economic status may be in steady decline.

So Locke's analysis of property constitutes a partial truth if viewed from the standpoint of justice, and it becomes even more partial when we factor in the ecological consequences of clearing land for monocultural farming; indiscriminately employing weed-killing chemicals and fertilizers; rearing large numbers of animals with their large-scale pollutants and their drains on the supply of grains that could be more efficiently used for human food than can the meats derived from their slaughter; mining and its rampant pollutions, dangers to miners, and mountain top destructions; oil and gas drilling and refining; profuse factory emissions and their effects on air, land, and water; destructions of forests and animal habitats by clear cutting without replanting; the resulting health and quality of life problems for humans and animals; and the like. As I indicated earlier, economics and ecology are inseparable, Locke and the founding myth to the contrary.

Despite the radical deficiencies of the founding myth of Western culture as Locke articulates it, there are still elements of truth in his assumptions and claims. We need to take these important elements of truth into account. In the first place, human beings, like all of the earth's species, are entitled to draw on the resources of their environments for the sake of their livelihood. In the second place, these resources obviously become of greater use to humans, even if not always to nature as a whole, to the extent that they are subjected to human labor and property entitlements and are brought within the orbit of the tools, techniques, discoveries, and theories of human beings.

In the third place, human population growth is not inexorable. It need not exceed the capacity of the earth to sustain it. It can be brought under control and kept in balance with the populations of the earth's other creatures by the right kind of planning and care. The resources of the earth are not limitless, but they are sufficient to sustain a viable human population in its relations to the earth and its nonhuman forms of life. In the fourth place, we can appropriate Locke's point about respect for the commons by extending this idea to include the land, air, and water that are common not only to us humans but to all the creatures of the earth. We should recognize that no human enterprise is entitled to inflict wanton waste or ruination on any aspect of the earth seen as the common "property" of us all, humans and nonhumans alike. This is true no matter what profit to some persons or corporations might be gained by such a practice.

In other words, we humans have every right, as do all of the earth's forms of life, to be here and to make appropriate use of the earth's resources. We need not be a blight on the face of the earth. To this extent, Locke is correct in his observations. He is onto some significant truths about our relations to the earth, but they are too unqualified and one-sided. The absence of qualification and the one-sidedness have continued to plague our thinking and acting as humans to this day. We humans do have skills and abilities that make us radically—although not totally—different from the millions of other life species on earth. These remarkable and inimitable skills and abilities, however, make inescapably evident our grave responsibilities to the earth and its life forms as a whole.

If we are not extremely knowledgeable, conscientious, and careful, we can wreak havoc on the earth, as our present looming ecological crisis makes abundantly evident. Locke seems to be cognizant solely of benefits and privileges the earth makes available to our species, as does, unfortunately, the deeply entrenched founding myth of the West as a whole. There are truths to be recognized or ferreted out from this myth. But there are aspects of dangerously seductive falsehood and delusion as well.

This is not to claim that every aspect of the current warnings of present and imminent ecological crisis and cries for appropriate changes in economic assumption and outlook is absolutely true either. The future may prove at least some of them wrong for factors or reasons we cannot know or be aware of today. Technological solutions as yet undreamt of might help to mitigate presently conceived dangers. But we need to weigh the available evidence and the current probabilities with great care. Given what is at stake, it is better to proceed with caution and with prompt and thoroughgoing changes of policy, procedure, and practice than to deeply regret that we failed to do so after it has become too late. Partial truths with significant levels of probability in the areas of our ecological dependencies and responsibilities can rightly and urgently demand bold new ways of imagining, thinking, and acting.

Now that we have looked at the partial truths in John Locke's economic outlook, as that is representative of a long assumed myth or set of generally unanalyzed assumptions about human beings, their economical beliefs and practices, and their relations to the rest of nature in Western thought, we can turn our attention to some other partial truths concerning economic ideas and their relations to ecological issues. Here are the five partial truths I shall discuss, in the order of their presentation. The first is the idea that free economic markets automatically and maximally benefit everyone. The second is the conviction that healthy economic systems always exhibit steady economic growth. The third is the notion that globalization is beneficial to everyone. The fourth is the view that government deficits are bad and should be avoided to the greatest possible extent. And the fifth is the belief that capitalism is always good and socialism is bad, and that any tendency or drift toward the latter should be avoided at all costs.

Each of these notions is at best a partial truth, as I now intend to show. And each is dangerously misleading and one-sided if assumed to be an absolute truth. In making these observations, I speak as a concerned citizen. I am not an expert on economic or ecological subjects. But as a philosopher I do feel responsible for incorporating reflections on these two subjects into my discussion of partial truths in view of the subjects' profound bearings on life in today's world. These five topics and their bearings illustrate in the realms of economics and ecology how distorting and damaging partial truths can be when their partiality is unacknowledged or unrecognized.

Free Markets Automatically and Maximally Benefit Everyone

The concept of the free market is that the forces of supply and demand are most likely to reach an optimal state where both sellers and buyers benefit to the greatest possible extent when economic transactions and economic systems are as little regulated, restricted, monitored, or controlled as possible by governments or any other agencies. The ideal economics, then, is a free market economics. And a basic principle underlying it is the importance of ensuring and maintaining unrestricted capitalistic competition. Buyers will benefit from the competition among sellers by being able to purchase goods at lower prices, and sellers who compete with one another will benefit when a particular seller is able to attract buyers with lower prices for that seller's goods. A similar benefit to particular sellers will result when sellers compete among one another for the quality of their goods, the best or perceived best quality at the lowest price attracting the greatest number of buyers. There is truth in the concept or ideal of the free market, but it is only a partial truth because it leaves out of account other important factors to be considered here.

One factor is the development of monopolies in particular economic sectors. One company may be so successful in its competitions with other companies that it either causes them to close down or becomes able over time to take them over. The result is that there is no longer the competition that would keep prices under control. Government anti-trust laws may be needed to avoid the development of monopolies. Another factor neglected in the free market scenario is collusion among companies to fix prices at a level maximally beneficial to all of the companies involved. Government intervention may be needed to avoid collusion, and especially collusion that occurs in secret, away from the public eye. In the absence of any kind of government oversight, companies may also condone serious deficiencies in worker health and safety, since not having to expend resources to attend to and ameliorate these conditions would help to keep at an attractive low level the company's prices for the consumer and corresponding greater consumer demand and profit for the company.

Workers could be deprived of a fair wage that takes into account the true value of their productivity when there is no government protection for labor unions. We should also note that in a completely free market, devoid of any kind of governmental regulation, there would be no such thing as laws pertaining to patents or copyrights—a serious disservice to inventors, writers, composers, performers, and the like. Moreover, in a market lacking any kind of government intervention into the market place, there would be no taxes on businesses beyond normal property taxes. And this would be in spite of deleterious effects a business might have on humans and the natural environment: effects such as degradations of the environmental commons and bad effects on the health of those in the vicinity of or perhaps even at considerable distance away from the business. With no government regulation or appropriate taxation, power plants, oil refineries, mines, factory farms, commercial fishing, and the like can inflict grave harm on the environment without recompense or reckoning for damage done to people, animals, rivers, seas, atmosphere, land, and other aspects of the natural world. There would be no government monitoring and regulation of polluting effects of business enterprises or requirements to clean up environmentally damaging effects of their operations at their own expense.

We also need to be open to the possibility that particular social and economic functions may be more fairly, efficiently, and wisely run and money spent, in at least some cases, by local, regional, or federal government programs than by private enterprises. Possible examples would include education, job training, prisons, mail delivery, power production, local transportation, disaster relief, legal aid, and health care—where the bottom line is people and their entitlements to government services rather than unrestricted profits. Assistance to the poor is another area of concern where government ought to have a role. Adequate taxes would need to be levied in support of appropriate government supervision and operation in these areas. A reasonably just progressive tax system would be of great benefit in these respects, enabling the prosperous to contribute relatively more to the wellbeing of the society as a whole than the less prosperous are required to do—a society, it should be well noted, that benefits and supports the former group in countless but often unacknowledged ways.

A radically free market can be a radically *irresponsible* market without appropriate government sanctions, protections, taxes, and laws. But it is also true that government policies and regulations can become too bureaucratic, complex, and burdensome and that they may need to be reconsidered, simplified, made more transparent, or revised whenever this problem presents itself. There is essential truth in the idea of the free market, with its beneficial workings of relatively unrestricted supply and demand. But this truth is partial and limited, as is shown by important factors such as those I have mentioned that need to be borne in mind and effectively addressed when necessary. Neither a completely unregulated market nor an overly regulated one is desirable. The truth lies in between these extremes. But this in-between region can vary over time or with changing circumstances. Market relationships are moving targets, not matters to be relentlessly and futilely fixed by obstinate ideological commitments on either side.

Healthy Economic Systems Always Exhibit Steady Growth

There are a number of problems with the blanket assertion that healthy economic systems always exhibit steady growth that show the assertion, in unqualified form, to be only a partial truth that needs to be brought into balance with other considerations. This need relates to the conventional way of measuring economic growth. The measurement is usually performed by ascertaining a country's gross domestic product or GDP, the value of the goods and services produced over a period of time (usually annually) by a given country. If GDP increases notably over time, the country in question is assumed to be exhibiting both essential and healthy growth and development. Absence of such growth is seen as indication that a country is in economic trouble. This assumption raises problems that need to be brought into view.

One such problem is that the GDP measures the *quantity* of economic transactions in a country but is no adequate measure of the overall *quality* of life in the country. The economic values may be so unequally distributed, for example—primarily benefiting the few rich rather than the many less rich or struggling poor—that a nation with a high rate of GDP growth may suffer from radical distributive injustice and be far from prosperous and flourishing in this crucial respect.

Another important problem with the GDP as an adequate measure of a country's wellbeing is that the economic growth of one country may be procured at the expense of severe economic decline in another country, as when a valuable resource is extorted from one country, resulting in that country's decreasing GDP but in considerable benefit to the extorting country's GDP. This problem is particularly glaring when the resource is non-replaceable, such as coal, oil, natural gas, diamonds, or gold. Here distributive justice of countries and their peoples in relation to one another is the point at issue, not just distributive justice within a given country—a factor not measured by a single country's GDP gauged in isolation from its effects on the GDPs of other countries.

Still another factor left out of account by GDP measurement alone is the amount of environmental endangerment and degradation produced by the economic enterprises of a country either within its own borders or in another country from which it obtains resources. Such destructive environmental consequences can include deforestation, mountain top removal, unattended mine tailings, methane and carbon dioxide pollution, bad grazing practices, destruction of arable land, flooding, endangerment of species, and depleting oceans and other waters of sea life and filling these waters with trash, industrial waste, or the contamination of industrial accidents. Overlooking such ecological consequences and failing to address them with both privately and publically funded strategies of prevention, melioration, or control can make a GDP measurement look good in the short run even though it may turn out to be extremely deleterious to a country or to the world in the longer run.

The deleterious consequences are or ought to be obvious and in need of timely remedy, but focusing on the GDP alone can distract attention from them in ways that harm the commons of particular countries or of the world as a whole while benefiting, at least for a time, the businesses, companies, and industries—whether private or public—that are allowed to ignore and leave out of account ecological outcomes of their policies and practices. These ecological outcomes will also turn out to bear closely on economic ones in the longer run, if not in the near future. Economics and ecology are close cousins, as we are at last beginning to recognize today. The same is true of economics and social justice. We need to consider the prices of unlimited and unregulated growth not only in economic but also in broader human and ecological terms.

We can legitimately question the idea that regular economic growth, however it may be measured or ascertained, is itself always or in all circumstances a desirable outcome. The economist Herman Daly argues that we should be more concerned in our time to bring about *sustainable* or *steady-state* rather than continuously *growing* economies. His endorsement of this position can help to bring to light the lack of complete truth in the alleged desirability of unrestricted economic growth as measured by a given country's GDP. The main conclusion of Daly's important book *Beyond Growth* turns on four key terms: *sustainability*, *equity*, *sufficiency*, and *efficiency*. He argues that economic growth "has become unsustainable. It has never been equitable in that some live far above sufficiency, while others live far below. And no system that uses resources at a rate that destroys natural life-support systems without meeting the basic needs of all can possibly be considered efficient."[6]

Another way in which Daly states this conclusion is reminiscent of Locke's view of the earth as a warehouse of resources to be claimed without reserve as rightful property for human use. Daly observes that the "vision of the earth as an alchemist's centrally planned terrarium, with nothing wild or spontaneous but everything base transformed into gold, into its highest instrumental value for humans, is a sure recipe for disaster."[7] In other words, we are creatures of earth among innumerable other creatures of earth. Nature does not exist merely to serve our desires and needs. It certainly is not subservient to insatiable greed and consumerist passion on the part of human beings. To think of nature in this way or to treat it in this way—as though we contain or are coterminous with nature rather than it containing and sustaining us—is to open the way to catastrophe and ruin not only for us humans but for other biological species and the natural environments on which we as well as they critically rely.

In contrast with this outmoded and untenable view, Daly proposes that we picture the human economy as a relatively small subsystem contained within the earth's encompassing ecosystem, which is a precise *reversal* of Locke's outlook. Locke and far too many people today seem to think of the human economy as somehow floating in empty space rather than being anchored in the vast ecosystem on which it, like everything else on earth, necessarily depends.[8] When we keep the more accurate and realistic picture in mind, we have to realize that the human population cannot be allowed and will not be able to swell at the present exponential rate forever, that the earth's resources are finite and not unbounded, that unrestrained technological and industrial despoliations of the earth must cease, and that respect for the integrity and viability of the ecosystem and all of its interdependent creatures—including us humans—is absolutely essential if we humans are to maintain an appropriate but limited place within it.

We are not lords of the earth and should not allow a shortsighted delusion of endless economic growth to beguile us into thinking that we can be so or can become so. And we should not tolerate the growing gap between rich and poor being accepted as the necessary consequence of unbridled capitalistic development. Economic justice has to be an essential factor in viable economic processes, and appropriate government regulation, restraint, and taxation policies are important ways of effecting and ensuring just distribution of wealth and due respect for the entitlement of all humans to basic health, prosperity, and wellbeing. Unbridled economic growth is not the be-all and end-all of just and equitable economic systems. For Daly, and I cannot help but agree, sustainability trumps mere growth. This is not to reject out of hand a role for certain kinds of growth as an aspect of healthy economics, but it is to object to the notion that everything else in economic systems or programs should be subordinated to growth or that steady, unrestricted growth should be regarded as the sole or principal determinant of prosperity and the quality of economic life.

Daly points to the heavy irony of continuing to defend a supposed invisible hand of free and unregulated market forces while failing to acknowledge that unrestricted economic growth threatens the very natural environment on which all macroeconomics depends. He argues that we are much more capable of limiting the rates of economic growth than we are of managing the entire ecosystem. Therefore, he writes, "Our limited managerial capacities should be devoted to institutionalizing an economic Plimsoll line that limits the macroeconomy to a scale such that the invisible hand can function in both domains to the maximum extent."[9] Otherwise, we will have to resort in the not too distant future to an unimaginable scale and amount of central planning required to avoid ecological disaster. Lack of appropriate *economic* management now will lead inevitably to the necessity of enormous degrees of desperate attempts at across-the-board *ecological* management later on.

Daly does not deny, nor do I, the importance of allowing market forces to work in appropriate ways. Not everything is in need of detailed government management or control, and too much of it—especially when adamantly fixed in place and not responsive to changing situations and different contexts—might well turn out to be as harmful and ill-advised as not enough management. But Daly does take issue with the notion that there should be no restriction of market forces and no need to balance them with other economic factors or critical considerations such as distributive justice and ecological responsibility. The claimed necessity or desirability of the free market alone in the economic arena conveys at best a partial truth, one in need of considerable qualification, balance, and correction. The significant truth in it is lost if it is regarded as an absolute principle from which all aspects of sound economic practice, to say nothing of ethically praiseworthy and vitally necessary social and ecological practices, will automatically flow.

An assumption closely related to the idea that the free market will work to ensure both economic and ecological wellbeing is the idea that as wealth grows apace, developments of efficient technologies can ensure that no lasting damage is done to the earth and its nonhuman creatures. In this optimistic vision, the whole earth can be brought under shrewd technological management and control even as market economics continues its steady and largely unimpeded growth. These two factors, it is held, will contribute to an ongoing stable relation between human economic progress and the sustainability of the earth as a whole. There is truth in the conviction that technologies can brought into play to allay some of the devastations of earth's ecological systems. Alternative sources of energy such as photovoltaic cells, wind-driven turbines, and the pressing need for improved batteries for effective storage of the energy produced by the first two technologies are important examples of this fact. The first two technologies are already beginning to play this role in various places as they substitute for the harmful effects on earth, sea, and the atmosphere of fossil fuel production and use.

But steady economic growth and technological applications and innovations alone are not at all likely to save the earth from ecological devastation. Much more fundamental to this urgent task is the *awakening of a moral sense* willing to make far-reaching changes in the ways humans view, act, and relate to the natural order. Included in this moral sense is frank acknowledgment that the ideal of the free market and the promise of technology contain only partial truths that need correction by appropriate basic regulations of economic policies and practices, by subjecting to profound question commitment to continuing economic growth, and most fundamentally by thoroughgoing alteration of attitudes that persist in assuming the human right of unbridled dominance over the earth and heedless exploitation of its resources. These changes would include reverting to much more modest estimates of the promise of technology—founded to a significant extent on recognition of the rampant damages unrestrained human technology has already inflicted and is continuing to inflict on the planet. The changes would also require concerted attention to the plights of humans and nonhumans whose livelihoods and futures are most immediately and direly threatened by these damages.

In his book *Technology and the Contested Meanings of Sustainability*, Australian scientist and philosopher Aidan Davison makes a compelling case for this kind of deeply critical outlook on the prospects for the earth and its creatures of the combination of the free market ideal of continuing growth and development, on the one hand, and the supposed adequately mitigating environmental effects of appropriate old and new technologies, on the other. He argues that continued growth is not compatible with genuine sustainability and that it cannot be made so merely by applications or advances of technology. To think that it can, he reasons, is to co-opt the concept of sustainability and rid it of meaning. It is to convert talk about sustainability into empty rhetoric that covertly if not overtly serves the interests of elites from the global North and South who benefit from unrestrained growth and development at the cost of non-elites, especially impoverished non-elites of the global South, and that works to the accelerating detriment of the natural environment.

Davison lays heavy stress on the need for the awakening of a radically new moral sense of obligation to the natural environment and its creatures that I referred to above. He warns that the specific shape and content of this moral sense is not easy to come by, noting that "sustainability is an essentially contested domain of meaning and practice. Moral concern with the ideal of sustainability demands that we pose difficult questions for ourselves, individually and communally, questions whose answers remain open to legitimate contestation and reformulation."[10] He also insists that we dare not simply take for granted answers to these questions proposed or presumed by global cultural and technocratic elites, thus ignoring the needs, experiences, situations, and wisdom of local non-elites.

The urgent and unavoidable need for this new moral concern casts into clear light the limited truth of the claim for ongoing economic growth and appropriate uses of technology as sufficient guardians of ecological sustainability and global distributive justice. Growth and technology may be useful and needed at particular places and times. But they are far from being a universal panacea for all the troubles of an ecologically endangered world and one in desperate need of economic policies and practices that can work effectively toward an equitable and sustainable distribution of its goods and services.

Globalization is Beneficial to Everyone

A careful weighing in the balance of the pros and cons of the current phenomenon of increasing globalization is needed, both in the long run and in the short run. We should not respond to the fast-growing globalization of cultures in our time with naïve complacency, unthinking optimism, or resigned pessimism. Globalization poses serious problems in the midst of its promise of bringing nations, peoples, and cultures into closer contact, providing economic opportunities such as industries and jobs not available to some of them earlier, and breaking down barriers of suspicion and hostility stemming from the older isolation of cultures from one another and the threatening strangeness of the peoples of one culture as viewed from the limited, uninformed perspective of another.

A serious problem with the ease of transport, communication, travel, and trade that globalization makes possible is the loss of jobs in one country because of the cheaper wages and less regulated working conditions in another. This process contributes substantially to the weakening of labor unions in the job-losing country and the resulting decline of workers' employment opportunities, salaries, and benefits. A further problem is the loss of needed tax funds in one country when its industries relocate abroad. Moreover, globalism tends to take the focus off of local governments and their appropriate concerns for the wellbeing of their citizens and to place economic practices more and more in the hands of international agencies such as the World Bank, the International Monetary Fund, the World Trade Organization, and the European Union. The result is the loss of a particular country's ability to protect its economic interests and those of its own people and to monitor and regulate its ecological and other affairs.

A country's progressive taxation that helps the poor and the nation as a whole by taxing the wealthy and well-to-do at a higher rate is jeopardized by competition in the world market where successful businesses and wealthy individuals and their capital tend to gravitate to countries or regions where taxes are relatively low and non-progressive. And the operations of special interest groups can become less transparent and more immune to effective regulation in the global arena where local laws are less easily enforced or do not apply. We should also note that globalization can work, and to date often has worked, to the benefit of the wealthy, well positioned, and influential few countries or individuals that are capable of acting on a global scale at the expense of the many that are less fortunate and less powerful. The managers of international banking and trade agencies such as those mentioned above are a case in point.

The ecological consequences of globalization must also be taken into account. Greater ease of travel and transportation made possible by the breakdown of national barriers can have the effect of increasing to a dangerous extent the pollution of the atmosphere produced by the burning of fossil fuels in ships, airplanes, and trucks. And global treaties can interfere with local environmental regulations, either by prohibiting their strict enforcements in particular countries or by opening up unfair and biologically destructive economic advantages to those countries whose environmental laws are judged to be less stringent and inhibitory of maximum profits.

The problems posed by globalization, such as those I have briefly indicated, are not so much problems with globalization per se as with how it is managed. The claim that globalization will automatically benefit everyone is a partial truth for the reason that the contingencies of its particular managers and management policies are critical factors in determining its beneficial or hurtful outcomes. Globalization may potentially benefit everyone more than it brings harm to them, and this remains to be seen. But this is different from saying that it will necessarily or inevitably do so. And we have to distinguish between short-term and long-term benefits of globalization, particularly in view of the severe short-term disadvantages and damages that can be inflicted and have already been inflicted on some countries and their governments and peoples by inept, short-sighted, or deeply biased global managers and regulators. One thinks, for example, of enticing but burdensome loans imposed on particular countries by transnational agencies, with austere and inflexible conditions for their granting and repayment, which can end up causing severe damage to their citizens and local economies.

On the other side of the ledger, however, globalism provides opportunity for dealing with problems and concerns that are global in character and cannot be properly or adequately dealt with by nation states or regional agencies alone. In this way, it can provide the possibility of benefit to every human being on earth as well as to earth's other species of life and their natural environments. Grave illustrations of the need for this way of thinking about globalism are the phenomena of global climate changes and ocean acidification. These are momentous threats to the health and wellbeing of the earth as a whole, and the high likelihood of their connections with unrestricted worldwide human use of fossil fuels and other aspects of human activity makes it incumbent on humans around the world to find ways to take all possible measures to reduce the rate of atmospheric and ocean pollutions to a nondestructive level.

R. G. Foster and L. Kreitzman indicate that current global climate change is altering the seasonal cycles, with the result that "the exquisite temporal sensitivities of living organisms, established over countless generations, that enable them to predict the regular rhythms in the environment and so synchronize their life histories to maximize reproduction, are being split asunder."[11] Global agencies and intensive global cooperation and planning are urgently necessary means for addressing worldwide environmental problems and working for the benefit and aid of all the creatures of earth. Globalism is clearly a mixed bag of actual and potential goods and evils, harms and benefits. It is neither to the exclusion of the other in an automatic or foregone sense. It sets many urgent tasks before us.

Government Deficits are Bad and
Should be Avoided to the Greatest Possible Extent

The notion that government deficits are bad is closely tied to the idea that deficits will bring about inflation by cheapening the value of the money supply and by having the interest and principal repayments on the deficits consume far too much of a government's tax income and annual budget. The issuance and sale of government bonds to other federal government agencies, individuals, businesses, state and local governments, and foreign governments, businesses, and individuals in order to fund government programs, increases a country's money supply, so the argument goes, and can create inflation by artificially putting more money in circulation and thereby lowering its unit value. Furthermore, since the loans by the government will have to be repaid in due time, the interest and principle of such loans—especially if many different loan amounts are allowed to accumulate without check—will increasingly take up a government's tax money that could have been put to more productive purposes or, even better, could have provided justification and incentive for economy-stimulating reduction of taxes on individuals and businesses.

Over time, such growing interest combined with unrepaid principle, the argument continues, is likely to consume an undesirable amount of a country's budget and might even expose it to possible default, with corresponding loss of confidence on the part of future possible lenders in the government's fitness to borrow needed money at reasonable interest rates. Issuing bonds and borrowing money is the easy part, so easy in fact as to tempt governments to borrow more than they can effectively and efficiently repay. Increasing deficits spell decreasing economic health of a country and decreasing confidence in a country's solvency. They can create ruinous inflation, according to this argument, a prospect haunted by the destructive inflation of the Weimar Republic in the aftermath of World War I.

This negative view of government deficits contains important truth. Deficits can get out of hand, and they are especially in need of caution and restraint in prosperous times when interest rates may be high, when rising inflation can be a serious problem, and when a country's existing money supply and other resources may already be adequate to meet its legitimate needs. But the need for such stated conditions or qualifications shows that the proposition under consideration in this section is at best a partial truth, one circumscribed by particular circumstances rather than being in all cases completely and unequivocally true.

When an economy is sluggish and interest rates are low, a government's taking on debt may make good sense, especially when low interest rates on the government's loans can be fixed for a considerable length of time. Such loans of money made readily available by low-interest indebtedness can be put promptly to use by government spending on such projects as infrastructure maintenance and repair and the jobs created thereby; job training or retraining programs; education funding; medical programs; food stamps, welfare payments, legal aid, and other help for the poor and needy; and alternative energy research and development and other environmental programs. Funding for such projects made possible by appropriate government deficits can contribute to the strength and recovery of an economy rather than detracting from it. A recovered and flourishing economy will have the resources to repay the deficits incurred when it was sluggish, and they can be repaid at the fixed low-interest rates taken on when they were incurred.

Government deficits are not the bugaboo they are sometimes made out to be. A government's taking on too much debt is certainly a matter of concern. But how much is too much and why this is so; at what interest rates; whether the rates are fixed and for how long a term they will run; for what uses are they to be devoted and how urgent or justified are these uses—these are among the important questions to be raised. Sensible, low-interest indebtedness can enable a government to do important things at a given time that it would not otherwise be capable of doing.

Relentless cutting back of deficits based on the idea that they are always bad and need promptly to be cut back as far as possible can be a reckless policy when its consequences are not carefully weighed. Drastic reductions or ill-advised privatizations of vitally needed government programs might be required in order to cut back deficits in short order. To think that this is always and under all conditions advisable is to succumb to the temptation to convert a partial truth into a whole truth. It is to fall victim to an ideology rather than retaining the ability to think through complex and changing economic issues in pragmatic, constructive, and helpful ways. It is to assume that there is some "single, best policy" for all sectors of society and for all economic situations and times.[12]

I can define an ideology as the thoughtless conversion of a large-scale partial truth into an absolute truth, with the consequence of ignoring conceptual considerations and empirical conditions that when taken into account should make its provisional, contextual, partial character readily apparent. We should also note that unrelenting, unqualified opposition to a government's deficit spending can be closely connected with other commitments, themselves sometimes if not often of an ideological character, such as the idea that government programs should be cut to the bone and turned over to private enterprises in the name of supposed greater efficiency, and that taxes should be drastically reduced, especially on businesses and the very rich. This latter idea is tied to the theory that if businesses and the rich are rid of tax burdens as well as strict government regulations, then their natural and unimpeded operations, purchases, goods, and services will maximally enrich and enliven the economy to the benefit of all.

The growing disparity between the rich and the poor, and the economic stagnation and decline of the middle class in the United States and elsewhere despite already instituted tax cuts and the absence of strong government regulations over banks and other private agencies, call this idea into serious question. Social justice and the wellbeing of all persons within a society are likely to be better served when tax systems are rid of numerous unfair loopholes that favor the few at the expense of the many and when they are graduated in accordance with respective ability or resources to pay them, so that the fortunate well-off can help to contribute to the quality of life of the less well-off. This practice is also suited to put more money into the general economy, as opposed to having the money squirreled away and not put to proper use. Money is by its very nature, after all, a means to ends and not an end in itself, and one of its principal ends should be the support of policies and provisions that can ensure fairness and justice for all.

Most relevant to the ecological as well as economic concerns of this chapter is the strong probability that private businesses or the very wealthy will not do much and generally have not done much on their own initiative to address the pressing ecological problems of our time because doing so would be more likely, in their perspectives, to jeopardize maximum profits or maximum accumulations of wealth.

Some businesses are historically notorious for their careless and often flagrant inflictions of ecological damages or neglects of the ecological consequences of their practices, in contrast with the illusion of their unmandated, unregulated readiness to recognize and address these damages and consequences. Moreover, wealthy investors in businesses are for the most part reluctant to have the business's profit margins threatened by governmental requirements for appropriate costly actions regarding their past and present environmental depredations or neglects. Free enterprise and responsible enterprise are not always synonymous despite the belief in some quarters that they are somehow magically conjoined, especially when it comes to social justice and ecological awareness and action.

There are of course poisonous ideological assumptions and beliefs among liberals as well as conservatives that need constantly to be guarded against. An example of too much tendency in a liberal, deficit-endorsing direction is the notion that deficits should never be a matter of great concern, that a government has the right or even the obligation to borrow endlessly to finance its projects, no matter what the current economic situation or how relatively urgent or non-urgent the need for such projects might be. This idea is as wrong-headed and one-sided as the one I am discussing in this section. Those of a more conservative, cautious persuasion are right to argue that government regulations, taxation policies, and practices need constant policing, lest they become unfair, overly burdensome, and out of control. The latter group is also correct in insisting that people should take responsibility for their own lives to the fullest extent possible and that governments should not be expected or required to do for others what they are entirely capable of doing for themselves.

The relevant qualifications implicit in all such statements and commitments need to be borne constantly in mind. Ideological partial truths are a constant menace against which we should always be on guard, whatever our economic or political persuasions. This assertion of the need to be on guard is not so much itself a partial truth as a meta-statement, a reminder to watch out lest we or our government leaders become too enchanted and ensnared by temptations to treat partial truths as absolute ones. This kind of diligence could do much to make disagreements and debates more congenial, open-minded, and productive in political, economic, environmental, and other areas of policymaking and procedure.

Capitalism is Always Good and
Any Tendency to Socialism is Bad

The partiality and one-sidedness of this claim turns to a significant extent on the meaning of the term *socialism*. Socialism is often associated with extreme collectivism and ruthless top-down government management of a country's affairs and of every detail of the individual lives of its citizens. It is often thought to be synonymous with total government ownership and control of industry and business. And it conjures up disturbing images of the repressive policies and practices of Soviet Russia, Red China, and the nations of the Soviet Bloc during the period of the Cold War. Even the policies of the Roosevelt administration during the excruciating time of the Great Depression are seen by some as deplorably socialistic, defined or thoughtlessly assumed to be defined in these extreme, inaccurate, and misleading ways.

I have already stated in this chapter that pure free-market capitalism needs to be restricted and qualified by appropriate economic, social justice, and ecological considerations. And I have given reasons for thinking this to be so. But this does not mean that I am endorsing the extreme kind of collectivism or government control described in the previous paragraph. There is such a thing as a proper balance between capitalism and socialism, and the championing of either to the total exclusion of the latter is to fall prey to a partial truth, one desperately in need of balance and correction. Some important measure of government management, enforcement, and control is required if there is to be such a thing as a healthy national economy, distributive and other kinds of social justice, and shared environmental awareness and responsibility.

Unbridled capitalism can be just as destructive of the peoples of a nation as unbridled socialism, and there is plenty of historical evidence to show this to be so. There are elements of truth in both, but significant elements of falsity as well. The greater truth resides in a proper and continuing tension or balance between them, a balance that needs to be continually monitored and regulated in the face of changing circumstances.

The monopolies and capitalistic excesses of the Robber Baron period in the United States in the late nineteenth and early twentieth century were in crying need of government oversight and correction, and urgent attention was required to the plight of workers whose basic rights and needs were overlooked and whose productivity was mercilessly exploited in that era. The moderately socialistic innovations, regulations, and programs in the time of the Great Depression were also needed to avoid economic calamity and to help steer the national economy in the right direction.

Many of these measures continue to work to the benefit of all in the United States, the Social Security system being one outstanding example. And as we have seen, the looming environmental crisis of the present day requires creative, thoroughgoing, and urgent national and international attention and regulation. This crisis cannot be adequately met with the blind hope or trust that private businesses, agencies, or individuals alone are competent or motivated in the right ways to deal with it. This is especially evident in light of the incontestable fact that there is much more to a nation's or the world's wellbeing than the bottom lines of profits and losses. The wellbeing of a nation's peoples in all the aspects of their lives matters too, as do the health and integrity of the natural environment and its creatures—the environment on which all of us, human and nonhuman alike, critically depend.

We need to stop thinking of either capitalism or socialism as things to be resisted tooth-and-nail. For example, a government owned and regulated medical program similar to those presently in place in other parts of the world might be better, on balance, for people of the United States than the present mixture of private insurance companies, with their profit requirements, and tax-supported government programs. We should at least be open to this possibility instead of rejecting it out of hand. Available evidence on both sides of the question should be carefully weighed. And we should avoid having unthinking ideological commitments blur our vision and inhibit consideration of possible changes of present practices.

An open mind is a mind alert to the ever dangerous possibility of partial truths being converted into whole truths, with the consequence that the latent or manifest truths in opposing views are lost sight of and peremptorily rejected. Philip Clayton and Justin Heinzekehr speak wisely when they argue for the need, across the world, for *hybrid* economic systems "that combine profit-making activities with regulations that are designed to prevent corruption, environmental abuse, and the inordinate acquisition of wealth by small numbers of citizens."[13] Such systems would not be purely capitalistic or purely socialistic but a reasonable and responsible blend of the best features of the two approaches.

Wheeling and Dealing

There are wheelings and dealings in government, business, and other enterprises and institutions that may have little to do with carefully considered economic or political principles and everything to do with the self-interest of those who stand to gain economically, politically, or in other ways. Let's take, for example, the principle of the free market. Business people might support the free market idea mainly for the sake of trying to avoid government regulation and taxation of business that threaten to diminish their profits and incomes from their investments. And politicians might encourage this support in order to gain contributions from businesses and business executives for their re-election campaigns and for the sake of their political party's influence and positions of power. Issues such as the threat of global climate change or fair distributions of a country's wealth can be placed out of bounds by these kinds of tacit negotiations and agreements between politicians, political parties, businesses, the powerful, and the rich.

On both sides of this kind of bargaining, the appeal to principles can be a smokescreen for self-interest. Principles may have little or nothing to do with such matters. For business, the bottom line is maximum profits and yields from investments; for politicians, the bottom line is re-election and party power. So it is not so much principles and their partial but important truths that are operative in such cases. Rather, principles are paraded before the public as distractions from and shieldings of more selfish concerns.

Consider all the groups, religious or otherwise, that may give vocal support for the free market or minimum government idea or other economically related ones, not on the basis of conviction and principle, but with the idea that if the government stays out of their activities or at least radically reduces its intrusions into them, then the self-interest of the particular groups can best be served. Tax-supported vouchers and relentless privatization of education, for example, would allow certain religiously based educational institutions to thrive without separation of church and state issues having to be raised, and without the constraint of government policies relating to hiring or firing of faculty, admissions or refusals to admission of particular students or classes of students, prayer and other religious practices, or the content of educational curricula.

"Support us in this," such religious groups might be inclined to say to government leaders, "and we will support your re-elections, your political party, and the non-intrusive economic and other kinds of policies you may be seeking to foster and enforce." Or, to state the issue more forthrightly, "You stay out of our bailiwick, and we will stay out of yours. Do what you wish (within assumed or stated parameters) and we will do the same." The resulting situation is one of *irresponsibility* on both sides. The government allows its publicly raised taxes to be used for discriminatory practices in the all-important field of education, and the religious group undercuts the long-established government tradition of a publicly funded, religiously tolerant and neutral, all-inclusive educational system.

To cite another example of wheeling and dealing, as opposed to clear-cut, reasonable debate about principles and their implementations, a policy of one-sided economic, weapons, and other kinds of support for the nation of Israel and consequent inattention to legitimate concerns of Palestinians and others in the Middle East might be endorsed or tend to be endorsed by leaders in a national government such as that of the United States mainly in order to garner political backing from influential Jewish citizens of the nation, and not primarily out of deep concern for the rights of all concerned in the Middle East.

Politicians might also encourage similar backing from certain right-wing Christians of a country, even though this group's concern for the fate of Israel may not be tied to a defensible *realpolitik* policy of the need for a balance of power between an even-handed American support for Israel and similar support for the other nations of the Middle East. Instead, the religious group's support may be motivated by the bizarre and extraneous conviction that the return of Jews to Palestine presages a biblically prophesied Battle of Armageddon on the plains of Palestine and the resulting return of Christ to judge and save the world.[14] Its concern may not be for even-handed justice for all but instead for escalation of a conflict it sees as inevitable.

"Support is support, wherever it comes from, and should be accepted so long as it bolsters a political party's policies and programs or furthers a particular group's interests. There is no pressing need to think critically about the reasons behind it or the consequences that may stem from it." This can sometimes if not all too often be the attitude and response of politicians and political parties, on the one hand, and of those who give their assistance to these politicians and parties with expectation of reciprocal advocacy and aid for their programs, on the other. Covert self-interest on both sides, and not conscious commitment to a broad, well-thought-out political or economic outlook, is what may really be operative. Concerns for the all-around wellbeing of one's country, regions of the world like the Middle East, the emerging global community, or the ecosystem on which we all—human and nonhuman alike—critically depend may not even enter in as relevant considerations. Statesmanship and the wide-ranging responsibilities of citizenship are often compromised for the narrow self-interest and advantage of parties, persons, or groups. In such cases, expediency rather than announced principles and policies, reigns.

Consider again the specific example of a government's policies relating to Israel. It is critically important that the government not allow itself to be guided by the idea that the situation in the Middle East is intractable and beyond all maneuverability and change. It must not assume that Israel alone is the victim of a tragic conflict of rights, interests, and values or that it is entitled to expand its territories without limit or constraint. It certainly must not be guided by the notion that warfare with the Palestinians or others in the Middle East is inevitable or divinely fated, or give any kind of encouragement or assurance to individuals or groups who are convinced that this is so, no matter how alluring or lucrative their support might be. Instead, a government must respect the rights of all concerned, Israelis and Palestinians alike, and work tirelessly for just resolution of their differences. There are partial truths on both sides of this tragic situation, and that awareness must be kept constantly at the forefront of government policy. Sober reflections like these are not directly related to the conceptual and theoretical issues of this chapter, but they need to be borne constantly in mind.

Partiality of Truths as Excuses for Inaction

I have given considerable stress so far in this book to the dangers of absolutizing partial truths in domains such as religion, the natural and social sciences, economics, and ecology. These dangers include tribal conflicts among, between, or within religious groups based on each party's claim to conclusive and exclusive knowledge in basic areas of religious thought and commitment. They include the degeneration of science into scientism or logical positivism, that is, the indefensible assumption that the only reliable route to truth in all domains of thought lies in the sciences, and that whatever resists or prohibits reduction to scientific ways of knowing is bogus, fanciful, and misleading. These dangers are also posed by attempts to confine the whole of moral life and thought within the parameters of a single moral theory. And in the areas of ecology and economics, failure to recognize the partiality of relevant claims, approaches, and procedures can lead to arrogant, inadequate, unjust, and destructive outlooks and practices.

Partial truths parading as completeness, finality, and absoluteness of assertion can quickly degenerate into obfuscating ideologies that slam the door against other points of view that may contain significant measures of plausibility and that may propose actions and reforms that need to be taken seriously into account rather than dismissed out of hand. Such ideological stances, far from containing all truth, bar the way to more comprehensive truths. And they are flagrantly blind to the finitude and fallibility of all things human.

Close-minded ideologies pose acute dangers to peaceful, orderly, and equitable human societies and to the ability of humans to address in effective ways formidable present threats to the intricately entwined fates of humans and nonhumans on this planet. Diversity of points of view should not be shunned on the untenable basis of appeals to claims to absolute truth. It should be welcomed because different angles of vision often illuminate different aspects of complex problems in need of resolution. To insist on only one path to truth is to ignore other promising paths, all of which taken together might converge into complementary and thus more comprehensive and adequate modes of understanding and acting. These are the kinds of danger that lurk in claims to absolute truths that I have highlighted thus far in this book.

But there is another kind of danger relating to partial truths that I have not yet brought into view. I want in this section to call attention to it. This is the danger of rejecting a truth solely on the ground that it is partial, thus implicitly ignoring my central thesis that all claims to truth are inevitably partial.[15] The mistake here is ignoring the marked difference in *degrees* of truth and falsity in such claims. There are those who reject the need for acknowledging or addressing the issue of global climate change, for example, because even though the vast majority of scientists today concur in its reality and imminent threat to our planet, and in the conviction that humans are contributing in important and regrettable ways to it, there are a few scientists who do not agree with this view. The degree of truth and evidence relating to climate change and to its anthropogenic character stemming from the Industrial Revolution to the present is extremely strong, but this truth and evidence are sometimes rejected on the ground that they are not absolutely binding. This is an example of a dangerous and irresponsible response to the partiality of all claims to truth.

Corporations that manufacture cigarettes or types of pesticides and herbicides and minimize their threats to health—to cite another kind of example—sometimes do so with the aid of hired scientific research- ers who insist that knowledge regarding these issues is not complete enough to warrant public warnings of these products' dangers or to justify taking them off the market. The corporate researchers may be in the small minority, but they can register their disagreement with the majority view as the basis for doing nothing or for delaying action until a later time. In the meantime, large numbers of people may die of smoking-induced lung cancer or of the poisoning effects of widely disseminated pesticides and herbicides. Since the probability of the threatening consequences I have mentioned in this section is high, as that probability is assessed by the bulk of the scientific community, it would be better to take the chance of being wrong about predictions of those consequences than to run the serious risk of turning out to have been right and to have done nothing.

When there is a large amount of truth in a given claim, it needs to be accepted and responsibly acted on. The claim should not be set aside just because a small minority out of a large number of those in a position to judge its truth or falsity—and with reasons to reject its truth that happen to accord with a corporation's concern for uninterrupted profits—insists on its rejection. The partiality of all claims to truth should not blind us to the responsibility of carefully weighing the different degrees of partiality in them and of accepting and working with claims, policies, and practices that are supported by strong—even if not absolutely conclusive—investigations, arguments, and appeals to relevant evidence.

Therefore, there are two major dangers in the inevitability of partial truths. The first is treating particular ones of them as absolute truths or insisting on the ones so selected as undebatable, uncontestable, incorrigible truths. In this way one closes one's mind to the contributions other claims to truth might make to one's knowledge and understanding of these matters, and thus to more adequate visions of the world. This close-minded, intolerant approach to truth can generate acrimonious and sometimes woefully damaging disagreements and conflicts of individuals and societies. And it can stand in the way of much-needed personal and social progress and improvement.

The second danger, and the one that is my principal focus in this section, lies in a myopic overlooking of the degrees of truth in given claims and rejecting any and all of them that are amenable to question or debate, even to the slightest extent. This is the considerable danger of converting the inevitable less-and-more of all claims to truth into a supposedly forced or unavoidable either-or. A crust is still a crust even though it is not the whole loaf, and sharing our crusts of truth with one another can expand our common resources and be mutually edifying and enlightening. We need not quixotically insist on "all or nothing" in the realm of truth. If probable truths do not suffice to guide our way, then there is nothing capable of doing so, given the fact that all claimed truths about the world about are probable at best. And if declared truths with little evidence in their favor do not merit rejection or critical reconsideration, then the whole issue of truth and falsity goes by the board.

Chapter 5

PHILOSOPHY

Rationalism never shakes off its status of an experimental adventure. The combined influences of mathematics and religion, which
have so greatly contributed to the rise of philosophy, have also
had the unfortunate effect of yoking it with static dogmatism.
Rationalism is an adventure in the clarification of thought, progressive and never final. But it is an adventure in which even
partial success has importance.

—Alfred North Whitehead[1]

The "static dogmatism" that mathematician, logician, and philosopher Alfred North Whitehead warns philosophers against in this
chapter's epigraph is another name for the fruitless pursuit of absolute
truth—or the illusory claim finally to have arrived at some version of
it—that I am describing and cautioning against in this book. When
Whitehead says that the adventure of philosophy can acknowledge
importance in "even partial success," he is asserting, in effect, that
partial truths as the outcome of philosophical analyses and investigations are not to be disparaged but should be welcomed and cherished
because of the significant amounts of truth they may contain—truth
that can contribute in important ways to ongoing philosophical inquiry.
Putative absolutes or unwarranted dogmatisms in philosophy arrest
inquiry rather than furthering it. They have the effect of abruptly
reining in philosophy, consigning it to premature and unfortunate
halts at critical junctures. They place artificial barriers in the way of
a philosophical adventure that has brought many improvements and
refinements of insight and awareness over the years but whose beacon
of tantalizing problems and issues will never grow dim or flicker out.

The philosophical enterprise is in all likelihood unending and forever lacking in complete certitude or closure because, among other things, it is always, at bottom, subject to the elusive uncertainties and possibilities of ever-unfolding experience and not just to the rigors of internally consistent and coherent logical reasoning. Logical clarity and precision each have their place in philosophy, and it is an undeniably important one. But if philosophical thought is to remain relevant to the world and to our lives in the world, its final appeal must be to experience. Even this claim, however, is at best only partially true, given the intricate and not always easily sortable relations of what precisely is the contribution of reason and what precisely is the contribution of experience, and given our necessary uncertainty about what future understandings might bring to this distinction and line of thought. I state the claim as a probability, not as a certainty.

In this chapter I shall highlight a number of philosophical claims to truth that sometimes parade as absolute truths but can be exposed as partial truths. Each of these claims has the form of an either-or statement or a rigid dichotomy, but none of them, in my view, can stand up under careful scrutiny. The first of these is a rigid opposition between facts and values. After discussing and criticizing this opposition, I will address in respective sections of this chapter the supposed sharp divisions between continuity and novelty, rationalism and empiricism, mind-body dualism or reductionism, and good and evil. Partial truths lurk in each of these distinctions, but they are often too sharply drawn, and none of them is absolute or unassailable.

Facts and Values

The eighteenth-century Scottish philosopher David Hume famously argued in his *A Treatise of Human Nature* that statements of fact, or "is" statements, are entirely different in their inherent logic and meaning from assertions of moral obligation or "ought" ones. There is no way, he insists, to deduce the second kind of statement from the first. The implication of his analysis is that factual statements and statements of value must be rigorously distinguished from one another. And Hume takes strong issue with those who tend to slide surreptitiously or unthinkingly from one to the other.[2]

The English philosopher George Edward Moore argued in his book *Principia Ethica*, first published in 1903, that the term *good* "denotes a simple and indefinable quality."[3] In keeping with this statement, he went on to insist that the moral goodness or badness of something cannot be rightly thought to be synonymous with or inferable from any factual or natural state of affairs. To reason in this way is to commit what he calls "the naturalistic fallacy." We cannot rightly say, for example, as John Stuart Mill and others have said, that *goodness* is synonymous with *pleasure* or that, as the English philosopher Herbert Spencer contended, the quality of goodness can be said somehow to be implicit in, derivable from, or definable in terms of the Darwinian theory of natural selection.[4] For Moore, moral goodness belongs to a class of its own and should not be confused with classes of factual or natural things or theories. In other words, values and facts are entirely distinct from one another, and it would be a mistake to think that the former can be derived from or based on the latter.

Later in the twentieth century, the Logical Positivist philosopher A. J. Ayer argued in his own fashion for the thesis with which I intend shortly to take issue, namely, the radical separation of values from facts. Ayer asserts that only those statements that can be scientifically verifiable or falsifiable can correctly be said to be true or false. Hence, only these statements qualify as factual. Since moral, aesthetic, or religious affirmations of value cannot be put to any conceivable scientific test, he insists, they are not only non-factual; they are not even statements. Instead, as pseudo-statements they are really expressions of emotion or appeals and incitement to emotion. In other words, facts can be stated and put to some kind of scientific test: this is what identifies them as facts. Values can only be felt or induced as feelings in others. Values as such cannot rightly either be claimed or disputed about in any scientific manner, and this observation shows them to be forever distinct from facts.[5] Ayer's view is similar to Hume's idea that morality "is more properly felt than judged of."[6] We saw in chapter 3 how Hume roots morality in sentiments rather than in reason.

The alleged impregnable wall between facts and values described by Hume, Moore, Ayer, and others can be broken down in a number of ways, as I shall now proceed to indicate. First, if the distinction between the two is as insurmountable as these philosophers allege, it should be impossible to reason from "ought" to "is," just as it is putatively impossible to reason from "is" to "ought." But if I say, "We ought to do this," implicit in my sentence is the assumption that we are *capable* of doing it. And is not the latter a factual statement, one that is susceptible, *pace* Ayer, of being put to an empirical test? If "ought" does imply "can" in at least some situations, then the two ideas are at some times more closely conjoined than the three philosophers discussed above are willing to allow.

Second, reasoning from "is" to "ought" is fallacious only so long as we think of nature just as a collection of bare facts devoid of inherent value. But in the perspective of my own Religion of Nature (as well as in many other religious and nonreligious perspectives), nature teems with values (and disvalues) as well as facts. For example, there is the sheer fact of the rare flower viewed as a biological phenomenon in need of scientific examination and explanation. There is also its distinctive value to someone appreciative of natural beauty who happens upon it by a frolicking stream or on a windswept mountain top. Even the curious biologist *values* the rare flower as an interesting fact inviting investigation, if not in other ways. In similar fashion, a bush loaded with succulent berries is not just a bare fact for the ravenous bear; it is a highly valued and inherently valuable fact. It is not just valuable because it is valued. It is valuable because it contains within itself the capability of satisfying the need of hunger and creating the delight of eating.

In all cases, the facticity and the value lie in the relation between the object and its perceiver or evaluator, not in either to the exclusion of the other. The flower has the potential to be recognized as a significant fact and/or as a thing of beauty, and the human mind has the capability to actualize both kinds of potentiality in its conscious awareness. In responding to facts or values, sentience or mind is not just aware of its own inner states but of something beyond itself recognized to have a certain character, whether in the way of fact or value. The beauty of the flower or value of the berries does not lie just in the mind of the beholder or consumer.

Do we just *construct* facts and values in our subjectivity, projecting these constructions on the world? I contend that we do not sheerly or arbitrarily construct either. There is considerable truth in the idea that we *discover* both facts and values. My third way of responding to the alleged rigid dichotomy of facts and values is to assert that we discover both of them via *interpretation*. We interpret and infer something as a fact in some context of interest, purpose, or inquiry, and we do the same with value. There is some use and partial truth in the metaphor of construction, however. What we interpret either in the way of facts or in the way of values is a kind of raw material presenting itself for interpretation. And the significance of such interpretations may vary somewhat from situation to situation. But there is no compelling reason to think that this significance must always be the outcome of mere construction or projection by the interpreter onto a featureless world. Just as bricks are more suitable than seaweed for constructing a wall, so some things are more amenable to some kinds of interpretation than others. This is true both in the realm of facts and in the realm of values.

To stretch the metaphor a bit further, bricks are not only, factually speaking, the sorts of things from which walls can actually be built; they are also of great *value* when available for this task. In other words, it is *good* to have them available if we wish to build a wall. None of what I have so far said is inconsistent with noting that facts are different from values or that discoursing and reasoning about the one is not the same as discoursing and reasoning about the other. It is only to argue that both result from interpretations and inferences about matters at hand, and that neither is always just made up with no critical connections with characters and qualities of things in the world. Neither facts nor values are simply "out in the world." Nor are they arbitrary projections on a faceless or featureless world. Both reside in the *relations* of interpreters with the things being interpreted. Neither is sheerly constructed, invented, or made. Values are no less actual or real than are facts.

To put my view succinctly, there are valuative facts as well as non-valuative ones of innumerable kinds waiting discovery and acknowledgment throughout nature. And even apprehension of something as a fact requires that it be capable of being *valued* as a significant fact in the context of some kind of discourse, expression, inquiry, activity, or experience. So we can strive to realize the many potential values and meanings in our experiences of the world as wholly natural beings capable both of discovering and contributing in numerous ways to the values and valuative opportunities of the world. We can live according to our character and capacities as a distinctive form of natural life and, in doing so, seek to contribute reverently to, and not to run roughshod over, the integrity and wellbeing of the earth and its creatures in our shared natural home. This earth is not just a congeries of facts. It is also a vast assemblage of inherent and discoverable values. The factual and the valuative aspects of the world are interfused, not radically separate from one another. We can make good use in this context of Whitehead's idea of a logical contrast, where "opposed elements stand to each other in their mutual requirement" rather than existing in rigid distinction from one another.[7]

A fourth line of argument against a rigid dichotomy of facts and values is the commonplace observation that every intentional act is, at least implicitly, an act of evaluation. I choose "A" over "B" because I value "A" more than "B," whether these be epistemic, aesthetic, moral, or religious alternatives. But is this not just a subjective matter, a mere creation of value by a subjective choice? I do not think so, because my body permits me to carry out the choice, and I am able to implement it in ways that have effects in the world. In other words, my body and the world beyond my body permit the choice to be made, meaning that they had the potentiality for the value to be activated. As I write these words, for example, I choose to place them on my computer screen. My computer is structured in such a way—thanks to the decisions of those who designed and manufactured it—that I am able to register my choices of words, phrases, paragraphs on the screen—put them out there in the world, so to speak, where I and others can read them.

Others can read my words—as you, the reader, are perusing and weighing them now—because they, like me, are participants in a common language whose meanings and possibilities of expression are publicly available. From something private there is produced by intentional acts and choices something public. In choosing words and phrases as I write, I am valuing some over others. That is, I have in mind values such as clarity and precision of presentation, felicity and attractiveness of expression, persuasiveness and soundness of argument. I may intentionally replace one mode of expression for another as I write, and I do so in light of such values. My mind and body are constituted in such a manner that these choices and their implementations are possible, and the same thing is true of the language in which I write and the computer where I commit my linguistic choices to its screen. Values flow into facts, and facts record values.

My intentional choices and the values routinely contained in them are registered in the world because they are already present as potentialities or relevant alternatives of the world. My subjectivity is in constant concourse with the world. I affect it, and it affects me. This is no less true in the realm of values than it is in the realm of facts. Both are interpretations of aspects of the world, a world whose potentialities include me and my capabilities of choice, evaluation, and action. This is not to say that facts and values are the same: to this extent the fact-value distinction contains relevant truth. But it is to say that facts and values are much more closely connected and conjoined than the alleged rigid fact-value dichotomy will permit. What counts as a fact is what is valued as such in some context of inquiry and interpretation, and the same thing is true of what counts as a value.

Without the innumerable *evaluative* interpretations implicit in scientific investigations, there would be no sciences, and without innumerable *factual* interpretations of the world carried out by the sciences, we would lack the vast assemblage of presumed facts that scientific investigations and interpretations bring to light. In chapter 2 I referred to this necessary correlation of facts and values in the sciences. Ayer's analysis of the relation of facts and values is especially blind to this necessary correlation as it relates to the methods and findings of the sciences, as he is to his own announced but highly questionable evaluation of the sciences and their methods as the sole sources of reliable facts in comparison with other modes of inquiry. His evaluation seems to be guided by the fact of there being such a thing as the sciences as he perceives them. Such guidance is inconsistent with his theory of the rigid separation of facts from values. And is his evaluation of the sciences a mere expression of emotion on his part and not a disputable assertion, as he staunchly claims all acts of evaluation must be? He seems to think otherwise because he devotes an entire chapter of *Language, Truth, and Logic* to arguments for what looks like a genuine proposition—and not a pseudo-statement—that the sciences should be valued as having the distinctive, non-valuative role he assigns to them. He values them for their assumed singular facticity and this tacit evaluation pervades the whole of his logical positivist outlook. It is not at all easy even for Ayer to keep scientific facts in quarantine, safe from contamination by what he regards as purely emotional values. The arguments of this section are intended to explain and defend the necessary intermixtures of facts and values, as opposed to their alleged isolation and separation from one another.

Continuity and Novelty

I have argued at length elsewhere for the essential bearing of the two notions of continuity and novelty on the natures of time, change, causality, chance, and freedom.[8] I shall argue here against the idea that the two are somehow completely opposed to one another, the idea that if one exists or is present, the other cannot exist or be present. In other words, the two are often held to be mutually exclusive. The thesis of causal determinism is sometimes defended in part by the argument that the only conceivable alternative to it is chaotic eruptions of chance happenings with no continuous connections to one another that would render absurd not only the relation of causes and effects but any meaningful conception of human freedom. For example, Hume argues this way in his A *Treatise of Human Nature*. He writes,

> According to my definitions, necessity makes an essential part of causation; and consequently liberty, by removing necessity, removes also causes, and is the very same thing with chance. As chance is commonly thought to imply a contradiction [to causality], and is at least directly contradictory to experience, there are always the same arguments against liberty or free-will.[9]

But I argue that temporal and causal continuity are unintelligible without at least some element of novelty and that novelty is unintelligible without at least some significant amount of temporal and causal continuity.

Let me begin with the first of these two allegations. *What would causal continuity look like with no element of novelty?* In the first place, it would not be a continuity of changes unfolding through time. And in the second place, it would not be an intelligible continuity of dynamic causes and their effects. There would be no change without novelty because there would be no differences between and among events of time. There would be no difference between past and present, or present and future, and thus no such thing as distinctive moments unfolding in a passage of time. There would be the kind of continuity or interrelationships of the features of a *spatial* configuration or drawing but no dynamic, processive continuity of flowing *time*. Were there no such thing as a unique, unrepeatable novelty, we could as easily conceive of putting the present before the past or the future before the present so as to arrange them in a different order. A flow of time requires unrepeatable, emergent, and thus novel presents. If this were not so, there would be no arrow of time pointing from the fixed past, through a new and at least somewhat different present occurrence, to an as yet indeterminate future.

Must the present be *completely* novel? Of course not. Were it completely novel, there would be no continuity from the past into the present, no carrying over of traits of the past into the present. The degrees of novelty in a present moment can and do vary. But the complete absence of novelty would also mean the absence of causal connection and continuity. Without some element of novelty, the so-called present collapses into a past from which it exhibits no difference. If continuity were the whole story of time, time would cease to exist.

By the same token, there must be some difference, however negligible or slight, *between a cause and its effects*. Elsewise, the two could not be distinguished from one another, and the cause-effect sequence itself would be rendered unintelligible. I could not meaningfully say, "This is the cause, and this is its effect," because there would be no distinction between the former and the latter. Novelty is thus as essential to cause-effect relations as is continuity. Neither is completely opposed to the other, either in fact or in coherent conceptionalization. The "necessity" Hume associates with causality and sternly opposes to any bit of chance or degree of meaningful freedom is a static necessity having little to do with either time or cause and effect relations unfolding in time.

Just as the flow of time and the relationship of causes and their effects require novelty for their intelligibility and adequacy to experience, so does novelty presuppose a context or background of continuity if it is to be properly understood. The novelty of the present moment consists in its contrast with the previous moment, now fixed in an unalterable past. But the present moment flows out of and is made possible by the moments preceding it. The past moments provide impetus for the emergence of the present moment, and they also provide determination for the range of possibilities within which the new moments can arise. The present moment is a transformation in some degree of moments of the past, at the very least by virtue of being a *new moment* of time. And were there no past to be so transformed or at least iterated anew, there would be no present moments by whose means they can be transformed or reiterated. Moreover, all past moments were once present ones, themselves transformations or iterations of previous moments—thus constituting a continuity of moments throughout the past.

This reasoning should serve to remind us that continuity and novelty go necessarily together. To speak of causality is to speak of a continuity or interconnected sequence of causes and their effects, and to speak of novelty is to speak of innovations or iterations continuously introduced through the course of that sequence. Slight differences early on can become the basis of major differences later as they are enhanced, expanded, and built on, moment by moment, over a span of time.

There is truth in the insistence on causal continuity, and there is truth in insistence on the reality of innovations made possible by chance and freedom. But these truths are correlative, so that either by itself is a partial truth—one side of the coin needs correction by the other side if a better approach to adequacy of conception and assertion is to be found. To seek for causal explanations of phenomena is an essential enterprise, one that lies at the heart of the scientific enterprise. Implicit in this enterprise and its striking successes is the partial truth in the idea that everything that occurs is explicable in terms of its causes. But to deny, in the name of absolute causality, the possibility of anything genuinely new ever occurring is a glaring mistake. It is a mistake made abundantly evident by all of the changes, many of them impressively unexpected, unpredicted, and even momentous, that have become manifest in the past and that continue to emerge against the background or within the context of cause-effect relations today.

The precise relations between continuity and novelty cannot be pinned down because these relations undergo constant changes over the passage of time and from situation to situation. But to deny their essential relationship altogether, as Hume and other advocates of causal necessity and determination have done, is to deny any role for novelty altogether and thus to make unintelligible the flow of time and even the necessary distinction between causes and their effects. It is to assume to be completely predictable in principle something that can never, by its very nature, be completely predictable in fact. And it is to freeze the flow of time. Causality is real, continuity through time is real, and novelty is real. These are interdependent principles, not opposed conceptions. The more adequate truth lies in the tensions among them, at least as each is commonly misunderstood, not in their opposition to one another. Causality does not cancel chance or freedom, and chance or freedom does not cancel causality, despite a relatively common assumption among many philosophers and scientists today that this must be so.

Rationalism and Empiricism

Rationalism and empiricism are approaches to the nature and extent of human knowing with ancient roots. But they became especially prominent in the modern era, which began in the seventeenth century. The chief exemplars of these two approaches are René Descartes and John Locke, and their theories of knowledge have been reference points for philosophical theories relating to epistemology from that time to the present.

A paradigm of rationalism is the theory of the French philosopher of the seventeenth century, Descartes, as laid out, among other places, in his Meditations on First Philosophy (1641 and 1642).[10] Descartes regards sensate experiences as hopelessly vague and confused, and thus not at all to be trusted as sources of dependable knowledge. He searches in his Meditations for clear and distinct or undeniable and determinate ideas of reason which lie innately within the mind and do not suffer from the shifting imprecisions and misdirections of the ideas of sensation. Descartes's method of systematic doubt is brought resolutely to bear in the Meditations, and his doubt is resolved when he is able to find convincing evidence in reason alone, quite apart from the senses themselves, of such fundamental propositions as that he exists, that God exists, and that material things exist. Descartes is convinced that, apart from the clear and distinct, wholly innate ideas of reason, the philosopher who searches for reliable knowledge is doomed to epistemic disappointment and despair.

The polar opposite of Descartes's theory of knowledge is the theory of the English philosopher Locke. In his groundbreaking book An Essay Concerning Human Understanding (1690),[11] Locke conceived of the human mind as a kind of blank tablet that is written on by discrete ideas derived from sensate experience. In other words, all of the ideas and operations of the human mind are ultimately based on and derived from sensation, and these ideas and operations include the simple ideas involved in the mind's reflections on or responses to its sensate experiences. The discrete simple ideas of sensation and reflection are then compounded in various ways by the mind, producing its complex ways of understanding itself and the world. We have reliable knowledge, Locke reasons, only to the extent that we can trace our claims of knowledge back to the input of our senses. Thus, there is for Locke no such thing as innate ideas. All reliable ideas concerning ourselves and the world are acquired through sensate experiences.

Neither of these extreme views was able to stand up under the critical scrutiny of future generations and they do not do so today. There is truth in both approaches to knowledge, but both are partial truths, each needing correction by the truth residing in the other. We do need our senses to be in contact with the world, as Locke argues, but we also require inherent capabilities and operations of the mind itself if reliable knowledge is to be gained. The epistemological theories of both Locke and Descartes end up in radical subjectivism or solipsism if each is not corrected by the other.

Locke confesses that he must believe in substances external to himself that have the causal powers to produce ideas in his mind via sensations. But there is no clear evidence in the discrete ideas of sensation that either such substances or causal powers exist. Belief in both is a function of the mind, not something wholly acquired through the simple ideas of sensation. The German philosopher Gottfried Leibniz, in a critique of Locke's *Essay* entitled *New Essays on Human Understanding* (1765), responded to Locke's contention that there is nothing in the mind or intellect which does not originally come from the senses with the apt rejoinder: "*Nihil est in intellectu quod non fuerit in sensu, excipe: nisi ipse intellectus*" (nothing exists in the mind which was not first in the senses except the mind itself). The states and operations of the mind are required, Leibniz is arguing, in order for any meaning to be found in the deliverances of the senses and for them to refer to anything beyond themselves. He notes that these states and operations include such things as "being, substance, one, same, cause, perception, reasoning, and many other notions which the senses cannot provide."[12]

Leibniz is calling attention in his own manner to the relational conception of knowledge I outlined when talking about the status of values in discussing the fact-value dichotomy. Truth and value lie in the relations of subjects to objects, not in either to the exclusion of the other. Were there no innate capacities and capabilities of the mind, there would be no such thing as knowledge of fact or value. The same holds true if there were no such thing as sensate experience. Overemphasis on the innate resources of the mind, with a corresponding neglect of the indispensable importance of sensate experience, as with Descartes, is also destructive of knowledge.

Descartes famously declares that he is incapable of being certain of anyone else's existence than his own because his thinking gives clear and distinct evidence only of his own existence ("I think, therefore I am"). He has to prove the existence of God and also to show that God is not a deceiver in other parts of his *Meditations* in order to prove the reliability of any and all of his clear and distinct ideas, including this one exhibiting his—that is Descartes's—own existence. But he can only prove the existence of God, and thus his own existence, by relying on the same clear and distinct ideas whose reliability God is supposed to ensure. So he is caught in a solipsistic circle from which there is no escape except by granting to sensate experiences indispensable roles as routes to knowledge. If everything must be finally certain in order for it to be confidently relied on, then nothing even approaches certainty except the momentary deliverances of an isolated, self-contained, non-referring mental substance or *res cogitans*. But concerning the *continuing existence* of such an underling mental substance there is still room for doubt.

Thus, both Locke and Descartes are right, each in his own way, but both are only partially right. Hume's epistemology of the eighteenth century, which is a relentless carrying out of Locke's program of basing everything on sensate experience, ends in complete skepticism, as he reluctantly has to admit. And the Jewish philosopher Baruch Spinoza's *Ethics, Demonstrated in Geometrical Order* (1677),[13] which carries out the rationalistic program of Descartes to its ultimate degree, culminates in an absolute monism wherein particular individuals of any sort and any kind of sensibly based contingency are entirely eliminated. In his philosophy, internal, mathematical-like rational coherence is the sole criterion and measure of dependable knowledge, and any need for appeal to day-to-day experiences of the world is dismissed out of hand. As with Descartes, rationalism trumps empiricism.

Immanuel Kant's attempted synthesis of Leibniz's (and Descartes's) rationalism with Hume's (and Lock's) empiricism in his *Critique of Pure Reason*, 2nd edition (1787)[14] has three troublesome defects. He denies any possible knowledge of an in-itself world, claiming that we know only a world of subjective sense experiences guided and ordered by certain innate principles, and he quite inconsistently has to take for granted the in-itself existence of human minds as all structured alike if his intersubjective epistemological program is to get off the ground and if he is to communicate his ideas to other human beings. The third defect is that some of the principles he regarded as innate and unchangeable, such as certain principles of Newtonian physics, Aristotelian syllogistic logic, and Euclidian geometry, were later shown to be alterable, dependent on debatable premises, or admissible of alternatives. But Kant at least calls firm attention to the need for a relational theory of knowledge, one that finds truth and value in the relations of sensate objects to the knowing mind, not in either to the exclusion of the other.

Now this might look like ancient history. But the problem of the relationship of sensate experiences and what look like innate capacities of the mind persists to this day. The clue to such innateness presumed by thinkers such as Descartes, Leibniz, and Kant is their certainty or undeniability. But Ayer, Bertrand Russell, Rudolf Carnap, and others in the twentieth century, following the lead of Hume in the eighteenth,[15] declare that all undeniably certain propositions are tautologies, and this includes all of logic and mathematics. But even if they are not mere tautologies but are part of the innate structures of the mind, the problem is posed of how they came to be such and how they relate to sensate experiences and to the world beyond the mind.

The best answer would seem to be that certain traits, operations, or capabilities of the mind that provide certainty as an epistemic state or conviction have been long ago acquired by evolutionary processes for their adaptive significance and value. An example of this way of thinking is provided by the contemporary philosopher Adam C. Scarfe, drawing on the work of the Austrian zoologist Konrad Lorenz. Scarfe argues that the presently innately certain belief in cause and effect, for example, which Hume was unable to account for on the basis of sensation alone, was probably implanted early on in the brains of sentient creatures by the evolutionary process of organisms interacting with their environments.[16] It functions as an indispensable means of adaptation and survival in the world. How would a sentient animal survive or thrive with no sense of what can be firmly depended on to be the source or cause of something else? It could not safely eat, drink, protect itself against predators, shelter itself from the cold, or confidently and efficiently explore and make use of any of the resources of its environment. The innate conviction of the relations of causes and effects and other innate features or functions of our human minds interact with our sensate experiences in order to give knowledge of ourselves, the world, and our relations as human subjects to the world. Hence, it is in the tensions between rationalism and empiricism that the more adequate truth is to be found, and not in either to the exclusion of the other.

Does this mean that there is absolute truth in the *tension*, then, if not in the *exclusion* of one view by the other? No, it does not, because there is no finally adequate theory presently available of the precise interrelations and workings of reason and experience, of how much we bring to the knowledge table and how much is served to us from outside ourselves. No one to date has been able fully and finally to explain, for example, how the purely deductive operations of high-level mathematical reasoning can have so many successful, insightful, and surprising applications to the experienced world—as they undeniably do in the natural sciences. All theories about this problem and other conundrums bearing on the interrelations of sensate experiences and the contributions of the mind are tentative and incomplete at best.

Mind-Body Dualism and Reductionism

Descartes opted for mind-body dualism, on the ground that mind and body are totally distinct from one another. Matter has for him the attribute of *extension*, with figure, magnitude, mobility, substance, duration, and number as its modes. And mind has the attribute of *thinking*, with its modes of doubting, understanding, affirming, denying, willing, refusing, imagining, and feeling.[17] These respective attributes and modes, he reasons, are so different from one another that they have to belong to radically different kinds of substance, the one physical, and the other mental. How these two entirely distinct and separate types of substance are able to interact with one another, Descartes is never able successfully to explain. He is right in believing that the respective characters and traits of mind and body, or consciousness and matter, are different from one another and that this difference needs seriously to be taken into account. This observation is the important partial truth in his view. But he is wrong, in my view and in the view of many other philosophers since his time, in concluding that the two must belong to entirely different orders of being. His inability to explain how they can relate to another—as they obviously do in everyday life—once he has so radically set them apart, is the principal symptom of this error.

If mind-body dualism does not work, then perhaps either resolute materialism or idealism will. In the first case, mind is reduced to matter, and in the second, matter is reduced to mind. These options were explored by others in the early modern period. Thomas Hobbes and Julien de la Mettrie developed materialistic outlooks on mind and world in the seventeenth and eighteenth centuries, respectively.[18] Mettrie provides a succinct statement of their materialistic philosophy when he writes that "the soul [or mind] is but a principle of motion or a material and sensible part of the brain, which can be regarded, without fear or error, as the mainspring of the whole machine, having a visible influence on all the parts."[19] Locke, who was not convinced by Cartesian dualism, allows in one place in his *Essay* that it is possible that matter can in some unknown manner think or at least be made to think by God.[20] But none of these three thinkers had anything close to a conception of matter adequate to explain how matter as conceived in their time could be capable of thought.

Bishop George Berkeley, for his part, opted in the eighteenth century for the view that matter does not exist. Matter is an abstract way of talking about collections of certain kinds of idea in the mind such as those Descartes lists as material modes, but there is no such thing as material substances existing in their own right, independently of the mind. Berkeley's theory had the pressing problem of explaining how sensate ideas in the minds of many different subjects can in many particular situations be commonly entertained by those subjects and of explaining how it is that we all seem to exist in an orderly and predictable world that gives every indication of being objective and separate from individual subjects. Berkeley's famous contention that we all somehow participate in ideas in the mind of God as the ultimate, all-inclusive thinking subject, is little more than a patently *deus ex machina* solution to the problem his idealism so forcefully poses.[21] Kant's so-called transcendental idealism, as I indicated earlier, leaves us with the skeptical conclusion that we can know nothing of the world as it is in and of itself, even though Kant does find it necessary to assume that our minds are all, in-themselves, structured alike, giving us a kind of intersubjective objectivity or commonality of experience and reference.

Each of these views, dualism, materialism, and idealism, states important partial truths. Descartes is correct in seeing that mind is not exactly the same thing as body (or matter), as shown by their radically different properties, and that neither can be simply reduced to the other. Hobbes and Mettrie are right in suggesting that the relation of mind to matter is much more intimate and deep-rooted than Descartes's dualistic theory suggests. Berkeley is right in suggesting that our conception of matter depends to a highly significant extent on ideas in our minds represented to us via our sensations. Kant is right in arguing for a relational conception of sensate experiences, on the one hand, and the inherent tendencies, predilections, and principles of the mind, on the other—as I noted earlier. He correctly contends that the world for us humans is an *interpreted* world.

However, it does not follow from Kant's observation that there is *nothing* of the in-itself world in our interpretations. He is right to an extent because our interpretations are limited to what is possible for creatures such as we are—with the epistemic abilities we possess in virtue of our five senses (and the supplementations of them with various kinds of technological inventions), our native feelings and intuitions, and the fertile reasoning capacities of our minds. But we humans are also members of a highly developed evolutionary species living in intimate relations with the world and equipped to interact meaningfully and veridically with it in countless ways. In consequence, we would appear to be capable of significant amounts of partial truths in our interpretations of the real world, despite Kant's adamant denial of this possibility.

It was not until the nineteenth and twentieth centuries that an important alternative to the by-then timeworn ideas of dualism, materialism, and idealism could present itself. This new idea, already hinted at in the previous paragraph, is that mind is an *emergent and not a primordial feature of the universe* and that it emerges with life itself in its more complex and elaborately organized forms. In this view, mind is a function of matter, but the kind of matter that is capable of producing mind is radically different from what could be envisioned by Newtonian physics of the early modern era or can even comprehended solely by the physics of today. It is organic matter, living matter, matter of an extremely complex type of evolutionary development that produces in varying degrees, depending on the type of organism, capacities of sentience and conscious awareness that did not exist and could not have existed earlier in evolutionary history.

In this view, mind is a new order of reality. It is radically dependent on matter and continues to be such, but it is not reducible to earlier, non-evolved, less complex types of matter. In a sense, it is a new form of matter, matter that is capable, as Locke divined, of thought. But since it is still something material or the emergent function of something material, it is not opposed to matter and is not some kind of substance entirely different from matter. A suggestive large-scale vision of the emergentist view of mind in its relation to matter is provided by the contemporary neuroscientist Terrence W. Deacon, in his book *Incomplete Nature: How Mind Emerged from Matter*.[22]

I think that it is a mistake to argue that mind can be reduced to matter in the manner of regarding sentient organisms as nothing more than extremely complex algorithmic machines or robots, or in claiming that mental functions and contents such as consciously entertained beliefs, intentions, choices, and creations are mere epiphenomena or illusions, and that only matter as described by contemporary physicists finally and really exists. Such models of mind may themselves contain useful partial truths, but they cannot tell the whole story of mentality in its wide-ranging capabilities, functions, and traits. At least no one to date has been able to show conclusively and convincingly that they can do so.

The evolutionary, emergentist, expansionist, and hence, nonreductive view of the relation of mind to matter or of mind and body is itself only a partial truth, however, attractive as it might seem to some, including this writer. It is only a partial truth because no one to date, scientist, philosopher, or other kind of theorist, has been able to explain precisely how matter is able to give rise to mind over the span of evolutionary history. The evolutionary and adaptive advantages of sentience and mind are abundantly evident. But no one as of the time of this writing is able to explain successfully or conclusively how life itself originated from matter, to say nothing of how matter could have given rise to the intricacies and mysteries of mind. There are theories aplenty on both of these issues, but none of them should be considered as setting forth absolute truth. After all of the discussions, debates, and arguments have subsided and the smoke has cleared, only partial truths of varying degrees of convincingness and adequacy remain on the natures and relations of mind and body or mind and matter.

Good and Evil

It might be thought that we can at least in some cases or with respect to some topics of discussion rightly brand some things as absolutely good and other things as absolutely evil, and in that way draw a hard-and-fast distinction between examples of either side of the spectrum of good and evil. But even in this area of thought, I contend that we can have at best only partial, not absolute, truths. Why do I think this to be so? I respond to this question by considering five conceptions, imaginings, or exhibitions of goodness or evil that are inevitably situated somewhere between rather than at the extremes of absolute goodness, on the one hand, or absolute evil, on the other. And this is so despite what is sometimes or even often thought to be the case. The first is the idea of God, the second is an imagined heavenly afterlife, the third is the character of nature, the fourth relates to particular examples of human beings, and the fifth addresses the issue of outlandish moral statements. In no one of these five areas can we find reliable claims to either absolute goodness or absolute evil. Instead, we find degrees of each, at least so far as what we can cogently analyze and understand is concerned.

1. The Idea of God

Jews, Christians, and Muslims hold it to be absolutely true that God is good. But the Book of Job in the Hebrew Bible reminds us that the goodness of God, if it can rightly be called that, far exceeds anything that humans can fully understand. God has created a world, according to these religious traditions, that God pronounces to be good, even though there are abundant natural evils in this world, and even though God's human creatures are guilty of many glaring acts of evil. If these facts are attributed to a supposed fall of human beings into sin, then God has created them with this susceptibility and surely could have been able to predict or foresee that they would succumb to it. Is God not then somehow complicit in the evils of nature and of human beings?

There is a paradox of good and evil in the conception of God that the Hebrew Bible, for example, makes no attempt to resolve. It is left standing as a reminder of the radical distinction between the assumed reality of God and human attempts to comprehend the ways of God, including trying to understand how God can allow so many evils to be present in the world and yet to assert with the Psalmist, "As for God, his Way is perfect" (Psalm 18:31). Jews of the biblical period had humbly to acknowledge the Prophet Isaiah's testimony regarding God, "my thoughts are not your thoughts, neither are your Ways my Ways, saith the Lord" (Isaiah 55:8). This Prophet even has God proclaiming in one place, "I form the light, and create darkness; I make peace, and create evil; I am the Lord, that doeth all these things" (Isaiah 45:7).[23]

The paradox I am speaking of here becomes even more pronounced when Paul, the author of the Epistle to the Romans in the Christian New Testament, says the following: "For God has consigned all men to disobedience, that he may have mercy on all. O the depth of the riches and wisdom and knowledge of God! How unsearchable are his judgments and how inscrutable his ways! For who has known the mind of the Lord, or who has been his counselor?" (Romans 11:32–34).[24] These are puzzling words, but they are no doubt meant to be so. God's unqualified goodness may be assumed, Paul seems to be asserting, but when it comes to trying to comprehend God's goodness and reconciling it with the unquestionable, pervasive reality of evil in the world and in human life, a failure of comprehension has to be admitted.

The gist of the matter, as far as human minds are capable of knowing and asserting, is that the goodness of God, if there be such a divine being, cannot be stated without paradox. It is one thing to affirm the absolute goodness of God but quite another to claim to understand it. God's goodness is thought to be beyond question but also to be somehow inextricably mixed with the perplexing mystery of the rampant and undeniable evils of the world. These thoughts take us back to those of the first chapter of this book, where we were brought up against the radical noetic transcendence, mystery, and elusiveness of the ultimate focus or object of faith in any adequate religious outlook on the world, whether that is Yahweh, the Christian God, Allah, Brahman, the Dao, nature, or some other religious ultimate.

2. The Hope of Heaven

In a number of religions, including Christianity and Islam, there is expectation of an afterlife awaiting the faithful, one where, in the words of the Book of Revelation in the Christian New Testament, God will "wipe every tear" from the eyes of the saved, "and death shall be no more, neither shall there be mourning nor crying nor pain any more, for the former things have passed away" (Revelation 21:4). Surah LVI, 1–56 of the Qur'an contains a vision of the afterlife where the faithful have been raised to everlasting life. They shall live in gardens of delight, with gushing water, refreshing shade, abundant fruit, and delectable meat of every kind readily available. They shall recline on couches inlaid with jewels and be waited on by immortal youths. They shall drink the finest wine and never become intoxicated. Fair virgins with lovely eyes shall be available as lovers and friends for the faithful males of the afterlife. In this heavenly paradise, there is no vain speaking, hatred, or recrimination. These two writings paint a vision of heaven as wholly and eternally good, with not even the slightest shadow of suffering or evil. The promise of its joys and delights for the saved is confidently affirmed as an absolute truth.

However, there are at least three profound problems with this affirmation. There is the problem of hell, the problem of an orderly world, and the problem of human freedom. Let me say a word or two about each problem in order to bring it into view. I once had a conversation with a conservative Christian who argued that, if I did not believe as he did, God would doom me to hell. He was a compassionate person, and I asked him how he could be happy in heaven if I, his friend, was writhing in hell. More fundamentally, we can raise the question of how a loving and merciful God could regard his purposes for humankind as having been fulfilled when many of his creatures are doomed to unending, pitiless, horrible suffering in the flames of hell. The Surah of the Qur'an I referred to above also draws a stark contrast between the unceasing delights of faithful Muslims in paradise, on the one hand, and the eternal torments of the infidels in hell, on the other. So the same problem of the seeming lack of fulfillment of divine compassion and purpose is posed. If the idea of predestination of some to heaven and some to hell is raised, as it sometimes is in both Christianity and Islam, this only compounds the problem. Why would a just, merciful, and loving God consign some of his own creatures to hell? And how can this idea or the idea of hell itself as eternal punishment for the unfaithful—whether predestined to be such or because of their own wrong choices—be reconciled with the goodness and mercy of God?

A second major problem with viewing the hope of heaven or paradise as an unqualified good is the seeming absence of natural order or natural law in this domain. Here God's (or Allah's) providential care is thought to guard the faithful against any kind of accident, misfortune, or pain. Suffering or deprivation of any kind is deemed to be impossible. But we can get no clear picture of how this could be the case. How could there be order and predictability in a realm where natural laws are inoperative, getting hurt is not possible, and fallibility and finitude pose no problems? The problem here with assertion of the afterlife for the faithful as an unqualified good is that we cannot really conceive such an afterlife. If we cannot conceive it, then the assertion of it as an unqualified good suffers from incoherence and unintelligibility.

The third serious difficulty with this assertion relates to human freedom. The absence of natural laws which can inflict misery, damage, or pain on the faithful would seem to mean that they are incapable of predicting the consequences of their actions. No matter what they choose to do or intend to do, it will always turn out to be good. This is a strange kind of freedom. Moreover, it is assumed by traditional proponents of the unqualified goodness of heaven or paradise that no mistakes can be made by the faithful and that no misdeeds can be performed by them. There is therefore nothing to be learned, nothing to be striven for, and nothing to be accomplished. Everything is already perfect. Everything is already complete. Human actions would seem to be superfluous in such an afterlife and nothing would seem to hang on human choices or responsibility. Most fundamentally, how could we humans be the same persons in this kind of afterlife as we were on earth? Once again, this is a strange, if not wholly unintelligible view of human freedom, and, again, it makes assertion of the goodness of an afterlife, so conceived, highly problematic and far from qualifying as an absolute truth.

3. The Character of Nature

Total, unqualified, uninterrupted goodness is sometimes attributed to nature. The idea is that the devastations of natural disasters such as storms, floods, volcanic eruptions, forest fires, mudslides, pestilences, plagues, tsunamis, predations, starvations, deformed births, and the like are aspects of nature that are somehow conceived to be swallowed up into the unqualified goodness of nature when the latter is seen as a whole. There is important partial truth in this idea, as I shall show. But there is falsity as well. Nature is a blend of the good and the bad, of the creative and the destructive. It is neither to the exclusion of the other. And it is by no means easy to imagine how it could be otherwise.

Can we envision a nature without natural laws? If not, and I contend that we cannot, then we have to acknowledge that natural laws can hurt as well as help on different occasions or in different circumstances. If I accidently ingest a poison, I may die. If a tree falls on me, I may be killed or wounded. A severe storm may wipe out a neighborhood. A raging forest fire may kill innumerable plants and animals. Predations are routine in nature; animals are sometimes torn limb from limb by their predators and the progeny of these animals deprived of their parents' protection. Natural laws make possible the sad and deeply regrettable births of deformed babies, just as they make possible the births of ones with no defects. A nature of natural laws—and what other kind of nature can even be conceived?—is an axiologically ambiguous nature, not one exhibiting either complete goodness or complete evil. But a nature of natural laws also provides the predictability and manageability of aspects of nature that are necessary for the survival of all forms of life and for the meaningful exercise of human freedom. Freedom would be useless, for its part, if there were no law-like nature amenable and responsive to its exercise.

The partial truth implicit in the idea of nature as absolutely good is that creation and destruction go hand-in-hand in a nature in which dynamism and change are routinely operative. If they were not operative, there would be no emergence of the present universe over eons of cosmological time. There would be no origin of the solar system and its planet earth and no evolution of the species of life on the face of the earth, including our own human species. There would be no warmth of the sun or the cooling refreshment of rain. There would be no food chain giving support to one species of life at the expense of another, thus cycling through living beings the essential energy of the sun.

We can rightly say that it is good for there to be this universe, this solar system and earth, and the multifarious species of earth and its complex systems of interdependence. And we can affirm the goodness of our own species, as part of the ecological community of living beings. But these and many other goods of nature must be kept in balance with the evils of nature that have made them possible. Predations are rampant, extinctions of species litter the path to our own evolution, and natural catastrophes often take place. Getting in the way of natural laws can be disastrous for humans and nonhumans alike. Interdependencies of biological species also entail their vulnerabilities.

Nature has a horrible, menacing, ugly side as well as one of delight, sustenance, and beauty. It is no more *altogether* good than it is *altogether* bad. The truth about it lies between these extremes. Nature as it is and as we experience it countenances neither nihilistic disgust and loathing nor gushingly sentimental *downplaying* of its ineliminable threats, tradeoffs, and destructions. It can be religiously right to reverence nature, but it would be foolish to deny its blend of goods and evils—a blend without which no conception of nature is imaginable.

4. Particular Examples of Human Beings

Has any human being ever been completely, unqualifiedly, unambiguously good? Alternatively, has any human being ever been totally evil, beyond redemption, deserving only of complete abhorrence and rejection? Can we draw a clear line in this area of thought and experience between absolute goodness and absolute evil? I argue that we cannot because all humans are by their very nature finite and fallible and because no human should ever be regarded as beyond the reach of renewal, rehabilitation, or redemption, or as being totally bereft of inner resources to make this process possible. Even more basically, none of us has sufficient knowledge or understanding to make such absolute assessments possible. We are not even able to assess the quality of our own motivations, beliefs, and actions with complete objectivity, clarity, and precision.

In traditional Judaism and Islam, there is firm resistance to any tendency to apotheosize the founders or great figures of their respective religious traditions. Moses, David, Isaiah, and Mohammad, for example, are viewed as men, not as God in human flesh. Moses quakes in fear in the presence of Yahweh and removes his sandals before Yahweh's ominous presence at the burning bush. He confesses himself unworthy and incapable to carry the divine message to his people in Egypt and to become their leader. The otherwise exemplary and heroic King David sins grievously and is shown in the Hebrew Bible to be far from divine when he takes Bathsheba to be his wife and sends her husband to die in the front line of battle. Isaiah in the temple, when he has the vision of Yahweh "high and lifted up," confesses himself to be "a man of unclean lips" (Isaiah 6:1-5). Even the Jesus of Luke's gospel, when addressed by a ruler as "Good Teacher," responds to him, "Why do you call me good? No one is good but God alone" (Luke 18:18). Mohammad is filled with trepidation and fear and at first wonders if he has gone mad when he begins to receive Allah's revelations in the cave in Mecca. There is never a question of his thinking himself to be Allah in human form, and Muslims would regard such an attribution as commission of the grave sin of *shirk* or idolatry.

The case of traditional Christianity's attitude toward Jesus of Nazareth is an interesting one in this regard. He was later claimed to be an incarnation of God and to be like God, having no inclination toward sin and even as being incapable of sin. The story of his being born of a virgin impregnated by the spirit of God rather than by a human father was cited as evidence of his being free from the condition of sinfulness that could be traced back to Adam and Eve. But how can a mere man exhibit the perfect goodness attributable only to God? How can this idea be reconciled with Jesus's stern reminder in Luke's Gospel that God alone is perfectly good?

Nestorian Christians of the fifth century attempted to sort out this mystery by claiming that the man Jesus was fully and completely human, but that the divine spirit that infused Jesus was not. So, by implication, whatever miscalculations or mistakes of judgment Jesus may have made and had to learn from in the course of his life from childhood to his death in his early thirties would be those of his human aspect, not of his divine one. The man Jesus could be born and suffer death on the cross, Nestorians held, but it was impossible for the divine spirit to do so.

The Nestorian view was branded as heretical by what came to be regarded as traditional or normative Christianity, the latter asserting that the divine and the human were two aspects of the one being Jesus. He was not a combination of divine and human beings, the one separate from the other.[25] The orthodox view turned principally on the view that if God did not suffer and die on the cross, then the sins of humans could not be forgiven and their sinful condition radically altered and redeemed by the sacrificial death and resurrection of the God-man Jesus.

In any event, we do not know nearly enough about the historical Jesus's life, and certainly not enough about his inner life, to conclude with certainty that he was perfect in every aspect. And if he was perfect, it is doubtful that and highly unclear how he could really have been a part of the finite, fallible human race. I earlier questioned, it will be recalled, even our ability to comprehend what the perfection of God (or Allah) would amount to and how it could with complete clarity and adequacy be assessed. A fortiori, it would seem impossible to imagine what a completely and unambiguously good human life—one entirely devoid of the slightest miscalculation, error, or sin from childhood to death—would look like.

What about the other side of the spectrum? Are there humans who are totally evil and depraved and, as such, undeserving of any kind of positive hope, approbation, or regard? At first glance, one might think immediately of people such as Joseph Stalin, Adolf Hitler, Pol Pot, or Ted Bundy, each of them of recent memory, who seem to belong to this alleged class of human beings. The nefarious characters and horrible deeds of each of these four persons are beyond contention. But who of us is competent to understand why they were capable of or disposed toward being so evil? Who of us is competent to know the heart and inner being of each one? Finally, who can claim to know with utter certainty that any of them is beyond the possibility of radical change and renewal?

To take another example, it tends in our time to be commonly assumed that those who prey sexually on the young suffer from some kind of fatal defect that can never be cured, and that such persons, once found guilty of such a crime, must be labeled as a chronically evil and imminently dangerous sexual offenders who should be ostracized and cut off from any location where children are present. But these are absolute assertions made in the face of what in the very nature of things cannot be certainties. To hold a person forever in the bondage of such a characterization, especially if based on a single deed perpetrated in adolescence, is to pretend to a completeness and certainty of knowledge that none of us, no matter how astute his or her psychological, biological, or legal training and experience might be, can possess. I do not question the need to make judgments relating to such persons; I only question the notion that such judgments can be anything but probably rather than absolutely correct or that they would never require correction at a later time.

A similar point applies to the idea of capital punishment which, in effect, assumes the certainty of guilt in cases where only probability may be available, where egregious mistakes have been made in judgments of guilt in the past, and where the person condemned to execution is deemed to be beyond rehabilitation. Is there such a thing as absolute, irremediable evil in human beings? I argue that even if there were, we would not be capable of knowing with absolute certainty that it is so, even in the most extreme cases we can cite or imagine. It may or may not be true that to know all is to forgive all. I am neither defending nor attacking this proposition. But I am insisting that none of us humans is capable of knowing everything that would be necessary for passing a final judgment of irrevocable, irremediable evil on another human being.

5. Outlandish Moral Claims

Under this heading, let me take the imagined case of someone saying, "It is morally permissible to boil babies in oil for fun. Whatever gives me pleasure is what I am entitled to pursue and to do."[26] On first glance, this looks like an absolutely false claim, but more careful examination of shows that there is residual truth in one aspect of the claim. The residual truth is that pleasure is a good. But of course not all forms of pleasure are necessarily good. To take pleasure in the suffering of another human being—or, I submit, in that of any sentient being—is morally reprehensible.

Aristotle rightly insisted that human desires should not be blindly obeyed but brought under the supervision and control of reason. And

John Stuart Mill plausibly argued that sympathy for the wellbeing of others is a deeply rooted natural trait in human beings that needs to be morally ranged alongside of and to stand in tension with that of self-regard. He viewed this observation as entirely consistent with his view that happiness or pleasure is the ultimate moral principle. He distinguished sensate pleasures from those of the mind or spirit and argued that the latter takes precedence over the former; and he refused to endorse the egoistic idea that any one person's pleasures should take absolute moral precedence over those of others. In other words, there is no reason to think that I am an exception to moral principles that in their very nature apply to everyone, including me.

Now a person, let's say he is a male, who seriously makes the outlandish claim quoted above is likely to be a psychopath or sadist who takes fiendish delight in the suffering of others, including innocent babies. He is right in thinking that personal pleasure can be a justifiable moral pursuit or good in some situations of choice and action, but he is wrong in applying this principle in an absolutistic, unqualified, wholly self-centered manner. He is wrong in thinking that only his pleasure matters and that the suffering of others is of no moral concern. He announces his claim, not with the thinking of a normal person but with the distorted attitude of a seriously sick one. He needs long-term counseling and/or drug therapy, not reasoned discussion of the tenability of his point of view. His is not a thoughtful assessment of moral responsibility but an obliviousness to this issue altogether. He may have no sense or understanding of moral obligation, in which case he is not in a position to make pronouncements concerning it. Still, he is a human being and as such worthy of moral respect. He is entitled, as all of us are, to appropriate pleasures of life. But he needs to be brought to an understanding—if this is possible—that he is not entitled routinely to pursue his pleasures at the expense of the pains of others.

Who knows what assumptions about his life and actions may lurk beneath such a person's statement? Beneath the distortions, there may well be assumptions that point in a promising direction and that can be steered through counseling and therapy in this promising way. At any rate, it is important to see that it is not at all likely that any serious moral thinker would endorse his view about the suffering of babies as a welcome source of personal pleasure. What lurks *beneath* his outlandish claim is another matter, and it may be found that there are lineaments of truth or elements of moral concern even in such a person's outlook on himself and the world that can be brought to the surface. We cannot know for sure that this is not the case.

His imagined claim as it stands is would appear to be patently false, but its rootage in his psychological makeup would need to be understood for all of its aspects and suggestions of meaning to be properly exposed to view. He may, for example, be passionately resentful of babies in general because of gnawing childhood jealousy regarding treatment of a sibling or siblings by his parents. And he is within his rights in having expected and yearned for equal treatment from the parents. Thus, his claim does not stand alone. It is rooted in a wider context of attitude, assumption, background, and biological, and psychological makeup—all of which should be taken into account. And its implications have clearly not been thought through by the claimant.

Is it a serious claim? I do not think that it is, at least not in the sense of having been clearly and responsibly arrived at by a competent thinker. It is more like the senseless ravings of a disturbed person. In any event, it and other imagined claims similar to it should not be regarded as exceptions to the thesis that all significant claims to truth are partial in varying degrees and that even patently false claims may implicitly contain or point toward elements of truth.

I have argued in this section that there is no way for us to know with absolute clarity and certainty or to hold as an absolute rather than partial truth that God, heaven, nature, and any human being is completely, unequivocally, and unambiguously good. We are similarly fallible when it comes to judgments about the character and extent of evil. The best we can do is to make probable judgments, and these judgments, if rationally made, will always turn out to affirm some seeming mixture of potential or actual goodness and evil, creation and destruction, susceptibility to error and soundness of judgment, or despicable action and lingering compassion and hope for the person or persons responsible for the action.

In other words, we humans are incapable in our very natures of anything other than partial truths in these areas. But this is not to deny the crucially important meta-statement running through the pages of this book that some claims can be far more true or false, justified or unjustified, than others. I do not deny the reality and recognizability of markedly different degrees of good and evil. I only deny our ability entirely to separate the one from the other, that is, clearly and unambiguously to conceive an utmost pole of unqualified goodness, on the one hand, or a diametrically opposite pole of irredeemable evil, on the other. Our judgments can and do approximate these poles in particular circumstances, but there is always room for reasonable doubt about claims to have arrived at either pole with absolute, indefeasible certainty. Just as the values of pi can never be exhausted, human thought is always somewhere along the spectrum of good and evil in its thinking, never entirely at either of the spectrum's opposite ends. Judgment must be mixed with compassion, and justice with mercy.

Chapter 6

HUMANITY

Nothing straight can be constructed from such warped wood as
that which man is made of.

Immanuel Kant[1]

Like Martin Luther King, Jr., in our own time, Immanuel Kant
had a dream in his time. He sets it forth in his essay entitled
Idea for a Universal History with a Cosmopolitan Purpose (1784). His
dream was of a federation of states that would inaugurate a new era
of universal peace and justice among human beings. Kant envisioned
three possible outcomes of the search for such a federation: first, that
it would happen entirely by chance; second, that it would come into
being by a natural process leading the human species gradually but
progressively from a lowest state of animality to its highest level of
moral, social, and political achievement; or third, that humans would
descend to a hell of unimaginable evils in an increasingly retrograde
moral, social, and political existence.

Stunted and Soaring Trees

In developing the idea of his dream, Kant draws on the analogy of
trees growing in a forest. One group of trees grows splendidly upward,
each tree seeking its access to the sun for its nourishment and development. These trees cooperate with one another, as it were. They do
not infringe on one another and, in consequence, all can flourish. But
in another group of trees, each tree extends its branches outward in

all directions, rather than upward. Therefore, it and the other trees around it have to struggle to survive, and they are crooked, twisted, and stunted as a result. This crookedness and stuntedness, Kant suggests, has marked humanity throughout its sad history of destructive self-centeredness, conflict, wickedness, and injustice.

In the epigraph to this chapter, Kant is noting how difficult it will be for his dream to be fulfilled, given the warped and crooked timber of humanity. He does not expect perfection. Steady progress toward ever closer approximations to the goal of his dream will do. But he recognizes the need to be honest and realistic about the prospects for the dream's realization. What it will take, Kant surmises, is three things: the correct conception of the moral development and system of political organization necessary to the dream's achievement and maintenance; relevant and ongoing experiences pondered and tested in the affairs of the world; and a human good will prepared to take fully into account, learn from, and put into practice the positive and negative lessons of these experiences.

Kant does not so much doubt the *capability* of human beings to develop steadily and progressively in the direction of this ideal. He has faith in their rational abilities and in the inherent power of their wills. But he warns of the great danger of their persistent *unwillingness* to draw upon this capability in effective ways. It will be inordinately hard, he is saying, for the warped and crooked condition of humanity, as made glaringly evident in its sad history up to the date of his writing in the latter part of the eighteenth century, to do anything as straightforwardly dedicated and upwardly striving as to work steadily toward the realization of his great dream.

Kant's dream has not died from his day in the eighteenth century to the present. But the hope of its realization has been disappointed again and again. This has proved to be the case as the nations of the world have continued to compete with each other for domination and supremacy, as new and horrible technologies of warfare have been developed, as competitiveness and greed have been allowed to triumph over compassion and mercy, and as racial and religious prejudice and hatred have continued to rear their menacing heads.

Adolf Hitler in the twentieth century had his own fond dream of a federation of European powers, but it was to be ruthlessly ordered and ruled as his thousand-year German Reich. The people in ascendancy in this so-called federation were to be those of the so-called Aryan race. Jews and other undesirables were being systematically annihilated in concentration camps in preparation for the Aryan reign, a reign to be free of "vermin" peoples infecting the purity and glory of the Reich. Hitler sought to enforce realization of his monstrous dream with the latest types of ingenious and rampantly destructive military technology, and his efforts were met with the lethal technologies of the Allies to the west of Germany and the Soviet Union to its east. Kant's nightmare of hell on earth came true during the years of World War II, not only in Europe but in nations of Asia, the Philippines, and the islands of the Pacific.

Japan's arrogant dream of domination of the nations of the far East and Pacific—a racist, totalitarian dream all too similar to that of Hitler in the West—was finally dashed by the hideous atomic bombing of two of its major cities, the peoples and properties of each reduced to cinders by the unprecedented technology of a single bomb dropped by a single airplane. Thus, the crooked timber of humanity wreaked havoc on the earth, binding nations into separate warring groups across the world rather than in peaceful coexistence and fervent pursuit of international justice and prosperity.

The horrors of World War II were preceded by the Napoleonic wars of the early nineteenth century, the American Civil War at mid-century, the French and Prussian wars, the Boer War, and the unbelievable carnage of the trench warfare of World War I. In the meantime, chauvinistic Western nations of the nineteenth century were devoted militarily, culturally, and economically to colonial exploitation and domination of the peoples of other lands such as India, Africa, and China. In addition, the cruel institution of slavery was widespread in the first two-thirds of the century after Kant's eighteenth century.

Implicit in these brief reflections is the burning question: Is Kant's confidence justified when he speaks of the *capacity* of human beings to achieve the kind of international peace and justice of which he dreams? Are we humans really capable of it? And can his hope for the *exercise* of this alleged capacity be rightly asserted in the face of all the terrible things that have happened and continue to happen from his time to the present? The raging wars and population displacements of peoples in Syria and other parts of the Middle East, based in part on seething religious intolerance and fanaticism as well as deep-seated resentment against condescending European colonialism and exploitation, are one prominent example at the time of my writing.

I claim in this chapter that Kant's assertion of this capacity and his hope for its progressive exercise can be affirmed, but only as partial truths that require sober qualification and correction by other critical considerations—the most relevant of which, as Kant observes, being the distorted, twisted, and corrupt attitudes and behaviors of humanity itself as made appallingly manifest through much of its history. But this history, as I shall argue here, is a mixed history, a combination of lessons of hope and lessons of despair, of achieved goods and heart-wrenching evils, of commendable progress and deplorable retrogression. The fact, at least by my reckoning, that this history is neither to the exclusion of the other gives support to Kant's dream, but it is a support that depends crucially on the human willingness to bring about a better world through its resourceful, out-of-the-box imaginings and persistent efforts.

To make the crooked timber of humanity entirely straight is, by all evidences impossible, as Kant admitted. But with the proper kind of care, it can perhaps be made much less misshapen and more productive of universal peacefulness, prosperity, and justice among human beings and other creatures of earth. This would seem to qualify at least as a partial truth. It is far from being an absolute truth, given the grievous evidences of human history. But I believe that the hope it expresses is justifiable and workable, even though it is also admittedly tentative and uncertain. We have the capacity of which Kant speaks, and we can exercise the will of which he dreams.

Straws in the wind can be signs of an approaching storm, but they can also provide indications of a storm's abatement. There are straws of our own time, some pointing to the possibility of growing worldwide disaster but others serving as signs of progressive attainment and hopeful assurance. I shall first discuss some unmistakable signs of imminent disaster, but in a following section I shall develop a basis for the optimistic and at least partially true proposition that we humans not only can but will find ways to work together to bring about a better world. The latter is not only Kant's dream but very much my own, and it should be the dream of all right-thinking and right-aspiring citizens of the world today. To abandon the dream and to despair of growing approximations to its noble goal is to make inevitable the nightmare to which it stands in stubborn opposition.

Signs of Approaching Disaster

There is considerable truth in the idea that the world of today is headed toward disastrous outcomes, and that these outcomes will become increasingly probable to the extent that humans pay no attention to their looming prospects and continue thoughtlessly and recklessly to foster and condone their actualization. We do not know what the future will bring, but we can be reasonably sure that such impending disasters pose serious threats to our future and the future of other living beings on earth. I take note in this section of four kinds of threatening disaster: the sweeping injustices of unchecked, unregulated capitalism; the unresolved cruelties and disruptions of religious conflicts; the development and threatening use of ever more sophisticated weapons of terror and destruction; and the woeful prospect and already rapidly increasing amount of regional and global ecological devastation.

These signs of approaching disaster are not infallible. We do not know with certainty what the future will bring. But if we weigh the dire probabilities attendant on being unconcerned with such signs and doing nothing about them, the need for keen alertness to the dangers they signify and the urgent demand for effective responses to these dangers should become abundantly evident. We cannot escape the responsibility that is ours as human beings to work together to the fullest extent of our capabilities for the wellbeing of all lives on this planet, including our own, and for the nurture, safety, and integrity of the natural environments on which all earthly lives depend. As we will to do so, we crooked-timbered humans may discover capabilities we were previously unaware of within ourselves, in our collective actions, and in appropriate uses and developments of our institutions.

1. Unchecked, Unregulated Capitalism

In chapter 4, I discussed some of the unfortunate tendencies and consequences of unregulated capitalism. I focus here more fully on one of these, namely, the increasingly yawning gap between the extremely wealthy and the other members of society, especially the relatively uneducated and unskilled and the extremely poor, but also to a growing extent the middle class. This gap is made possible by several things.

One is the sheer, unmerited luck of large amounts of inherited wealth attained by the few and their enjoyment of the interest, rents, and other opportunities and gains made possible by this inherited wealth. Another is complex tax systems with numerous loopholes and exceptions that favor the rich at the expense of the less rich. A third is the unequal access and influence the rich gain through their financial support for politicians and the consequent favorable political treatments and policies relating to themselves, their investments, their other business enterprises, and the favorable tax status they gain thereby. A kind of feedback loop is established by this process. The wealthy bestow their financial largess on the politicians' campaigns and elections; the politicians respond by enacting or allowing programs favorable to the wealthy, enabling the latter to become ever more wealthy; their increasing wealth gives them even greater political influence and clout; and so on—with the result that the disparity between the wealthy few and the non-wealthy many becomes ever more pronounced.

A final factor is the devotion of more and more of the productivity of large businesses to the salaries, stock acquisitions, bonuses, and benefits of their top executives—a productivity that could have been more justly and equitably distributed to the lower-tiered workers who made that productivity possible. The process of unregulated, non-interfering, favorably taxed (or untaxed), special treatments of the rich at the expense of the less rich—all greased by covert and inequitable political influence—threatens increasingly to produce a small coterie of the extremely rich empowered to direct the affairs of the world in ways that benefit their own narrow self-interest and give little or no consideration or aid to the needs of others.

The threat, in a word, is creation of a powerful, dominant, extremely wealthy *oligarchy* that by virtue of its wealth and influence—much of it untaxed, unregulated, and unmerited—comes to dominate the economic, political, and social affairs of the world. All of this can be allowed to occur under the cover of policies and practices that pretend to be just, fair, and even-handed on the ground of their alleged consistency with a free market ideal. This kind of creeping, oligarchic capitalism is a severe danger to the justice and fair-dealing of the world that needs to be kept in mind along with the fears of creeping socialism kept alive by ardent proponents of *laissez-faire* capitalism, themselves sometimes often covertly or even unconsciously self-interested rather than being genuinely principled in their outlook.

The self-interest of the wealthy few can, if unrecognized, unacknowledged, and unchecked produce widespread indifference toward and violations of the rights and legitimate needs of the unwealthy many—particularly those on the lowest rungs of the economic ladder. The threat of this emerging situation, accompanied by the evidence for strong current trends in its direction, is a serious one. It could be highly detrimental to the general wellbeing of the world's peoples.[2] It could warp the timber of humanity to a grotesque degree and be a major cause of instability and unrest within and among the nations of our planet.

French economist Thomas Piketty notes that between 1977 and 2007 in the United States "the richest 10 percent appropriated three-quarters of [the country's] growth. The richest 1percent alone absorbed nearly 60 percent of the total increase of US national income in this period. Hence for the bottom 90 percent, the rate of income growth was less than 0.5 percent per year." He adds, "It is hard to imagine an economy and society that can continue functioning indefinitely with such extreme divergence between social groups."[3] The pressures created by such divergence are like those of tectonic plates slowly encroaching on one another. Sooner or later, they have to fracture and explode, with calamitous results. This is the dark portent of increasing worldwide economic inequalities if they are allowed to develop without relief.

As I indicated in chapter 4, the greater truth lies in the search for justly achieved and maintained tensions or balances between the extremes of a completely free market, on the one hand, and that of an unrelenting collectivist control of economic affairs, on the other—and in neither one to the exclusion of the other. Under-regulation is no less a threat to world peace, prosperity, and justice than over-regulation. Thoughtful, sustained deliberation on the carefully calculated less-and-more, with a view to the just and equitable effects for all concerned, is much more advisable in both the short and long run than unreflective, unrestrained, impulsive resort to an ideological either-or. In the concluding section of this chapter, we will look at some signs of progress in this more balanced direction.

2. The Cruelties and Disruptions of Religious Conflicts

Religion can be a tremendous force for good or evil. Indication of the second possibility is the fact that about eight million casualties resulted from the Thirty Years' War of 1618–1648, a war that was initially provoked by religious conflicts between Roman Catholic and Protestant states in central Europe. Political factors figured in as well, but a major impetus for this war was religious. It carried forward the conflict between Catholics and Protestants dating from Martin Luther's posting of his controversial "95 Theses" in 1517.

The City-State Geneva that came to be dominated by the stern and highly influential Protestant Christian John Calvin in the 1500s is an example of the kind of radical intolerance of opposing religious points of view and consequences of this intolerance that came to mark aspects of the Protestant Reformation and the Catholic Counter-Reformation. Only one strict way of thinking and acting was deemed to be acceptable in Protestant Geneva at this time. Calvin claimed that his carefully reasoned and clearly written interpretation of the Christian scriptures in his magnum opus *Institutes of the Christian Religion* was not one helpful interpretation among others but the only accurate and defensible way of understanding what he took to be the absolute truths of those scriptures. If one wanted to live in Geneva, one had to abide by the Calvinistic interpretation of the Christian faith in both outlook and practice or face penalties of banishment, imprisonment, or execution.

The Spanish theologian Michael Servetus, to cite one example, was convicted of heresy and burned at the stake in Geneva, in accordance with Calvin's personal instructions, for daring to question Calvinistic orthodoxy (and orthopraxis). The same fate befell the Italian Dominican friar, philosopher, and astronomer Giordano Bruno in the same century when he dared to question commonly accepted beliefs concerning God, Christ, and the universe and was convicted of heresy by the Roman Catholic Inquisition. When partial, debatable, tentative religious truths are converted into absolute ones, as in these two instances, great danger and possible vicious treatments are in the offing for those who presume or feel compelled in all honestly to think or act differently.

In the present century, the most prominent and tumultuous conflict over religious convictions is taking place in the Middle East. Here various Islamic groups with different religious outlooks are battling for influence, territory, and supremacy. For many if not most of these combatants, religion plays the dominant role in defining their sense of selfhood, social identity, purpose, and place in the world.

Religion also drives their long-term resentment against nations of the Christian West that have colonized them, exploited them, and tended to treat them with contemptuous prejudice and condescension over many years.

A central bone of contention among Muslims of the Middle East is the nation of Israel, a nation representing among other things the religious outlook of Judaism, which has established itself in Palestine and displaced and subjugated large numbers of Palestinian peoples, most of them Muslims. The people of Israel, in their turn, are in Palestine largely because of the notorious Nazi attempt to exterminate Jews in the Holocaust of the twentieth century but also because of a long history of recurrent pogroms—fueled by the prejudice and animosity of people calling themselves Christian—against the Jews in Europe.

The principal antagonists of the current wars of the Middle East are the Sunna and Sunni sects of Islam, the former represented most prominently in terms of population by Saudi Arabia and Egypt, and the latter represented by Iran, but also to a considerable extent by Iraq, with two-thirds Shiites. The wars attracting the most attention at the time of this writing are the civil war in Yemen between Sunni and Shia sympathizers and the one in Syria and Iraq largely orchestrated by ISIS or the Islamic State, a group of fanatical Jihadist warriors spawned by al-Qaida in Iraq and bent on setting up a radical, right-wing Sunni Caliphate in parts of Syria and Iraq.

The war in Syria involves Western nations such as the United States and Russia, these two on opposing sides, as well as other Western and Middle Eastern states. It has produced widespread carnage and a huge wave of immigrants trying to escape from the terrors and disruptions of wartime Syria through Turkey and countries of the West. A radically intolerant religious outlook is the driving force of ISIS, setting it adamantly and violently against any and all other religious views. In ISIS we have the spectacle of the crooked timber of humanity in lamentably twisted and gnarled form, and we are brought up against the vicious destructive effects of close-minded, tunnel-visioned, absolutistic religious commitments.

Why are religious conflicts potent forces for violent animosity, destruction, and evil? They become so when partial truth is converted into total truth, and when that so-called total truth is affirmed and defended at all costs, with no holds barred, and in the face of all opposing views—allowing for no compromise, no negotiation, or no peaceful settlement and justifying the use of any means for a religious group's unconditional supremacy and success.

Social anthropologist Scott Atran analyzes the factors underlying the total commitment of members of religious groups such as ISIS to their causes, goals, and ideals and concludes that such groups are entirely *deontic* or duty-driven in their outlook and approach, with little or no concern for the consequences of their actions to themselves or others. Their obedience to their religious mandate and conviction, when regarded as unquestionable, unconditional, and absolute, drives them relentlessly onward, regardless of imminent danger to their own lives and without regard to any other kind of prudential consideration.

Religiously oriented and motivated groups of this type are committed to inviolable sacred values such as, in the case of ISIS, the triumph of their version of Islam and the establishment of a Caliphate in the Middle East analogous to that of earlier Islamic civilization. The Caliphate would rule strictly—and, if need be, with uncompromising brutality—by the teachings, principles, and laws of the Qur'an and Sharia tradition as these two are viewed by the ISIS leaders. The indifference of members of religious groups of this kind to dangers to property or possessions, life or limb, personal prosperity or family wellbeing, and their willingness to sacrifice everything to their cause makes them formidable adversaries. They are not likely to be countered or vanquished by the cautionary, prudential stratagems of conventional warfare. This is particularly the case when such religious groups have the firm assurance of an ultimate reward for their ardent valor and uncompromising commitment in an afterlife of everlasting bliss.[4]

The radically unsettled, war-like character of the Middle East is a threat to the entire world. Major world powers have become embroiled in the conflict. It reminds us of the unsettled condition and nationalistic aspirations of the Balkan states prior to World War I that, especially in the case of Serbia, soon ignited that terrible war. Religious conflict in the Middle East today is a central part of the volatile mix of resentment against the West, nationalistic fervor, hostility toward Israel, Israeli responses to that hostility, and determination by some Muslims to restore the former glories and achievements of Islamic civilization. This combination of factors is like a lighted match waved over an open keg of dynamite, not only with regard to the Middle East itself but in relation to the world as a whole. This is a chilling portent. A third World War of unimaginable horror and destruction could have its impetus here. The ghastly scenario of a possible calamitous future for the world painted in this subsection contains a lot of truth, but it is partial truth. It is partial because it is contingent on what human beings do or fail to do. I shall make this claim more evident in the final section of this chapter.

3. The Development and Use of Increasingly Sophisticated and Rabidly Destructive Weapons

The threat of civil unrest and violence in the world is greatly augmented by the radically destructive weapons available to warring groups. The development of weapons has proceeded apace throughout human history, but in the twentieth and twenty-first centuries it has become especially gruesome in its actual and potential effects on human populations. Poison gasses, machine guns, and shrapnel-spewing heavy artillery inflicted widespread carnage on land combatants in the First World War. Submarines sank large numbers of defenseless merchant ships. And airplanes were used for the first time for reconnaissance and artillery spotting, dogfighting with machine guns firing through synchronized propellers, and light bombing.

The Second World War brought blockbuster and incendiary bombs that reduced whole cities to rubble; the enormous, heavily armed airplanes to carry the bombs; and the long range fighters to accompany and protect the bombers. Late in the war the Germans were able to produce rocket-powered guided missiles launched from German soil that bombed London, Antwerp, and Liège; and they created the first jet planes. Late in the war, the United States developed the atomic bomb, and its awesome destruction of two Japanese cities finally brought the terrible war to an end. Prior to the atomic bomb attacks, hundreds of airplanes with conventional bombs had already wreaked unspeakable destruction on the cities of Germany and Japan.

Today, thousands of ballistic missiles with nuclear warheads are positioned in Russia and the United States, as well as in sites in Europe. They are also carried by submarines fueled by nuclear energy and capable of staying underwater and undetected for long periods of time. These submarines have strategic areas of possible enemies' countries already plotted and ready for ballistic missile deployment. The nuclear warheads themselves are far more sophisticated and deadly in their destructive power than the atomic bombs of World

War II. Other countries have been able to acquire their own nuclear capabilities. These include countries such as Britain, France, China, North Korea, India, Pakistan, and Israel. The temptation to use such horrible weapons can be very strong when a country feels that its back is against the wall because of the threat of another country's aggression or when a country might decide to employ one or more of the weapons in an attempt to achieve its ends. I think of present-day North Korea in the latter case. The timber of humanity is always dangerously susceptible to further warping.

The knowledge required to make small and relatively simple nuclear weapons is now readily available. Imagine, just to cite one possible example, that members of the violent Jihadist group calling itself the Islamic State (ISIS) were able to obtain sufficient amounts of nuclear material to design a suitcase atomic bomb that could be smuggled into a major city such as New York. The actual explosion of such a bomb would produce unbelievably widespread destruction of lives, buildings, and infrastructure in the city and would precipitate a reaction by the United States government that could rapidly lead, by successive steps, to an escalating conflict in which opposing groups, not only in the Middle East but throughout the world, would become involved. This sort of thing has happened before, and we should not put it past the all-too-flexible and easily bent wood of humanity in the present or future.

But even if the suitcase atomic weapon were not detonated, a publicly announced possession of such a weapon and its possible use by ISIS or some other group could give that group an incredible amount of bargaining power to be used in the pursuit of its own ends—perhaps, to take an extreme example, forcing the United States to use the threat of its own enormous technological prowess to dominate and repel the enemies of ISIS, thus enabling the latter to set up its cherished Caliphate in the Middle East. Such an agreement—if it could be achieved—would probably be unstable, short-lived, and perilous, as other nations continued to brood resentfully over the newly established Caliphate, plan how to bring it to an end, or perhaps even make use of the instability it would create for dark machinations of their own devising. The forcefully instituted Caliphate would be a festering focus of unrest, surrounded by potential enemies on all sides. Its position would be analogous to that of Israel today. Such unrest can be a serious threat to the peace of the world, a threat we already witness in the Middle East of today. It is a threat greatly exacerbated by the formidable weapons of destruction possessed and widely traded among or covertly smuggled into nations across the world by groups intent on benefitting from the alluring profits they promise.

Weapons are a big business, and huge proportions of the budgets of nations like the United States and Russia are devoted to their development, improvement, production, and deployment. Recently invented drones are already being used by the United States to kill perceived enemies in faraway places by remote control, and the drones sometimes produce considerable so-called collateral civilian deaths. Hospitals and wedding parties have been intentional or unintentional targets of these drones. What if the peoples being routinely attacked by such drones were able to develop drones of their own and to use them in retaliation against selected cities of the West? What could be the result? I shudder to think about the dangers to world peace and stability posed in this scenario—a scenario made possible by yet another newly designed, devilishly sophisticated weapon.

4. Regional and Global Ecological Devastation

The greatest threat to ecological health and wellbeing in our time is global climate change. But before warnings of its devastating effects became prominent, there were already such ecological damages and horrors as widespread species losses and endangerments, the rampant destructions of animal habitats, the trashing of landfills and oceans with plastics and other kinds of non-biodegradable debris, across-the-board deforestations and their environmental consequences, hideous removals of mountaintops and grievous pollutions of their nearby streams, commercial fishing with its callous disregard for overfishing and the fate and ecological consequences of discarded by-catches, and industrial and agricultural large-scale pollutions. Methane from the burping, flatulence, and defecation of billions of pigs, chickens, and cattle raised for human food—especially in huge factory farms—is also an important factor. The recently publicized prospect of global climate change makes these more familiar and long recognized kinds of ecological calamities fade in comparison.

Glaciers are melting, ice-sheets are shelving, the earth's waters are becoming warmer and more acidic, and the levels of ocean waters are beginning to rise. The amount of carbon in the atmosphere has begun to rise steadily, and methane levels in the atmosphere are increasing—some of the latter due to long frozen vegetation in the soil being allowed by its thawing to emit methane gasses into the air. Methane is also emitted into the atmosphere by natural gas burn-offs and other industrial processes, and coal-burning factories and power plants are notorious sources of carbon pollution.

All of the things I have mentioned in the previous two paragraphs cry out for government regulation and collective action. Why have we humans of the twenty-first century not responded to this glaringly urgent and increasingly frightful prospect with appropriate laws, policies, and procedures? Climate reporter and activist Naomi Kline answers this question by referring to what she terms "three policy-pillars of the neo-liberal age" which she reasons to be regnant today. These pillars are "privatization of the public sphere, deregulation of the corporate sector, and the lowering of income and corporate taxes, paid for with cuts to public spending. . . ." These three factors, Kline goes on to say, "form an ideological wall that has blocked a serious response to climate change for decades."[5]

The free market outlook whose partial truth (and partial falsity) I discussed and critiqued in chapter four lies at the basis of the ideological wall that Kline brings into view. It eschews the kind of robust collective action required for effective response to the threat of global climate change because it flies in the face of a deeply entrenched worldview. This worldview assumes the dominance of the profit motive and disdain for governmental interference, as well as presuming a basic human egoism, consumerism, self-aggrandizing competitiveness, and inevitable enrichment of the few at the expense of the many—nonhuman as well as human—that run against the grain of any kind of presently effective action to meet the ominous challenge of accelerating climate change.

The crooked timber of humanity bends decidedly toward this regnant worldview of our own time, and it poses a dire threat to the ecosystems of earth and to all who depend on them, we humans emphatically included. We are not separate from nature but an integral part of it, and its sufferings, losses, and devastations are, or are soon to become, ours as well. We need in our time to take this alternative worldview to heart and to do everything we can to bring about the thoroughgoing revolution of attitude, thought, and action that it requires. Will we do so in time? Perhaps not; and if not, dread consequences are likely to follow.

In this section, I have looked briefly at four ways in which we might be tempted to succumb to despair and to be forced to acquiesce in the conception of a timber of humanity fated to be ever more twisted and gnarled beyond repair, and even to the breaking point. But in the next section I call attention to some less frightful and more hopeful straws in the wind. These remind us—again in the words of Kline—"there is a reason for social organizations to exist" and "it is not to accept dominant values as fixed and unchangeable but to offer other ways to live—to wage, and win, a battle of cultural worldviews."[6] History richly and hopefully illustrates the kind of revolutionary collective social actions and changes of which she speaks. With this encouraging idea in mind, let us look again at each of the four straws of pending doom discussed in the previous section and see if we can find in these areas warrant for a more optimistic outlook and hopeful prospects. Perhaps the crooked timber of humanity is not as hopelessly crooked and beyond straightening and repair as the previous section has suggested. If so, then the threats posed by its tendencies contain only partial truths—truths to be contemplated and responded to with urgent and active seriousness, not with moods of resignation and despair.

Signs of Hope

What basis can we find for counterresponses to the four signs of approaching disaster listed and discussed in the previous section? How can the partial truths of these ominous straws in the wind be met by more hopeful truths on the other sides of the issues they pose? Let us look in turn at each threatening sign with this question in mind.

1. Unchecked, Unregulated Capitalism

What is at stake with regard to this sign are not only particular modes of institutional organization and action but the worldview that underlies them. It is a worldview that justifies zero-sum and even cut-throat competitiveness; the search for every possible advantage to particular individuals and businesses regardless of the consequences for other individuals and businesses; near-exclusive fixation on profits and wealth; allowance for the profits and wealth to flow inexorably toward the few at the expense of the many; refusal to countenance collective responsibility for the poor, needy, and marginalized people in society; endorsement of the privatization of such things as schools, hospitals, prisons, and legal aid on the ground of claimed efficiency and generation of profits; and resistance to anything more than minimal taxation combined with work for many different kinds of tax loopholes and exemptions favoring businesses and wealthy individuals.

Studied indifference toward the harmful effects of business and industry on the natural environment is a prominent feature of the worldview of free market capitalism. It is a worldview that tends strongly toward minimizing or denying serious environmental endangerment and despoliation and toward outright denial of anthropogenic global climate change in particular. Acknowledging either would require recognition of the need for large-scale government oversight and regulation of businesses and industries, even to the extent of phasing out grotesquely polluting and harmful, if immensely profitable, industries and practices—especially those that require the unearthing and burning of fossil fuels that add enormous amounts of carbon and other heat-trapping gasses to the atmosphere and contribute to accelerating climate change.

The threat of unregulated capitalism can be met by attacking it at its root, that is, by bringing forcefully to light and subjecting to critical analysis the worldview that undergirds it. Free market capitalism is not set in stone. It is not part of the furniture of the universe. It is one extreme economic outlook ranged against the opposite extreme of the radical collectivism that reigns in some other parts of the world today. Neither should be regarded as an absolute truth. And neither is an all-or-nothing, either-or option. Furthermore, there are established models in places like the British Isles, Western Europe, and Canada today that do not have recourse to either of these two extremes. The relative advantages and disadvantages displayed in the practical enactments of these models can be carefully weighed against those of either of the two extremes. These advantages and disadvantages can be analyzed, not just in terms of profits, losses, and economic efficiency but in terms of fairness, justice, and benefit for all. Frantic competition and self-seeking can be replaced by a spirit of cooperative work focused on the wellbeing of others. The economic productivity of a society can then be shared in more equitable ways rather than being directed primarily toward the benefit of a small number of persons or groups.

The free market model of economics and society is deeply entrenched. It is kept prominently in view and ardently defended especially by those who stand to benefit most by it. Its beneficiaries represent a powerful oligarchy that will not easily be dislodged from their positions of extraordinary privilege and power. But Abraham Lincoln's vision of "government of the people, by the people, and for the people" is a powerful counterpoint to the all-too-selective benefits of the free market economic theory. The demands of mercy, justice, and environmental wellbeing can be ranged against a presumed bottom line of profits and wealth. Tenacious elements of pretense, ideological fixation, and covert egoism can be exposed as furtive parts of the idea of unregulated markets that need to be brought to light.

They can be brought forcibly to light in a democracy, especially one that is guided by effective, visionary, courageous leaders backed up by concerned and active citizens. We are not doomed to the deprivations of unregulated economies. Revolutionary over-turnings of powerful and persuasive social models have taken place in the past. Examples are the Protestant Reformation, the end of feudalism, the creation of democratic institutions, abolishment of the slave trade in the Western world, and civil rights legislation. None of these seemed to hold much promise of success at its outset. The much-needed revolution in economic thinking and acting can take place today. This is a partial truth that deserves focused consideration and hopeful action devoted to exhibiting its inherent plausibility and practicable realization. The free market ideal is a useful corrective to the claimed need in some quarters for relentlessly centralized, extremely regulated economies. But it suffers from glaring deficiencies of its own that can be and urgently need to be acknowledged and corrected.

2. The Cruelties and Disruptions of Religious Conflicts

When introducing this topic earlier in this chapter, I noted that religion is a powerful force that can be used for good or evil. This means that its power for goodness can be drawn upon to counter its power for evil. Not only has this often been the case in the past; it can also be the case in the future. Religious persons and institutions have frequently shown susceptibilities to arrogant close-mindedness and intolerance to opposing points of view. They have given ardent support to violent suppression of different religious outlooks while turning a blind eye to their own corruptions and imperfections.

But at the same time, religious persons and institutions have often worked effectively for the betterment of the world and given desperately needed support to the improvement and maintenance of the positive aspects of human civilizations. Religious inspiration has motivated and guided persons and institutions who have helped to produce revolutionary changes for the better in human societies.

William Wilberforce's religiously motivated and ultimately successful effort in England to bring about abolishment of the notorious evil of slavery by acts of Parliament, Bishop Desmond Tutu's passionate work for a peaceful end to *apartheid* in South Africa, and Martin Luther King's intensely religious devotion to the goal of eliminating legal enforcement of the evil of racial discrimination in the United States by congressional actions are good examples. In general, religions have kept alive the dream of compassion, mercy, and justice toward all persons and—even toward all sentient beings—even as they have at times suffered serious deficiencies and defects of their own that needed to be exposed and remedied by the efforts of reform-minded religious persons. The crooked timber of humanity has deeply regrettable exemplifications in the field of religion as in all other fields of human endeavor. But the powerful religious mode of thought and action is also an important resource for straightening and correcting the warped temperaments and tendencies of human beings.

The actual number of violent Islamic Jihadists such as those fighting to establish a Caliphate in the Middle East is quite small compared to the population of Muslims around the world, which numbers about one and a half billion persons. My friend Monte Palmer, who is a recognized and widely published scholar of the Middle East, having lived there for many years, suggests that the Muslim Brotherhood in this region, which is far larger in number than the members of ISIS, is less backward looking and much better equipped by temper and outlook to draw on the positive resources of Islam in order to achieve laudable goals. It is capable of doing so by demonstration, negotiation, and relatively peaceful action, in contrast with the gruesomely violent tactics of ISIS. So there is hope from this quarter.

There are rich resources in the Qur'an itself for inspiring and motivating effective social, political, and economic changes that need to be made, without recourse to close-minded violence and wanton destruction. Examples are those passages that stress the justice and mercy of Allah; his profound concern for the poor and downtrodden; the obligations of Muslim citizens and leaders to maintain safe, orderly, and peaceful societies bound by law; and Allah's revelations to Jews and Christians, meaning that they are to be acknowledged and respected as Peoples of the Book. Similarly, the scriptures of these other two religions speak of a just and merciful God whose concern for all peoples stands in judgment over all human institutions and practices that behave intolerantly toward others; inflict needless suffering on others; or do not attend patiently, kindly, and effectively to the needs of others. Religion is an undeniable part of the problem in the Middle East. But it can also be a significant part of the solution. The latter is a partial truth, one that is by no means guaranteed because it depends on visionary utilization of the ample resources for good in existing religious traditions and on the inspired leadership of exemplary spokespersons within those traditions. A two-edged sword like religion need not cut in only one way. It can be a formidable force for good instead of evil, empowering humans in their age-old struggles toward just societies and a peaceful world.

3. The Development and Use of Increasingly Sophisticated and Rabidly Destructive Weapons

A message dated October 5, 2016, from ABC News reports the poignant death of a four-year-old girl named Iman in Aleppo, Syria.[7] She and two of her older sisters had gone out to play near their house. They came across what they thought was a toy ball. The four-year-old picked it up and it exploded, wounding all three children. The four-year-old child died not long after from her terrible wounds, and the two others were badly injured. What the children believed to be a toy to be innocently picked up and played with was actually an undetonated bomblet, one of many scattered across their area by the grisly weapon called a cluster bomb.

These bombs are dropped from airplanes, fired from guns, or sent aloft with rockets. They are designed to explode when close to the ground and to spread numerous bomblets that explode on impact in their turn, with destructive effects for any persons, animals, or things nearby. Sometimes the bomblets malfunction and do not immediately explode on impact, thus posing a grave danger to anyone who happens later upon one or more of them, as did the three innocent Syrian children. Cluster bombs are in this way a great hazard not only for their immediate targets but also because of the unexploded bomblets that may be left behind. They pose the threat of explosion and con-sequent injury or death for the unwary long after the battles in which they were used may have ended. But even if the cluster bombs perform exactly as they were designed to do, they can still cause widespread carnage that affects not only military targets but civilian populations and the children among them who lie in their path.

Cluster bombs have been used in Syria, Yemen, the Ukraine, and Libya. Israel used them some time ago in Lebanon, and the United States used them in Cambodia, Laos, and Vietnam. Saudi Arabia has employed them in Yemen, and Russia and the Syrian government have used them in Syria. Great Britain and the United States have sold them to Saudi Arabia. The United States Department of Defense announced in August of 2016 that it will be building and selling 1,300 cluster bombs, worth 641 million dollars, to Saudi Arabia.[8]

The manufacture, transfer, sale, and use of these bombs, and their woefully destructive effects on human lives are but one powerful indication of the evil tendencies of the crooked timber of humanity. The fact that companies and individuals are driven by the fond hope to profit handsomely from the sale of these weapons, with little regard for the consequences of their use, only underscores the malicious malalignment of the human spirit. This is a straw in the wind that bodes ill for us as a species, as do the recent creation and use of many other kinds of rampantly destructive instruments of conflict and war.

It is a partial truth that we are all too likely to ratchet up the scale of our conflicts and the wanton usages of such weapons in them to the point of a worldwide conflagration, misery, and calamity of such ghastly proportions as to make the two previous world wars seem mild by comparison. Millions of children like the hapless Syr-ian four-year-olds would be its innocent victims, along with hordes of other innocent persons.

But fortunately, not all the current straws point in this direction. I want to mention here two signs of hope as these relate to cluster bombs and, by implication, to other fearsome weapons of recent times. The two signs of hope are a significant international treaty and a notable vote by the House of Representatives of the United States. This treaty and vote give indication of the possibility of humans proceeding clear-headedly toward greater world amity, peace, and prosperity instead of moving with increasingly unalterable momentum along the path that leads to mutual catastrophe and misery.

The international treaty I have in mind is the Convention on Cluster Munitions that prohibits the use, transfer, and stockpiling of cluster bombs. By April 2016, a hundred states had ratified it. The treaty still allows for some similar weapons, but only those that incorporate a specified very small number of explosive devices that are designed to explode much more dependably and immediately after their release from the main body of the weapon. This is admittedly not a complete ban, but it moves hopefully in the right direction and has the growing support of many nations. Unfortunately, as of the date of this writing, neither the United States nor Saudi Arabia has signed the treaty. China and Russia have also not signed it. Much more progress toward the goal of eliminating this dreadful weapon is still needed.

The encouraging vote I indicated above took place in the United States House of Representatives on June 16, 2016. An amendment was proposed that would ban the sale of U.S.-made cluster weapons to Saudi Arabia. It lost by only a narrow margin, more than two-hundred House members having voted in favor of it. These members did so despite the fact that the Department of Defense strongly opposed the amendment, arguing that it would "stigmatize" cluster weapons, which the Department claimed to be highly effective and to provide significant advantages against a wide range of targets. The Conference of Catholic Bishops, Human Rights Watch, and Amnesty International endorsed the amendment. Its advocates felt after the vote that the small margin by which the amendment lost was an extremely promising sign, one signifying major progress toward ending cluster-bomb trade and use.[9] The close vote is indeed a hopeful straw in the wind. It shows that the trees of humanity are capable of aspiring upward together and not just of becoming twisting, entangling, competing branches that serve only to drag one another down and to contribute to one another's increasing endangerment, suffering, and misery.

4. Regional and Global Ecological Devastation

Dutch chemist Paul J. Crutzen won the Nobel Prize in 1995 for sharing in discovery of the effects of ozone-depleting compounds.

This discovery led to increasingly successful endeavors to put an end to the use of such compounds and thus to save the earth from the effects of an ozone hole that would eventually have encompassed the earth instead of being confined, as before, to Antarctica in the spring. The ozone layer protects Earth and its creatures from the extremely harmful effects of ultraviolet rays from the sun. This discovery can be considered a step toward increasing human awareness of the profound effects of their technologies and practices on the vulnerable ecological conditions of the earth.

Crutzen made another important contribution to raising this awareness when in 2002 he published a short paper in *Nature* where he argued that we should replace the term *Holocene*, used up to that time to designate our geological epoch which began about twelve-thousand years ago, with the new term *Anthropocene*. The latter term is needed, in his view, to call attention to the massive geologic changes humans are producing around the world.[10] Debate about the appropriateness of this idea among geologists continues to the date of this writing, but the allegation that we humans are now living in a new epoch has attracted widespread attention.

Elizabeth Kolbert, a staff writer at *The New Yorker*, provides us with a list of geologic-scale changes humans have brought about, as indicated in Crutzen's brief *Nature* article. This list includes the human transformation of somewhere between one third and one half of the planet; diversion and damming of most major rivers; production of more nitrogen than is fixed naturally; removal of more than a third of the coastal oceans' primary fishery production; and human use of more than half of the world's readily available fresh water. To these five factors Crutzen also added a sixth crucial one I mentioned earlier in this chapter: because of fossil fuel combustion and deforestation, humans have increased the amount of carbon dioxide in the air by 40 percent over the past two centuries, and the amount of methane has more than doubled.[11] He concludes his article by observing that "mankind will remain a major environmental force for many millennia. A daunting task lies ahead for scientists and engineers to guide society toward environmentally sustainable management during the era of the Anthropocene."[12]

Our question here is this: Will humans rise to the challenge of this daunting task quickly enough and effectively enough to avert what Kolbert refers to as a sixth massive extinction event to parallel the other five extinction calamities that have marked the earth's earlier history? There are many signs that this extinction event is by now well underway. I shall site four examples among many that could be noted. The African elephant population has been reduced from 1.3 million in the 1970s to only 350,000 remaining today. The major causes of this 30 percent decline are malicious poaching for the ivory of the elephants' tusks, extensive habitat loss, and conflict with newly established human communities in their traditional areas. Elephants' slow breeding rates make their future in Africa look especially precarious.[13]

Kolbert cites the fates of chimpanzees in the wild; mountain and lowland gorillas; and Sumatran orangutans. The chimpanzee population has dropped over the past fifty years to about half. The same rate of decline applies to mountain gorillas, and lowland gorillas have declined even more precipitously, by 60 percent. In the case of the orangutans, decades of political unrest followed by a surge in legal and nonlegal logging have brought these wonderful creatures to the point of near-extinction.[14] Such deeply disturbing straws in the wind can cause caring humans to be brought close to the point of despair, but happily there are indications of some progress in attempts to reverse the trends toward a sixth extinction epoch and other effects of anthropogenic threats to the earth's regional and global environments that can be a basis for hope for further progress in the future.

The crooked timber of humanity is not by now so radically deformed in its attitudes and practices toward the natural environment and its creatures as to make such progress impossible. To conclude that it is, is at best to affirm a partial truth—one based on the many threatening evidences and tendencies to date. However, we also need to consider evidences and tendencies on the other side of this issue. Kolbert's book helps us to understand and find encouragement in some of these hopeful straws in the wind of our present century and in the later parts of the preceding century. Among other things, she mentions Rachel Carson's 1962 book *The Silent Spring* that played a major role in banning the use of DDT in 1972. This ban probably saved the emblematic American bald eagle from extinction. Kolbert also notes the Endangered Species Act passed by the U.S. Congress in 1974 and the considerable work that has been done since then to protect creatures listed in the Act. Extensive meticulous efforts to save condors and whooping cranes are other examples Kolbert cites, and she takes note of the many environmental groups that have been founded in recent years that call forceful attention to the need for protecting endangered species, lay heavy stress on the importance of working steadily for such protection, and devote themselves to soliciting adequate funding for its accomplishment.[15]

We can add to Kolbert's list the development of photovoltaic systems and windmills for generating electricity without the burning of fossil fuels. There is increasing use of these technologies around the world. Moreover, there is the Paris Agreement, adopted on December 12, 2015, which commits nearly 200 countries to cut greenhouse emissions over a period of years and to seek to restrict the increase in global warming to no more than 2 degrees Celsius. Many obstacles, financial and otherwise, lie in the path of this goal, but at least it is a notable start toward a low carbon future. As of October 5, 2016, 86 Parties out of 197 Parties to the Agreement have ratified it, but significant progress toward its implementation is uncertain and will at best be slow. The Agreement unites the nations of the world in the daunting task of tackling climate change for the first time in history.[16]

Perhaps the most encouraging aspect of Kolbert's frank and far-reaching book is her observations concerning the remarkable skill, resilience, and imagination with which members of the species *Homo sapiens* have sought to solve innumerable problems they have encountered in the course of their history. In this regard, they put their close relatives the Neanderthals, to say nothing of their more remote relatives the chimpanzees, in the shade. Modern humans were early on capable of producing such things as projectiles for more effective hunting; ships for exploring and settling distant lands across the sea; languages and alphabets for communicating, thinking, and recording; and unambiguous attempts at works of art. Human children have also shown themselves to be notably adept at collective or shared problem solving, a skill that chimpanzees, with all of their other traits of intelligence, seem to lack.[17]

If we add to these examples such things as the development of agriculture; animal domestication; city building and administration; empire building; the construction of wheeled vehicles; the creation of stories, paintings, statuary, music, temples, cathedrals, mosques, and other works of art; the development of religious traditions; the works of philosophy and science; and all of the artifacts and creations of the Industrial and Computer Science Revolutions, then we begin to get a sense of the marvelous creative and problem-solving abilities manifested by human beings throughout the millennia of their existence on earth. If humans can do all of this, are they not capable of responding in constructive, imaginative, creative, and effective ways to the ecological crisis of our time? I strongly suggest that they are, if only they have the will to do so and to continue to confront and critique the forces within our present culture—economic, political, religious, ideological, inertial, and the like—that stand stubbornly and dangerously in the way.

We humans have the inherent ability and the freedom of choice to honor, preserve, protect, and restore the wonders of the natural world, and not to continue to ignore, neglect, and betray our profound responsibilities to it. But proof of this ability and of the resolute exercise of our freedom in this regard lies in the future, meaning that the claim to it is always only a partially tested truth, a promise in need of ever more convincing confirmation and fulfillment. Palpable and increasingly sizable augmentations of the amount of truth in this promise are desperately needed in our time. They lie ahead of us, in future choices and actions intent on reversing our past grotesque desecrations of our earthly home and ushering in a new era of reverent, responsible, and effective ecological care.

Novelist Zadie Smith, in a talk given in Berlin on the occasion of her receiving the 2016 Welt Literature Prize, wisely remarks that "there is no perfectibility in human affairs." Her life as a citizen of the United States and as a black woman born to a white father and black mother, she notes, made this idea readily apparent to her. She is well aware, in other words, of what Kant meant by his metaphor of the crooked timber of humanity. Yet for her this realization is not a reason for despair. She acknowledges that

> in this world there is only incremental progress. Only the willfully blind can ignore that the history of human existence is simultaneously the history of pain: of brutality, murder, mass extinction, every form of venality and cyclical horror. No land is free of it; no people are without their bloodstain; no tribe entirely innocent. But there is still this redeeming matter of incremental progress. It might look small to those with apocalyptic perspectives, but to she who not so long ago could not vote or drink from the

same water fountain as her fellow citizens, or marry the person she chose, or live in a certain neighborhood, such incremental change feels enormous.[18]

Smith's sober but also encouraging comment, one eloquently reflective of both her personal experience and of her awareness of humanity's mixed history of admirable progress and deplorable failure, makes evident the partial truth on either side of the ledger of hope and despair. Neither extreme should be allowed to overshadow the other. Both should be kept constantly in mind as we fallible humans aspire to make incremental progress in all areas of our lives in the world.

Chapter 7

PERSPECTIVES

Our life is an apprenticeship to the truth that around every circle
another can be drawn; that there is no end in nature, but every
end is a beginning; that there is always another dawn risen on
mid-noon, and under every deep a lower deep opens.

Ralph Waldo Emerson[1]

I hold a plain porcelain cup in my hand. Surely, the statement,
"This is a cup" is not a mere partial truth. Instead, it seems to be
an absolute even if admittedly trivial truth, one beyond any shade
of vagueness or ambiguity. And could we not multiply examples like
this one indefinitely and within countless different aspects of our
experiences of and reflections upon ourselves and the world? But stop
to think about all we have not said in our simple declaration, "This
is a cup." We have not described and could not describe all of the
possible perspectives or points of view from which it could be viewed
and interpreted by a human being, to say nothing of it as experienced
by such nonhuman organisms as microbes, ants, spiders, or squirrels.
A large-muzzled dog, for instance, would no doubt regard the cup as
an unwieldly vessel from which to drink.

We have not described the multiple uses to which the cup could
be put in addition to holding a liquid from which to drink. It could
be for one person a cherished work of art to be proudly displayed on
a shelf or for another the inspiration for creation of a work of art;
it could be hurled as a makeshift weapon in anger or self-defense; it
could be a useful weight for holding down a sheaf of papers; it could
serve as a vase for a flower; it could be melted down or ground into
powder to create a new artifact; and so on. For an archeologist of

a distant future, it would perhaps serve as an interesting relic of a bygone culture. This cup, as among other things a physical object, exerts a minute gravitational force of its own, even as it is affected by the gravity of the earth and that of distant astral bodies.

Moreover, we draw on all of the resources of our language—such things as its vocabulary, syntax, pragmatics, and history—when we utter and expect to be readily understood the simple statement, "This is a cup." And we implicitly rely on our memories of all of the past things which we construed to be cups, despite the great variety of colors, sizes, shapes, weights, designs, and the like of such things. The construal of this object now before me as a cup makes tacit reference to such past experiences and our interpretations of them. Objects do not just present themselves immediately and certainly as cups but through a whole train of inferences and judgments concerning their respective statuses as such. The former notion would qualify as a sup-posed unmediated *intuition* of an object as a cup, in contrast with an inferential interpretation of it as a cup. But there really are no such supposed intuitions, devoid of judgment, inference, or interpretation.

Every time we fit an object into a category such as the category of a cup, we are making an inference and thus assigning conceptual meaning to some aspect of our experience. Apart from the judgment, inference, or bestowal of meaning, there is only the bare experience and the affirmation of nothing regarding it. "This is a cup" is an inferential judgment and part of a train of such inferential judgments. And as an inferential judgment, it is subject to error. On a given occasion, we could misjudge an object as a cup. But even at best its assumption or claim to be such is a partial truth, one arrived at on the tacit and underlying basis of everything—experiential, linguistic, mnemonic, conceptual, and inferential—that gives it meaning and status as an explicit claim to truth.[2]

But we need not stop here. We could also begin to think about all that has gone into the cup's history, including such things as when such a thing as a cup might first have been conceived, the different materials out of which cups might have been fashioned, and the vari-ous ways in which they have been designed in the past. We could also compare in some detail this cup's design with that of cups from the ancient past. We could be reminded of Christ's cup of suffering agonizingly awaited in the garden of Gethsemene or of the knightly quest for the Holy Grail.

We might think about the culturally dictated proprieties for correctly holding a cup and drinking from it. Slurping from it would be frowned upon in many cultures, while this act might be welcomed and applauded as a gesture of appreciation in others. We could also consider the kinds of cups to be used on different occasions. And when we identify something as a cup we are also making a tacit judgment about what it is not, since the complement of any set or class is all of the things not contained in that set or class. Determining what a cup is not, even if only by implication, raises the issue of borderline cases, things that might or might not qualify as cups in particular cases. This can be quite a tangled issue, one not at all easy to unravel. Must a cup have a handle? Clearly not, since some vessels designed to be cups and drunk from do not have handles. Is a small bowl also a cup? How large, then, would it need to be to become a bowl instead of a cup?

Custom and habit have important roles to play in addressing questions about what does or does not fit into an assumed category of description or representation. Philosopher Nelson Goodman uses the example of so-called representational painting in making this point:

> According to the more frequent usage, a picture is realistic to the extent that it is correct under the accustomed system of representation; for example, in the present Western culture, a picture by Dürer is more realistic than a picture by Cézanne. Realistic or right representation in this sense, like right categorization, requires observance of custom and tends to correlate loosely with ordinary judgments of resemblance, which likewise rest upon habit.[3]

As will become clear later in this chapter, I do not agree with Goodman's assertion, earlier in the chapter from which the above quotation is taken, that the difference between realism and idealism "is *purely* conventional" and that "if we abstract from all features responsible for disagreements between truths we have *nothing left* but versions without things or facts or worlds."[4]

Goodman's way of putting the matter is too much like the *constructivist* theory of truth I shall be critical of later when arguing in favor of a *perspectival realist* theory. Convention has an important role to play with regard to questions of truth or falsity, as Goodman rightly points out. But in my view, more than convention is ultimately involved. He is partially right in emphasizing the important role of convention, but the perspectival realist theory of truth I share with Ronald N. Giere is in my judgment the more nearly correct or defensible one. It can take convention appropriately and seriously into account while not reducing truth to convention. I'll say more about this subject later.

Issues like the ones raised here might sound like quibbling, but they can help to illustrate how a seemingly simple and undebatable assertion like "This thing before me is a cup" actually alludes to a whole host of other things connected with and warranting the idea of its being such a thing as a cup, including some things that might be problematic and uncertain if subjected to careful analysis. "This is a cup" might well qualify as a truth, but its necessary relationship with many other putative truths shows it to be, at best, only a partial truth rather than the whole truth. The same kind of analysis would apply to the person being sworn in as a witness who promises to "tell the whole truth and nothing but the truth." There would never be sufficient time to tell the whole truth in its intricate web of necessary connections, but the witness can tell enough of the truth to serve the needs of the court. In similar fashion, the assertion that this thing before me is a cup functions quite well in the ordinary situations of daily life. It does so despite being, on careful analysis, a partial truth in the respects I am elucidating here.

I recall one occasion when I had cupped my hands to drink from a lavatory faucet after brushing my teeth. My very young grandson was watching, and he asked, "What are you doing, Grandpa?" I showed him how I was making a cup with my two hands, and he, with quick recognition of something new and interesting to him, exclaimed, "Your hands can make a big cup; mine can be a little one!" Maybe in this way, the idea of fashioning a cup from available materials was originally born. We do not know this to be the case, but it is fascinating to think about it.

Beyond all of these types of example, there is the issue of what the cup is like or can be conceived to be like at the molecular level, the atomic level, and the subatomic level. In the eye of the chemist or particle physicist, it is something quite different from the way we regard it and make use of it in ordinary life. Moreover, the universe itself is not static. It continues to change. We cannot have complete knowledge today of what an open and unpredictable future might bring. Even as we unlock, or think we have unlocked, one level of mystery in nature, we more often than not open new and unexpected others to be contemplated and inquired into.

To say, "This is a cup" is to scratch the tip of an iceberg reaching down into the depths of a sea of fascinating and inexhaustible mystery. It is the beginning of wisdom to acknowledge that this is so and not to pretend to anything other than partial truths, however important to us these may be as we make our way in the world. Every truth is a partial truth because it is an incomplete truth, one that inevitably fails to take into account all of the implicit connections and overtones of plausibility and meaning that help to qualify it as a statement of truth.

But what about outright lying? Where is the partial truth here? There is truth to be uncovered in such things as the motivation for the lying; the circumstances in which the lie takes place and in those preceding it; the emotions underlying the act of lying; and the background, character, beliefs, and intention of the person doing the lying. The lie does not stand in isolation or by itself. Moreover, a lie is only possible when it stands in opposition to an act of truth-telling that is recognizable as such, and to all of the appropriate considerations that count to make something true rather than false. An articulated lie also presupposes, of course, the intricately complex resources of ordinary language. In other words, a lie is parasitical on truths, or assumed truths, of many different kinds. Just as truth, on examination, is no simple thing, the same is true of lying. If everything were false in a lie, then lying would not even be possible.

Ralph Waldo Emerson, in the epigraph to this chapter, rightly reminds us that around every circle of knowledge and intelligibility or recognition and description we may draw we dimly discern another larger circle that beckons us on. To speak of all truths as partial, at least in important and inescapable ways, is to keep Emerson's ever enlarging circles—similar to the expanding ripples resulting from a stone's throw into a pond—forever in the forefront of our minds. The endlessly widening circles implicitly surround all pursuits and domains, whether in areas such as the sciences, the arts, philosophy, religion, morality, politics, historical accounts, or daily life, and it would be folly to overlook or ignore them. They have done so and in all likelihood will continue to do so throughout the history of human thought and endeavor.

To drop a stone of ardent investigation into the well of the world's mysteries, to change the metaphor, is never to hear a splash that announces the end of need for persistent questioning, wondering, and searching. There may be important indications of partial truths as our imagined stone of inquiry bumps against roots or rocks of significance extending from the sides of the bottomless well on the way down, but it is foolish to yearn for or to expect a final theory of everything. It is critically important that we keep constantly in mind what the French philosopher Gilles Deleuze calls "the unrecognized in every recognition."[5] Still, it makes good sense for us to work together for more adequate ways of feeling, thinking, and acting, and thus to strive to move in the direction of more fruitful and fulfilling partial truths.

German physicist Werner Heisenberg adds to our understanding of the inevitable partiality of all claims to truth when he observes that "just as the human eye is capable of precise observation only in a small area of the retina and is always unconsciously directed toward the most important aspect of the image, similarly, human thinking focuses on a specific, small segment of subject matter which then enters into the clearest light of consciousness while the remaining content of the idea appears only in obscure semi-darkness." The depictions of language and the thought accompanying language, he therefore insists, "cannot be complete or accurate."[6] In other words, they are always partial. Heisenberg is speaking here specifically of technical language and thought, but his observation pertains to all sorts of language and thought.

To admit that a given claim to truth can be at best only partially true is an essential part of what is required for us to keep aspiring toward more adequate and inclusive understanding. Philosophy, like everything else, not only begins in wonder. It ends there as well, even when it has done its dead level best to analyze, describe, and comprehend. But of course philosophy, like all other human fields of investigation, never really ends. It is lured ceaselessly on by the hope of ever more accurate and more comprehensive ways of interpreting and understanding the world. There is always a wider circle, and endless ones beyond that one, to be acknowledged and explored. This is why the genius of philosophy is much more than pitting one fixed set of arguments and assertions or alleged final truths against others of like kind. It is an endless process of dialogical searching with no absolute stopping points.

This is not to say that progress cannot be made. I believe that much progress has been made in the history of philosophy as new arguments, new points of view, new insights, and new levels of understanding have been gained. These achievements have done much to enrich, encourage, and stimulate the ongoing dialogue among philosophers and others, but the achievements do not and cannot constitute final or absolute truths. The spirit of endless searching is where the larger truth always lies.

Plato, surely among the greatest if not the greatest philosopher of the Western World, understood this proposition well. His philosophy specializes in the raising of probing questions and the tenacious critical examinations of answers to these questions proffered by concerned interlocutors. It does not presume to provide or even to think us humans capable of finding final answers to the deepest conundrums and mysteries of life. A sometimes heavy note of irony suffusing many of Plato's dialogues helps to guard against such presumption. There really is no end to questioning all of the nuances, associations, and perplexities opened up by even the seemingly simple and straightforward statement, "This is a cup." Once one understands this to be the case even for the most ordinary and routine things of life, one's vision of the world will in all likelihood become more reflective and curious, and more radically enriched and transformed.

What I have said so far in this chapter falls under the head of the many different perspectives from which such a thing as a cup can be regarded. Since no one perspective can do justice by itself to all of the other perspectives from which it could be regarded, any single perspective on it has to be recognized as a partial truth. The cup will be experienced differently by a person, insect, or nonhuman animal, for example. It can be put to multiple uses. The idea of it as a cup draws on a complex texture of linguistic, mnemonic, and inferential associations. Drinking from it takes place in a context of cultural proprieties. To view it as a cup implicitly contrasts it with all the things that are not cups. The scientific attitude toward the cup as a physical object is generally quite different from that of a person casually drinking coffee from it in the morning. And yet, the cup is in some sense all of these things, more than all of them taken together, and more than we can readily imagine. The same is true of each and every aspect of our experience and thought.

If we think of the idea of partial truths as calling attention to the myriad different perspectives from which any one of these aspects could be regarded, then we can reinterpret the idea of partial truths as the idea of the unavoidable perspectivity of all claims to truth. And this idea brings to mind what philosopher of science Ronald N. Giere calls *perspectival realism*.[7] Giere's analysis of this position is itself a helpful and useful perspective on the inevitability of partial truths and the importance of understanding the implications of this inevitability. His analysis is focused on scientific thought, but a lot of it can be extended to the whole range of claims to truth, as I shall now proceed to show.

Perspectival Realism

I have entitled the whole of this chapter "Perspectives" because I want to emphasize that partial truths are such principally by virtue of their being a single perspective or at best a set of limited perspectives on matters of interest, and because of the impossibility of capturing all of the possible and yet relevant perspectives on such matters with any particular judgment or assertion. To say that all claims to truth are *partial* is closely related to the claim that they are all *perspectival*. Giere defends the latter claim by taking issue with two different but also highly influential current outlooks on claims to truth. The first one is constructivism, and the second one is absolute objectivist realism.[8] The second position is of special interest to us here, since it directly countermands all that is being said in this book about the inescapability of partial truths in all domains of experience, thought, or expression. But the first one is also of interest because it denies even the partiality of truth, if truth is regarded as consisting, even to some extent, in outlooks or affirmations concerning a world lying outside of or to any extent beyond the range of human subjectivity or human devising.

For Giere, constructivists are wrong in denying any sort of objective, that is, clearly even if only partly reliable scientific references to a real world beyond the creations of individual or social selves, while absolute objectivist realists are wrong in thinking at least some scientific claims to be unequivocally and absolutely objective—that is, unqualified, non-contingent, non-debatable, and non-perspectival—in contrast with what for Giere they actually and inevitably are. His perspectival realism, in contrast to these two views, allows for the possibility of objectively true statements about the world but also insists that such statements are always going to be perspectival and thus contingent, restricted, or limited in that sense. But if truth does not lie exclusively in the self and its creations or in completely objective references to a world existing beyond the subjectivity of humans, where does it lie for Giere? It lies for him, as it does for me, in the *interactions* of humans with the world. In other words, the truth lies in the relations of what is "out there" with what is "in here." Or, to put the point differently, there is no such thing as a pure in-here, and there is no such thing as a pure out-there so far as human thought is concerned.

The mind is in constant interaction with the world. The brain requires many other aspects of the complex human body in order to function, and the body requires constant interactions with the world in order to function. Mind, brain, body, and world are systematically connected with one another and function together as an intricate system. Constructivism artificially tears apart mind-brain from body-world. To use a simple example, my taste of the pudding is not merely in me, nor is it merely in the pudding. I would not have the taste without the pudding, and there is no taste in the pudding apart from its tasters. To say, "I like the taste of this pudding" is to make reference both to me and to the world beyond me. The same analysis applies to the statement, "This pudding is good." The statement may be debatable, but it is not just about me. My perspective is certainly involved in both of these statements, but it is a perspective on some aspect of the world, not just on my inner states of conscious sensation and reflection.

A similar analysis can be applied to scientific claims, as Giere views them, and I cannot help but agree. Let me try to flesh out his argument for perspectival realism in more detail. I can begin to do so by making reference to the epistemology of Kant that I discussed in chapter 5. It will be recalled that Kant argues that we humans are capable of intersubjective consensus, that is, of agreement on central claims of such things as science and morality, on the basis of our sensate and moral experiences as filtered through certain principles he took to be *synthetic a priori*. But he also insisted that we can have no experiences of, or reliable ideas concerning, the in-itself world.[9] He was thus a kind of constructivist, even though contemporary constructivism allows for changes through time in even our most fundamental expectations and beliefs as human beings in a way that Kant's philosophy does not. For Kant we are locked into our subjective selves despite the fact that our subjective selves are also joined collectively together by presumptive common and unchanging features of our respective minds.

Kant thus defends a kind of intersubjective idealism, in contrast with the kind of extreme idealism that would locate everything in the minds of particular individuals. In the latter view, consensual acknowledgment of and seeming experience of a common world is an inexplicable mystery, while Kant explains it on the ground of certain common, fixed structures and modes of operation of all human minds. But there is a contradiction in Kant's view, as I pointed out in chapter 5. The only way to argue successfully for the idea that all of our minds are alike in basic respects is to assume that we are talking about something that is objectively true rather than being subjectively relative. Kant's critical notion of consensual minds has somehow to take into account the seemingly objective truth—crucial to his whole philosophy—of the common structures and operations of all human minds.

Once we have allowed for at least this degree of objectivity or pan-consensual subjectivity, why not allow for its extension to other aspects of a world presumed to exist beyond individual human subjects? Kant's theory is a kind of perspectivism. We see the world from the perspective of our commonly constructed human minds, and we do this on the basis of alleged indisputable certainties of judgment made possible by these minds. But the world we experience is only a world of consensus made possible by this commonality. It is not the world as it is in itself. It is not a supposed God's-eye or objectively veridical view of the world.

Giere's perspectival realism takes implicit issue with this Kantian view in at least two fundamental ways.[10] The first, and this is also his basic objection to constructivism, is that we do have at least partially adequate and reliable access to the real world in our modes of thought, and in particular, those that are constrained by strict scientific rules and procedures of investigation and validation. And second, there is no such thing as absolute certainty in our claims about the nature of the world or anything else. All claims are perspectival and in that sense limited or uncertain to some degree. This statement applies even to the most firmly held scientific conclusions of any given time. Giere rejects "appeals to a priori claims of any kind." In contrast to Kant, he contends that "all claims, however well-grounded empirically, are [to be] regarded as fallible."[11] This is a resounding statement of the idea of all truths as partial truths that I am defending in this book. There are no absolute truths about the world because all human claims are partial and defeasible, if not evidently so on the surface, then invariably so at their deepest levels of meaning and support.

The perspectives that Giere has in mind and on whose basis we interpret and understand the world are not just those of the five human senses—restricted to only five and each having its own characteristic limitations of range and detection—or the limited capacities and operations of our reasoning, feeling, and choosing minds as they react to, explore, and endeavor to comprehend themselves and the world. Our models and mappings of the world assist us in understanding it, but they are abstractions from its details as are other kinds of limited perspective in addition to the perspectives of sensation and relatively unassisted or unmediated reasoning. The same thing goes, according to Giere, for our theories, with their principles and laws. These too are perspectival ways of seeing and comprehending. Our methods and instruments are such as well. None of these means of knowing exists in one-to-one correlations with the world. Our languages also, whether ordinary or technical, verbal or mathematical, help to shape our interpretations of the world. And finally, our purposes and intentions, exercised in particular contexts, provide lenses through which we view the world.

By way of example, I note how Giere treats images of the brain as produced by CT-Scan or MRI instruments. These are incapable of showing how the brain really looks, he argues: "scientific observation does not simply produce images of the brain. One has images *as produced by CAT or MRI or so forth.* One cannot detach the image from the perspective from which it was produced."[12] The perspective represented in a particular image is one among many possible other ones, not only those that might involve different kinds of instrument but also those involving different available choices of how best to make use of the options provided by the instruments in producing the desired images. Such instruments can provide important kinds of knowledge, but only partial or perspectival knowledge of what they are designed to detect and analyze.

All of the modes of access I have mentioned and that Giere discusses at length are perspectival and thus partial and limited. There is always involvement of the subjective knower in the known, just as there is involvement of the objectively known in the knower in any case of veridical knowing. But this involvement never reaches the point of the *unification* of knower and known. There is always a distance between the two even as they are brought into meaningful and reliable relationships with one another. This is the truth in constructivism as Giere sees it, despite its indefensible rejection of the possibility of coming to know an objective world. Absolute objectivist realism allows for perspectival realism's insistence on the possibility of genuine knowledge of such a world but tends wrongly to regard at least some of this knowledge as beyond reasonable dispute, as non-perspectival, and as all-inclusive.

If what Giere says of science even in its most disciplined and rigorous forms holds true, as I think it does, then his perspectival realism surely holds for less demanding ways of knowing. He wisely acknowledges that his theory of perspectival knowing must apply reflexively to itself. He does not ignore the possibility that this theory as well might turn out to be false or at least alterable in some respects in as yet unrealized ways. But he defends his theory as fully and convincingly as he can.[13]

So far, this is all well and good. But what about the way the world is in and of itself, the world as it truly is apart from all our attempts to comprehend and know it? Surely this world transcends all of our perspectives or partial beliefs about it, and surely this world must be known as such by the all-seeing eye of God, if there be such a being as God. But I now intend to show that a non-perspectival, non-limited view of the world would be impossible even for God, just so long as something other than or distinct from God is assumed to exist.

The Necessary Perspectivity of a
Supposed God's-Eye View of the World

In religions such as Judaism, Christianity, and Islam, God is often thought to have the attributes of omnipotence, omniscience, and omnipresence. Implicit these attributes is the idea of God's all-seeing eye, an eye that has no limitations of any kind, including the limitation of being one perspective—however large and encompassing—on the world among many others, human or nonhuman. The logical starting point of this view of God is the idea that God is all-powerful, meaning that nothing anywhere or at any time lies beyond the reach of God's anticipation and control. But if God is presumed to be all-powerful, then God must also be all-knowing because God cannot control what God is unaware of. And God must be everywhere if God is to have control over whatever happens throughout the universe.

Thus, no restrictions or limitations of any kind can be associated with God, including limitations of power, knowledge, or location. God's eye is all-seeing and thus beyond any kind of perspectival limitation. And the universe is what it truly and completely is *only as it is viewed by God*. We humans are restricted by our inevitably partial although in many ways shared perspectives on the world, but this restriction does not apply to God. Since God is believed to have created the world and to sustain it moment-by-moment by absolute power, God's knowledge of the world cannot be interrelational or interactive in the restrictive manner Giere claims all knowledge to be. God's vision of the world is not in any way limited with respect to the world's aspects or details, however massive, minute, complex, or intricate these might be. The world is exactly and through-and-through as God infallibly knows it to be at any given time. All truth about the world lies finally and completely in God's vision of it. God's *vision* of the world and the *reality* of the world coincide absolutely.

On careful examination, this conception of God is incoherent. It is so for a number of different reasons, but the one I want to concentrate on here is that the conception makes it impossible for there to be anything in existence other than God. By the reasoning I have just outlined, no other perspectives than God's perspective can exist. Why would this have to be the case? The answer to the question is that since God's perspective is all-comprehending and all-inclusive, it would have to *exhaustively contain* any and all other presumed perspectives. This would mean that God's perspective would have to include all the limitations and particularities of those perspectives which, by implication, it clearly *could not*. If God is believed to have one perspective on the world among others, no matter how broad and comprehensive God's perspective might be, then it not only follows that this divine perspective is distinct from all the world's finite perspectives. It also follows that God's perspective cannot completely include such finite perspectives as part of its knowledge.

To state the point perhaps more clearly, an unlimited, all-inclusive perspective is by definition no particular perspective at all, and if there are other existing perspectives to be included in God's outlook on the world, then God cannot view the world *from those perspectives* in any complete or all-inclusive sense. Something must be left out, and that is the finitude of those perspectives, in contrast with the supposed unrestricted reach of God's own perspective. If nothing is left out, then there is no such contrast, and the particularity, integrity, and inwardness of those finite perspectives cannot be said to exist. In other words, an infinite perspective cannot also be a finite one or experience the world in the ways that a finite one does. If it is infinite in power, comprehension, and presence, it must wipe out or ontologically exclude the possibility of any and all non-infinite ways of seeing, experiencing, and knowing. An absolute God's-eye vision of the world would erase the integrity and distinctiveness of other possible perspectives and the very existence of the world's sentient creatures.

The only alternative to this conclusion is to say that it is limited perspectives all the way down and all the way up. A hypothetical God's perspective is by necessity also limited, although not nearly to the degree of other perspectives, just as long as those other perspectives and their possessors can be acknowledged to exist. God can be imagined to sympathetically envision the perspectives of creatures of the world *but not to be those creatures*, which God would have to be if God's knowledge is exhaustive and all-comprehending. If the creatures are not swallowed up into God, then they and their perspectives impose some appreciable limit on the divine perspective.

An analogy will help to make this critical point. A close friend may be said to know me in some respect or respects better than I know myself. But this friend cannot be privy to all of my introspective awareness without becoming me. The untenable assumption of an inaccessible but all-comprehending God's-eye view of the world should not, therefore, be allowed to be an insurmountable barrier to the possibility of objective knowledge or a warrant for sheer constructivism or subjectivism of any kind. And it should not be thought to conflict with the perspectival realism Giere defends and I heartily support. The thesis of varying degrees of partiality or perspectival limitation of all truthful outlooks, including even a supposed God's-eye vision of the world, remains intact.

Epistemic Norms

Nothing I have said in this book about the partiality of all claims to truth should be taken to imply that there are no reasonable criteria or norms of truth that can be used in adjudicating the cogency or plausibility of specific claims or the relative degrees of reliability in different claims respecting the same or similar problems or issues. These criteria include consistency, coherence, simplicity, adequacy to experience, replicability, usefulness, and heuristic power or the furtherance of ongoing research into areas of thought under investigation. There are also publicly shared values to which appeals can be made. These values are usually enshrined in public traditions of long standing.

The criterion of usefulness pertains not merely to technological uses but to valuative ones as well. Truth and value are not the same, but the valuative implications of claims to truth are important aspects of investigations into their general usefulness. They may be adequate to a narrow range of experience but inadequate with respect to larger empirical issues. It is one thing, for example, to say that X-rays should routinely be put to use in determining foot sizes in a shoe store, as they were in an earlier time. And it is true that they can be so used. But it is another thing to say that they should be used indiscriminately for this purpose, given the now-known dangerous health consequences of such wide use. The large, commonly assumed value of human health and wellbeing trumps the narrow value of an indiscriminate use of foot X-rays.

Issues of consistency and coherence relate not only to truth and falsity but to the very meaning of proposals for truth. A radically inconsistent statement is not even a candidate for truth or falsity because its meaning is not at all clear. Consistency with previously established knowledge is also an important consideration. A claim that is radically out of kilter with what one already knows to be true can be questioned on that ground. But of course such anomalies could also point the way to possible deeper understanding of points at issue. In such a case, the anomaly may have heuristic significance and be entitled to consideration as a possible truth on that basis.

A coherent theory or one in which various parts of the theory give mutual support to one another is preferable to one in which this is not the case. And a radically incoherent theory or outlook lacks clear meaning, making assessment of its truth difficult. Of two theories that are equally adequate to some sort of relevant experience, the simplest one is best because it encompasses the data to be explained more concisely and elegantly. The more complex theory is also more cumbersome and difficult to use. The replicability of studies of the truth or falsity of hypotheses is a critical part of their assessment and a reminder of the fact that responsible adjudications of truth and falsity must be put to repeated public and not merely private tests.

Much more could be said about such epistemic norms. But satisfactory discussion and illustration of them here would take us too far afield. However, I do not want the reader to be left with the impression that such norms are unimportant or somehow irrelevant to my discussion of partial truths. Perspectival realism of the sort that I am defending in this chapter is not at all the same thing as an "anything goes" epistemological relativism. Degrees of truth and falsity in assertions can and should be carefully gauged on the basis of such criteria as those I have mentioned and with any other relevant ones as well. My insistence on the partiality of truths is not the same thing as arguing that there is no such thing as truth or that truth is whatever one thinks it to be or wishes it to be at any given time. There are publicly shared and commonly assumed or explicitly applied standards of truth to which all claims to truth of whatever kind or scope must be held responsible. These standards are necessary for assessing the relative degrees of truth and falsity in particular claims to truth.

Concluding Comments

I have argued throughout this book that all claims to truth are, at best, partial, and that the range of this argument extends from even relatively trivial claims to momentous ones. No such claim can be entirely isolated from its larger context or from the complex levels or overtones of meaning it presupposes. Each claim is a circle necessarily nested in or related to other circles, to refer again to Emerson's metaphor. And these circles are ever-widening and ever-narrowing at the same time. There is no limit to their upward, downward, inward, or outward reach. And yet, each claim, to extent that has at least some kind of warrant, reasonableness, or support, is to some extent true. And the amount of truth in respective claims can vary, and sometimes greatly, although no claim can be said to be completely or absolutely true in isolation or in and of itself.

If all claims to truth can only be partially true, it follows that they are also partially false. The degrees of truth or falsity in particular claims will vary, and sometimes they will vary to a large extent. Should we respond positively in any way to what seem to be patently false claims, then? I think we should endeavor always to be open to whatever elements or aspects of truth they may contain or imply. Just as there is honor among thieves, so there will be some amount of truth lurking in false claims, at least to the extent that they are intelligible. To be alert to this amount, however small it may turn out to be, might enable us to begin at least to understand why the largely false claims are being made. And this understanding can be a basis for critiquing false claims in a manner that is intelligible, pertinent, and helpful to both the claimants and the critics of their claims.

All significant disagreement rests on a basis of much larger areas of agreement, as the American philosopher Donald Davidson has pointed out. He provides an illuminating example of this point. If two persons are looking toward the sea and a sailboat passes by, one might exclaim, "What a beautiful yawl!" The other person might say, "It's not a yawl; it's a ketch." They both look through their binoculars at the boat and find themselves agreeing on the position of its masts, which is critical to determining the type of sailing vessel being viewed. The only conclusion to be drawn, then, if they continue to disagree, is that one of them has a different understanding of the term *yawl* and of the implications of that term than does the other.[14] Their agreements in such a case are necessarily greater than their disagreements, and the agreements can provide a basis for meaningful discussion of their disagreements. If a disagreement among two or more persons is a significant one for them, then they can search together for the grounds of their disagreement in the context of their larger underlying agreements and perhaps adjudicate their disagreement in positive and mutually helpful ways.

Such a scenario presupposes, of course, that participants in the discussion are open minded and rational in their approach and do not stubbornly insist on the truth of their claims despite all evidence, lexical or otherwise, to the contrary. Their disagreement can be a starting point for their eventual agreement or at least for better understanding of the basis of their disagreement. And it can lead to an enrichment of their understanding of the presupposed beliefs on which the disagreement depends for its significance. In at least this sense, then, a false claim can also imply elements or aspects of truth that it is eminently useful to recognize, explore, and keep in mind.

In similar fashion, it is important to recognize that all claims to truth without exception are only partially true at best, but in varying degrees, for the reasons I have developed in this volume. This recognition can provide a basis for discussion among two or more persons of the extent of truth and falsity in their respective claims and open their minds to the possibility of expanding the truth and reducing the falsity in their respective claims and arguments. It can also, in at least some situations, enable the holders of different beliefs about matters in dispute to recognize that there may be important elements of truth in views that are equally responsive to the available evidence despite their being in conflict with one another. The concept of partial truths can in this way give support to a pluralistic approach, especially to complex or wide-ranging issues, as opposed to the idea that only one of the views has to be the single right one.[15] It may turn out later that one claim is recognized to be truer than another or others in contention, but it is also possible that this will not prove to be the case.

In the meantime, allowance for a plurality of perspectives could point the way to eventual greater understanding, while insistence on there being only one right point of view could be a formidable obstacle to attaining such understanding. If participants in a group insist adamantly on the complete and final truth of their respective judgments or assertions in all contexts of disagreement, their discussion will either be brought abruptly to a close with no advance in mutual understanding, or it will soon degenerate into emotional close-mindedness as their claims are petulantly pitted against one another. Even worse, such close-minded disagreements on matters of small or great import can lead, and unfortunately often have led, to intractable hatred, cruelty, and violence.

There are occasions where it may be best to agree to disagree on disputed matters at least for a time, but in many cases pursuit of the disagreement in an open-minded, mutually respectful manner can contribute to enlarged recognitions of truth on both sides and to eventual reconciliations among those who take opposing points of view. One party to a dispute can learn more about its limited perspective by daring to enter into the limited perspective of another. And the perspectives of the two parties can each gain a greater amount of truth and understanding by such a process.

Factors of rivalry, competitiveness, and power also often underlie disagreements, and it is important to be cognizant of these and take them into account. In a novel about Egypt in the latter part of the twentieth century, Monte Palmer has one of his characters, an astute student of the Middle East, realize "that the important thing was what the Arabs believed, not its accuracy. They were not responding to the world as the United States saw it, but to the world as they saw it. Both were vague approximations of reality, dream worlds in which each saw what they wanted to see."[16] The Arabs want various things, including freedom from foreign domination and varying degrees of Islamic, or secular, but eventually just, stable, and prosperous forms of society, while the United States wants, among other things, to guard its own self-interest, protect itself from the threat of terrorism, avoid worldwide conflict, and exert significant influence on the affairs of Egypt and the Middle East as a global power. Meaningful negotiation would require frank recognition of the partial truths and legitimate concerns resident in these two very different perspectives and in the sub-perspectives contained in each one. Simply hunkering down into one of them with no due regard for the other is a recipe for stalemate at best or violence at worst.

The peace of the world, as well as the stability and order of any given society, rests primarily on agreements—some written and others tacit and unwritten—about how to resolve threatening and gnawing disagreements. This process will often require compromise on competing claims rather than outright abandonment of one in favor of the other. Compromise need not just be a prudential strategy. It can also involve sincere determination by one party to enter as best it can into the perspective of the other, and vice versa. Doing so would not only help to resolve a dispute; it would also enlarge the perspectives and understandings of the different disputants to the mutual benefit of them all. The thesis of partial truths that runs through this book, if widely recognized and accepted, could be an important contribution to a more orderly, amicable, and just world.

Relations among people and nations also involve necessary considerations of power, of course, not just ones of rational persuasion. Workable laws require the threat and application of their means of enforcement. But the key word in this observation is "also." It need not be the one to the exclusion of the other. Considerations of power have to be weighed as well as those of assent to truth or of expanding mutual horizons of truth, and there will be varying levels of truth and falsity regarding the accuracy and predicted effects of such weighing. But above all, what is required is the attempt to see the world as the other sees it and to humbly acknowledge in suitable situations the partiality of one's own claims to truth, no matter how persuasive, compelling, or comprehensive these claims may appear to be at a given time.

It is by no means the case for either me or Giere that all truth claims are *equally* credible or veridical, partial or defeasible. That is not the point. Some claims and outlooks are more reliably true than others and should be acknowledged and defended as such. But none should be seen as absolutely or unqualifiedly true in all relevant respects and in all situations or contexts. And none should be regarded as independent of any and all perspectives, each of the latter being inevitably restricted and partial in some degree. Objective truth is available, and it is contained, although in the final analysis only incompletely or perspectively, in statements or outlooks that can rightly be said to be true. The thesis I am supporting in this book should not be viewed as a weakening of the concept of truth or an underestimation of its singular importance. It is an insistence instead on such things as the entanglement of particular beliefs with underlying networks of tacit assumption; the consequent complexity and depth of any particular claim to truth; the unavoidable perspectival character and limitation of these claims; and the susceptibility of present putative truths to possible future criticism, alteration, or rejection.

If there are no absolute certainties in which we can take our rest, there is the ever-beckoning hope of new and more dependable and comprehensive ways of understanding ourselves and the world. Such improved ways of understanding—achieved through mutual cooperation, empathy, and support—could contribute in presently unexpected or unimagined ways to our learning how to live more justly, compassionately, and peacefully in our human communities and in the larger community of all of the earth's creatures.

Notes

Preface

1. David Brooks, "The Governing Cancer of Our Time," *The New York Times*, February 26, 2016. http://www.nytimes.com/2016/02/26/opinion/the-governing-cancer-of-our-time.html?
2. See Aristotle, *De Interpretatione*, chapters 7 and 9; *Metaphysica*, III. 2: 996b, 26–30; IV, 7: 1011b, 26–27, in Aristotle, *The Basic Works of Aristotle*, ed. Richard McKeon (New York: Random House, 1941), pp. 43–48, 719, 750.

Chapter 1

1. Karen Armstrong, *Twelve Steps to a Compassionate Life* (New York: Anchor Books, 2010), 118.
2. Armstrong, *Twelve Steps to a Compassionate Life*, 118.
3. Ninian Smart and Richard D. Hecht, eds., *Sacred Texts of the World: A Universal Anthology* (New York: Crossroads, 1982), 292. The earliest unearthed text of the *Daodejing* is about the late fourth century BCE.
4. For this discussion of Islam I have drawn on the entry "Allah" in H. A. R. Gibb and J. H. Kramers, eds., *Shorter Encyclopedia of Islam* (London: E. J. Brill and London: Luzac & Company, 1961), 33–42: 37–38.
5. This point is brought home with special clarity and convincingness by theologian Marjorie Suchocki in her book *Divinity and Diversity* (Nashville, TN: Abingdon Press, 1994).
6. Qur'an 2: 109.
7. R. A. Nicholson, ed., *Eastern Poetry and Prose* (Cambridge, UK: Cambridge University Press, 1922), 148; quoted by Armstrong, *Twelve Steps to a Compassionate Life*, 155.
8. In *Nature as Sacred Ground: A Metaphysics for Religious Naturalism* (Albany, NY: State University of New York Press, 2015), I develop and argue

for a metaphysics (or conception of reality) that gives prominent place to this claim. The claim is also a crucial aspect of the case for religious naturalism or what I call Religion of Nature that I develop in *A Religion of Nature* (Albany, NY: State University of New York Press, 2002).

9. I defend these ideas at some length in *Nature as Sacred Ground*. See chapter 1: "Being and Nothingness" and chapter 3: "Permanence and Change."

10. I spell out these three aspects and their meanings for Religion of Nature in the last chapter of *Faith and Reason: Their Roles in Religious and Secular Life* (Albany, NY: State University of New York Press, 2011).

11. For example, physicist Max Tegmark insists that "everything is in principle understandable to us," meaning mathematical physicists. See his *Our Mathematical Universe: My Quest for the Ultimate Nature of Reality* (New York: Alfred A. Knopf, 2014), 365.

12. In the novel Roquentin tries to resign himself to the inescapable truth (for him) that "the world of explanations and reasons is not the world of existence." Jean Paul Sartre, *Nausea*, trans. Lloyd Alexander (New York: New Directions, 1964), 174.

13. See in this connection my book *The Extraordinary in the Ordinary: Seven Miracles of Everyday Life* (Albany, NY: State University of New York Press, 2017).

14. On the fundamental role of nondiscursive symbols for evoking religious awareness and understanding, see my book *More Than Discourse: Symbolic Expressions of Naturalistic Faith* (Albany, NY: State University of New York Press, 2014).

15. Job 19:25–27, *The Holy Scriptures According to the Masoretic Text: A New Translation* (Philadelphia, PA: The Jewish Publication Society of America, 1952).

16. Paul Tillich, *The Courage to Be* (New Haven, CT: Yale University Press, 1952). See especially chapter 6.

17. Martin Heidegger, *Being and Time*, trans. Joan Stambaugh (Albany, NY: State University of New York Press, 1996). On the difference between being-itself and particular beings, see pp. 33–34 and *passim*.

18. Paul Tillich, *Systematic Theology*, vol. I (Chicago, IL: University of Chicago Press, 1951), 205.

Chapter 2

1. Hans-Georg Gadamer, *Reason in the Age of Science*, trans. Frederick G. Lawrence (Cambridge, MA: The MIT Press, 1981), 12.

2. See, for example, the *MIT Technology Review* item, "Super Physics Smackdown: Relativity v Quantum Mechanics . . . In Space:" https://www.

technologyreview.com/s/428328/super-physics-smackdown-relativity-v-quantum-mechanicsin-sp.

3. See Thomas S. Kuhn, *The Structure of Scientific Revolutions*, 3rd edition (Chicago, IL: The University of Chicago Press, 1996), especially chapter 3.

4. Donald A. Crosby, *The Specter of the Absurd: Sources and Criticisms of Modern Nihilism* (Albany, NY: State University of New York Press, 1988), 26–27, 32–33.

5. Donald A. Crosby, *The Philosophy of William James: Radical Empiricism and Radical Materialism* (Lanham, MD: Rowman & Littlefield, 2013). Rorty's view is developed and defended in *Philosophy and the Mirror of Nature* (Princeton, NJ: Princeton University Press, 1980).

6. See James Bogen, "Theory and Observation in Science," especially section 4, in the online *Stanford Encyclopedia of Philosophy*. https://plato.stanford.edu/archives/sum2014/entries/science-theory-observation/.

7. I recently had an experience of a correlation that initially looked like a causal relation but turned out not to be so. A lecturer at an academic conference was suddenly interrupted in his talk by a loud racket. He reached over to a small speaker on the lectern that he had earlier used to broadcast a part of his presentation and pushed a button on the speaker. The noise immediately stopped. I wondered how the speaker could have caused the raucous noise as he continued his talk. It turned out later that a large fan on the far side of the room had produced the noise and had ceased doing so at the exact point when the lecturer touched the button on the speaker. What had looked like a cause-effect relation was actually only one of correlation. For Hume, there is ultimately no such distinction. A cause-effect relation is one in which some particular thing stands in the relations of precedence, contiguity, and constant conjunction with another thing. The first is the cause, and the second, the effect, and these three correlations constitute the whole meaning of cause and effect relationships. See David Hume, *A Treatise of Human Nature*, 2nd edition, ed. L. A. Selby-Bigge and P. H. Nidditch (Oxford, UK: Oxford University Press, 1978), Book I, Part III, Section 14, pp. 155–72.

8. Compatibilism is the view that causal determinism and human freedom are entirely consistent with one another. I am "free," according to this view, when there is nothing *external* constraining me from acting or causing me to act, and when I act in accordance with my own *internal* desires, inclinations, motivations, and the like. These inner impulses and the choices resulting from them, however, are themselves held to be completely determined. For elaboration and criticism of this view, see my book *Consciousness and Freedom: The Inseparability of Thinking and Doing* (Lanham, MD: Lexington Books, 2017), especially chapter 1.

9. Kuhn's *The Structure of Scientific Revolutions* is devoted throughout to defense of this thesis.

10. A study of Einstein's religious views and their relations to his scientific thought is the book by physicist Max Jammer, *Einstein and Religion: Physics and Theology* (Princeton, NJ: Princeton University Press, 1999). Jammer and Einstein were friends. See also my article, "Einstein's Religion," in *The Midwest Quarterly*, XXXV, 2 (Winter 1994), 186–97.

11. An insightful book devoted to the Einstein-Bergson debate on the nature of time is Jimena Canales, *The Physicist and the Philosopher: Einstein, Bergson, and the Debate that Changed our Understanding of Time* (Princeton, NJ: Princeton University Press, 2015). See also chapter 2 of Bergson's book *Time and Free Will: An Essay on the Immediate Data of Consciousness*, trans. F. L. Pogson (Whitefish, MT: Kessinger Publishing Company, n.d.). In this chapter Bergson takes issue with the identification of time as directly experienced (*durée*)—and for him time in its real or metaphysical character—with measurable or clock time.

12. See Justus Buchler, *The Metaphysics of Natural Complexes: Second, Expanded Edition*, ed. Kathleen Wallace and Armen Marsoobian, with Robert S. Corrington (Albany, NY: State University of New York Press, 1990), 11–24.

13. See Galen Strawson, "Consciousness Isn't a Mystery. It's Matter." In *The Stone, New York Times*, May 16, 2016. http://www.nytimes.com/2016/05/16/opinion/consciousness-isnt-a-mystery-its-matter.html?mwrsm=Email&_r=0.

14. Einstein initially denied the expansion of the universe, even though his own theory of general relativity implied it. He later regarded this mistake as the "biggest blunder" of his scientific career when evidence for an expanding universe became available. See chapter 10 of Mario Livio's book *Brilliant Blunders: From Darwin to Einstein* (New York: Simon and Schuster, 2014).

15. Friedrich Schelling, *Die Weltalter in den Urfassungen von 1811 und 1813* (Nachlassband), ed. Manfred Schröter (Munich: Beck, 1946), I/8, 208–09; quoted by Jason M. Wirth, *Schelling's Practice of the Wild: Time, Art, Imagination* (Albany, NY: State University of New York Press, 2015), 84.

16. Wirth, *Schelling's Practice of the Wild*, 83.

Chapter 3

1. Mary Mothersill, *Ethics* (New York: Macmillan, 1965), 22.

2. See Aristotle, *Nichomachean Ethics*; trans. Terence Irwin (Indianapolis, IN: Hackett, 1985) and John Stuart Mill, *Utilitarianism*, ed. Oskar Piest (Indianapolis, IN: Bobbs-Merrill, 1957).

3. "Flourishing" is a better translation and has a less purely hedonistic ring. "Blessedness" is a translation closely related to the etymological meaning of *eudaimonia*.

4. The distinction between these two kinds of happiness in Mill is crucial; it shows that he does not have in mind an indiscriminate sort of pleasure but one where the pleasures, enjoyments, and challenges of the mind take precedence, for those experienced in both kinds of pleasure, over the pleasures of the body. Aristotle endorses a similar view.

5. Thomas Hobbes, *Leviathan: The Matter, Form, and Power of a Commonwealth Ecclesiastical and Civil*, in *The English Philosophers from Bacon to Mill*, ed. Edwin A. Burtt (New York: Modern Library, 1939), 129–234.

6. Philip Clayton and Justin Heinzekehr, *Organic Marxism: An Alternative to Capitalism and Ecological Catastrophe* (Claremont, CA: Process Century Press, 2014), 156.

7. David Hume, *A Treatise of Human Nature*, 2nd edition, ed. L. A. Selby-Bigge and P. H. Nidditch (Oxford: Clarendon Press, 1978), Book II; *An Enquiry Concerning the Principles of Morals*, ed. J. B. Schneewind (Indianapolis, IN: Hackett, 1983). Norman Kemp Smith's book *The Philosophy of David Hume: A Critical Study of its Origins and Central Doctrines* (London: Macmillan, 1966) has been a useful aid for me in explicating Hume's views on morality.

8. Immanuel Kant, *Groundwork of the Metaphysics of Morals*, trans. H. J. Paton (New York: Harper Torchbooks, 1964).

9. John Rawls, *A Theory of Justice* (Cambridge, MA: Harvard University Press, 1971), 52; see also 50.

10. Rawls, *A Theory of Justice*, 17.

11. Terry Tempest Williams, "America's Evolving Idea," *Sierra*, July/August, 2016, 32–35 and 63.

12. J. Baird Callicott, *Thinking Like a Planet: The Land Ethic and the Earth Ethic* (New York: Oxford University Press), 2013.

Chapter 4

1. Naomi Klein, *This Changes Everything: Capitalism vs. the Climate* (New York: Simon & Schuster, 2014), 159.

2. John Locke, *The Second Treatise of Government*, ed. Thomas P. Peardon (Indianapolis, IN: Bobbs-Merrill, 1952), 17.

3. Locke, *The Second Treatise of Government*, 25.

4. Locke, *The Second Treatise of Government*, 26,

5. Locke, *The Second Treatise of Government*, 22.

6. Herman E. Daly, *Beyond Growth: The Economics of Sustainable Development* (Boston, MA: Beacon Press, 1996), 219

7. Daly, *Beyond Growth*, 11.

8. Daly, *Beyond Growth*, 6–7.

9. Daly, *Beyond Growth*, 59.

10. Aidan Davison, *Technology and the Contested Meanings of Sustainability* (Albany, NY: State University of New York Press, 2001), 60.

11. R. G. Foster and L. Kreitzman, *The Rhythms of Life: The Biological Clocks that Control the Daily Lives of Every Living Thing* (London: Profile Books, 2009), 243; quoted in Adam C. Scarfe, "The Question of the Objective Basis of Whitehead's Theory of the Rhythm of Education: Homeostasis Research and Chronobiology," in *Interchange: A Quarterly Review of Education*, 47/3 (June 2016), p. 21 of Adam Scarfe's personal Springer Press copy of his essay that was made available to me.

12. Joseph E. Stiglitz, *The Price of Inequality: How Today's Divided Society Endangers our Future* (New York: W. W. Norton, 2013), 331.

13. Philip Clayton and Justin Heinzekehr, *Organic Marxism: An Alternative to Capitalism and Economic Catastrophe* (Claremont, CA: Process Century Press, 2014), 236.

14. This example is based on conversations with political scientist and Middle Eastern expert Monte Palmer.

15. I owe this important observation about partial truths to philosopher and religious scholar Michael Hogue.

Chapter 5

1. Alfred North Whitehead, *Process and Reality: Corrected Edition*, ed. David Ray Griffin and Donald W. Sherburne (New York: The Free Press, 1978), 9.

2. David Hume, *A Treatise of Human Nature*, ed. L. A. Selby-Bigge and P. H. Nidditch, 2nd edition (Oxford, UK: Clarendon Press, 1978), 469–70.

3. George Edward Moore, *Principia Ethica* (Cambridge, UK: Cambridge University Press, 1971), 10.

4. George Edward Moore, *Principia Ethica*, 47–58, 59–109.

5. Alfred Jules Ayer, *Language, Truth and Logic* (New York: Dover, 1946), 102–20.

6. David Hume, *A Treatise of Human Nature*, 470.

7. Alfred North Whitehead, *Process and Reality*, 348.

8. Donald A. Crosby, *Novelty* (Lanham, MD: Lexington Books, 2005); *Nature as Sacred Ground: A Metaphysics for Religious Naturalism* (Albany, NY: State University of New York Press, 2015), 45–56 and chapter 4; *Consciousness and Freedom: The Inseparability of Thinking and Doing* (Lanham, MD: Lexington Books, 2017), *passim*.

9. Hume, *A Treatise of Human Nature*, 407.

10. René Descartes, *Meditations on First Philosophy*, in Descartes, *The Philosophical Works of Descartes*, trans. Elizabeth S. Haldane and G. R. T. Ross, vol. I (Cambridge, UK: Cambridge University Press, 1967), 131–99.

11. John Locke, *An Essay Concerning Human Understanding: Complete and Unabridged*, ed. Alexander Campbell Fraser, 2 vols. (New York: Dover, 1959).

12. G. W. Leibniz, *New Essays on Human Understanding*, trans. and ed. Peter Remnant and Jonathan Bennett (Cambridge, UK: Cambridge University Press, 1982), 110.

13. Benedict de Spinoza, *Ethics in the Geometrical Order*, in *The Chief Works of Benedict de Spinoza*, trans. R. H. M. Elwes, vol. II (New York: Dover, 1951), 43–271.

14. Immanuel Kant, *Immanuel Kant's Critique of Pure Reason*, trans. Norman Kemp Smith (London: Macmillan, 1958).

15. David Hume, *A Treatise of Human Nature*, 463; *An Inquiry Concerning Human Understanding*, ed. Charles W. Hendel (Indianapolis, IN: Bobbs-Merrill, 1955), 40.

16. Adam C. Scarfe, "Skepticism Concerning Causality: An Evolutionary Epistemological Perspective," *Cosmos and History: The Journal of Natural and Social Philosophy*, 8/1 (2012), 227–88.

17. Descartes, *Meditations*, 154, 164.

18. Thomas Hobbes, *Leviathan*, in *The English Philosophers from Bacon to Mill*, ed. Edwin A. Burtt (New York: Modern Library, 1939), 129–234; Julien Offray de la Mettrie, *Man a Machine*, trans. M. W. Calkins and others (La Salle, IL: Open Court, 1912).

19. Mettrie, *Man a Machine*, 135.

20. Locke, *Essay*, II, 193–98.

21. George Berkeley, *Principles of Natural Knowledge*, in Berkeley, *Principles of Human Knowledge/Three Dialogues*, ed. Roger Woolhouse (London: Penguin, 1988), 32–113; see especially 53–64.

22. Terrence W. Deacon, *Incomplete Nature: How Mind Emerged from Matter* (New York: W. W. Norton, 2012).

23. All of these quotations are from *The Holy Scriptures According to the Masoretic Text: A New Translation* (Philadelphia, PA: The Jewish Publication Society of America, 1952).

24. This quotation and others from the New Testament are taken from *The Oxford Annotated Bible: Revised Standard Version Containing the Old and New Testaments*, ed. Herbert G. May and Bruce M. Metzger (New York: Oxford University Press, 1962).

25. Shiite Muslims had a similar view of the Imams who descended from Ali ibn Abi Talib, the cousin and son-in-law of Mohammad. See Karen Armstrong, *A History of God: The 4,000-Year Quest of Judaism, Christianity and Islam* (New York: Ballantine Books, 1993), 177.

26. I owe this example to my deceased colleague at Colorado State University, Daniel Lyons. He used it frequently in his classes as a way of showing the untenability of radical moral relativism. My wife Pam, who took one of his classes, reminded me of his use of this example.

Chapter 6

1. Immanuel Kant, *Idea for a Universal History with a Cosmopolitan Purpose*, in *Kant: Political Writings*, ed. H. S. Reis (Cambridge, UK: Cambridge University Press, 1997), 41–50: Proposition 6, p. 46.

2. For detailed discussions of this trend and for its threatening implications, see Thomas Piketty, *Capital in the Twenty-First Century*, trans. Arthur Goldhammer (Cambridge, MA: Belknap Press of Harvard University, 2014), especially Part Three "The Structure of Inequality"; and Joseph E. Stiglitz, *The Price of Inequality: How Today's Divided Society Endangers our Future* (New York: W. W. Norton, 2012).

3. Piketty, *Capital in the Twenty-First Century*, 207.

4. See Scott Atran, "The Devoted Actor: Unconditional Commitment and Intractable Conflict across Cultures," *Current Anthropology*, 57, Supplement 13 (June 2016), S192–S203. These brief remarks owe much to Atran's insightful and well-researched essay.

5. Naomi Klein, *This Changes Everything: Capitalism vs. the Climate* (New York: Simon and Schuster, 2014), 72–73; see also 19.

6. Klein, *This Changes Everything*, 61.

7. Lena Masri, "Girl Dies in Aleppo After She Mistakes a Cluster Bomb for a Toy."http://abcnews.go.com/International/girl-dies-aleppo-mistakes-cluster-bomb-toy/story?id=42596933.

8. Cary L. Biron, "Arms Control Advocates are Decrying a new U.S, Department of Defense Announcement that it will be Building and Selling 1,300 Cluster Bombs to Saudi Arabia, Worth Some 641 Million Dollars." North America Interpress Service: http://ipsnorthamerica.net/news.php?idnews=4850.

9. Catherine Thorbecke, "House Oks Ongoing Cluster Bomb Sales to Saudi Arabia, Saying a Ban Would 'Stigmatize' the Weapon." http://abcnews.go.com/US/house-oks-ongoing-cluster-bomb-sales-saudi-arabia/story?id=39931315.

10. Crutzen's paper "Geology of Mankind" was published in Volume 415, January 3, 2002, of *Nature*. It is available at http://www.readcube.com/articles/10.1038/415023a.

11. Elizabeth Kolbert, *The Sixth Extinction: An Unnatural History* (New York: Henry Holt and Company, 2014), 108.

12. Crutzen, "Geology of Mankind." See the "readcube" reference above.

13. See the article "She's Just 7" that refers to the future of a young female African elephant born in Kenya in 2009. http://www.awf.org/campaigns/countingelephants/?utm_campaign=fy17fall&ms=B17A08E03M&utm_source=1610fall1adv&utm_medium=email&utm_content=15700048&s

pMailingID=15700048&spUserID=MTkyNTk1ODM5MDI3S0&spJobID=88
1564265&spReportId=ODgxNTY0MjY1S0.

14. Kolbert, *The Sixth Extinction*, 254.

15. Kolbert, *The Sixth Extinction*, 261–62.

16. Unfortunately, the administration of President Donald Trump in the United States has decided to leave the Paris Climate Agreement. This is an extremely discouraging straw in the wind. However, some states in the country are passing legislation and making plans to sharply reduce their uses of fossil fuels and to take other steps as states to combat global climate change. This is an encouraging straw.

17. Kolbert, *The Sixth Extinction*, 249–52.

18. Zadie Smith, "On Optimism and Despair," *The New York Review of Books*, LXIII, 20, December 22, 2016, 36, 38.

Chapter 7

1. Ralph Waldo Emerson, "Circles," in *Collected Works of Ralph Waldo Emerson* (New York: Greystone Press, 1941), 102.

2. My thinking in this and the preceding paragraph is guided by philosopher Justus Buchler's ruminations on the thought of the eminent nineteenth-century American philosopher Charles Sanders Peirce. See Buchler, *Charles Sanders Peirce's Empiricism* (New York: Harcourt, Brace and Company, 1939), 6–9, especially 8–9.

3. Nelson Goodman, *Ways of Worldmaking* (Indianapolis, IN: Hackett, 1978), 130.

4. Goodman, *Ways of Worldmaking*, 119 (the italics are mine).

5. Gilles Deleuze, *Difference and Repetition*, trans. Paul Patton (New York: Columbia University Press), 152; quoted in Jason M. Wirth, *Schelling's Practice of the Wild* (Albany, NY: State University of New York Press, 2015), 108.

6. Werner Heisenberg, *Reality and its Order*, 1942. German Title: *Ordnung der Wirklichkeit*, in Werner Heisenberg, *Gesammelte Werke*, Abteilung C, Piper Verlag, München. An English translation this work can be accessed at http://www.heisenbergfamily.org/. The quotation is on p. 9 of the translation.

7. Ronald N. Giere, *Scientific Perspectivism* (Chicago, University of Chicago Press, 2006), 5.

8. As an example of a constructivist Giere cites philosopher of science Bas van Fraassen, and as an example of an absolute objectivist realist he points to Nobel Laureate in physics Steven Weinberg. See Giere, *Scientific Perspectivism*, 4–5, 10. See also his discussion of the two views in pp. 4–11 of his book.

9. See Kant, *Immanuel Kant's Critique of Pure Reason*, trans. Norman Kemp Smith (London: Macmillan, 1958), A614, B642, p. 514.

10. Giere does not explicitly discuss Kant, but since I did so in chapter five, I think it useful to relate his perspectival realism to Kant here. Doing so will help to clarify the similarity as well as two important differences in the two positions.

11. Giere, *Scientific Perspectivism*, 11.

12. Giere, *Scientific Perspectivism*, 56.

13. Giere, *Scientific Perspectivism*, 15, 95.

14. Donald Davidson, "On the Very Idea of a Conceptual Scheme," *Proceedings and Addresses of the American Philosophical Association*, Vol. 47 (1973–1974), 5–20: 18. This essay can be accessed at https://www2.southeastern.edu/Academics/Faculty/jbell/conceptualscheme.pdf.

A ketch has its mizzen (smaller) mast stepped *forward* of the rudder post, while a yawl has its mizzen mast stepped *aft* of the rudder post.

15. Philosopher Robert McKim makes a similar point in speaking about what he calls the *ambiguity* of the types of evidence relied on in making a case for important religious claims in various religious traditions. He writes, "The explanation of how it is that different groups are reasonable in interpreting a certain situation or phenomenon in different ways may in some cases be that it can correctly be described in those different ways—even in ways that seem incompatible. This may be so in the case of some issues and not in the case of others." Robert McKim, *On Religious Diversity* (New York: Oxford University Press, 2012), 151.

16. Monte Palmer, *Egypt and the Game of Terror* (Lincoln, NE: iUniverse, 2007), 102.

Works Cited

Aristotle. 1941. *The Basic Works of Aristotle*, ed. Richard McKeon. New York: Random House.

——. 1985. *Nichomachean Ethics*, trans. Terence Irwin. Indianapolis, IN: Hackett.

Armstrong, Karen. 1993. *A History of God: The 4,000-Year Quest of Judaism, Christianity and Islam*. New York: Ballantine Books.

——. 2010. *Twelve Steps to a Compassionate Life*. New York: Anchor Books.

Atran, Scott. 2016. "The Devoted Actor: Unconditional Commitment and Intractable Conflict across Cultures," *Current Anthropology*, 57, Supplement 13 (June), S192–S203.

Ayer, Alfred Jules. 1946. *Language, Truth and Logic*. New York: Dover.

Bergson, Henri. N. D. *Time and Free Will: An Essay on the Immediate Data of Consciousness*, trans. F. L. Pogson. Whitefish, MT: Kessinger Publishing Company.

Berkeley, George. 1988. *Principles of Natural Knowledge*, in Berkeley, *Principles of Human Knowledge/Three Dialogues*, ed. Roger Woolhouse. London: Penguin.

Biron, Cary L. "Arms Control Advocates are Decrying a new U.S, Department of Defense Announcement that it will be Building and Selling 1,300 Cluster Bombs to Saudi Arabia, Worth Some 641 Million Dollars." North America Interpress Service: http://ipsnorthamerica.net/news.php?idnews=4850.

Bogen, James. 2014. "Theory and Observation in Science," *The Stanford Encyclopedia of Philosophy* (Summer), Edward N. Zalta, ed. https://plato.stanford.edu/archives/sum2014/entries/science-theory-observation/.

Brooks, David. 2016. "The Governing Cancer of Our Time," *The New York Times*, February 26.http://www.nytimes.com/2016/02/26/opinion/the-governing-cancer-of-our-time.html?

Buchler, Justus. 1939. *Charles Sanders Peirce's Empiricism*. New York: Harcourt, Brace and Company.

———. 1990. *The Metaphysics of Natural Complexes: Second, Expanded Edition*, Kathleen Wallace and Armen Marsoobian, eds., with Robert S. Corrington. Albany, NY: State University of New York Press.

Callicott, J. Baird. 2013. *Thinking Like a Planet: The Land Ethic and the Earth Ethic*. New York: Oxford University Press.

Canales, Jimena. 2015. *The Physicist and the Philosopher: Einstein, Bergson, and the Debate that Changed our Understanding of Time*. Princeton, NJ: Princeton University Press.

Clayton, Philip, and Justin Heinzekehr. 2014. *Organic Marxism: An Alternative to Capitalism and Ecological Catastrophe*. Claremont, CA: Process Century Press.

Crosby, Donald A. 1988. *The Specter of the Absurd: Sources and Criticisms of Modern Nihilism*. Albany, NY: State University of New York Press.

———. 1994. "Einstein's Religion," in *The Midwest Quarterly Review* (Winter), 186–97.

———. 2002. *A Religion of Nature*. Albany, NY: State University of New York Press.

———. 2005. *Novelty*. Lanham, MD: Lexington Books.

———. 2011. *Faith and Reason: Their Roles in Religious and Secular Life*. Albany, NY: State University of New York Press.

———. 2013. *The Philosophy of William James: Radical Empiricism and Radical Materialism*. Lanham, MD: Rowman & Littlefield.

———. 2014. *More Than Discourse: Symbolic Expressions of Naturalistic Faith*. Albany, NY: State University of New York Press.

———. 2015. *Nature as Sacred Ground: A Metaphysics for Religious Naturalism*. Albany, NY: State University of New York Press.

———. 2017. *The Extraordinary in the Ordinary: Seven Miracles of Everyday Life*. Albany, NY: State University of New York Press.

———. 2017. *Consciousness and Freedom: The Inseparability of Thinking and Doing*. Lanham, MD: Lexington Books.

Crutzen, Paul J. 2002. "Geology of Mankind," in *Nature*, vol. 415 (January 3). It is available at http://www.readcube.com/articles/10.1038/415023a.

Daly, Herman. 1996. *Beyond Growth: The Economics of Sustainable Development*. Boston, MA: Beacon Press.

Davidson, Donald. 1973–1974. "On the Very Idea of a Conceptual Scheme," *Proceedings and Addresses of the American Philosophical Association*, vol. 7: 5–20

Davison, Aidan. 2001. *Technology and the Contested Meanings of Sustainability* (Albany, NY: State University of New York Press, 2001).

Deleuze, Gilles. 1994. *Difference and Repetition*, trans. Paul Patton. New York: Columbia University Press.

Descartes, René. 1967. *Meditations on First Philosophy*, in Descartes, *The Philosophical Works of Descartes*, trans. Elizabeth S. Haldane and G. R. T. Ross, vol. I. Cambridge, UK: Cambridge University Press.

Emerson, Ralph Waldo. 1941. "Circles," in *Collected Works of Ralph Waldo Emerson*. New York: Greystone Press.

Foster, R., and L. Kreitzman. 2009. *The Rhythms of Life: The Biological Clocks that Control the Daily Lives of Every Living Thing*. London: Profile Books.

Gadamer, Hans-Georg. 1981. *Reason in the Age of Science*, trans. Frederick G. Lawrence. Cambridge, MA: The MIT Press.

Gibb, A. R., and J. H. Kramers, eds. 1961. *Shorter Encyclopedia of Islam*. London: E. J. Brill and London: Luzac & Company.

Giere, Ronald N. 2006. *Scientific Perspectivism*. Chicago, IL: The University of Chicago Press.

Goodman, Nelson. 1978. *Ways of Worldmaking*. Indianapolis, IN: Hackett.

Heidegger, Martin. 1996. *Being and Time*, trans. Joan Stambaugh. Albany, NY: State University of New York Press.

Heisenberg, Werner. 1942. *Reality and its Order*. German Title: *Ordnung der Wirklichkeit*, in Werner Heisenberg, *Gesammelte Werke*, Abteilung C, Piper Verlag, München. An English translation this work can be accessed at http://www.heisenbergfamily.org/.

Hobbes, Thomas. 1939. *Leviathan: The Matter, Form, and Power of a Commonwealth Ecclesiastical and Civil*, in *The English Philosophers from Bacon to Mill*, ed. Edwin A. Burtt. New York: Modern Library.

Holy Scriptures According to the Masoretic Text: A New Translation. 1952. Philadelphia, PA: The Jewish Publication Society of America.

Hume, David. 1978. *A Treatise of Human Nature*, 2nd edition, ed. L.A. Selby-Bigge and P. H. Nidditch. Oxford, UK: Oxford University Press.

———. 1983. *An Enquiry Concerning the Principles of Morals*, ed. J. B. Schneewind. Indianapolis, IN: Hackett.

Jammer, Max. 1999. *Einstein and Religion: Physics and Theology*. Princeton, NJ: Princeton University Press.

Kant, Immanuel. 1958. *Immanuel Kant's Critique of Pure Reason*, trans. Norman Kemp Smith. London: Macmillan.

———. 1964. *Groundwork of the Metaphysics of Morals*, trans. H. J. Paton. New York: Harper Torchbooks.

———. 1997. *Idea for a Universal History with a Cosmopolitan Purpose*, in *Kant: Political Writings*, ed. H. S. Reis. Cambridge, UK: Cambridge University Press.

Kemp Smith, Norman. 1966. *The Philosophy of David Hume: A Critical Study of its Origins and Central Doctrines*. London: Macmillan.

Klein, Naomi. 2014. *This Changes Everything: Capitalism vs. the Climate*. New York: Simon & Schuster.

Kolbert, Elizabeth. 2014. *The Sixth Extinction: An Unnatural History*. New York: Henry Holt and Company.

Kuhn, Thomas S.1996. *The Structure of Scientific Revolutions*, 3rd ed. Chicago, IL: The University of Chicago Press, 1966.

Leibniz, G. W. 1982. *New Essays on Human Understanding*, trans. and ed. Peter Remnant and Jonathan Bennett. Cambridge, UK: Cambridge University Press.

Livio, Mario. 2014. *Brilliant Blunders: From Darwin to Einstein*. New York: Simon and Schuster.

Locke, John. 1952. *The Second Treatise of Government*, ed. Thomas P. Peardon. Indianapolis, IN: Bobbs-Merrill.

———. 1959. *An Essay Concerning Human Understanding: Complete and Unabridged*, ed. Alexander Campbell Fraser, 2 vols. New York: Dover, 1959.

Masri, Lena. "Girl Dies in Aleppo After She Mistakes a Cluster Bomb for a Toy." http://abcnews.go.com/International/girl-dies-aleppo-mistakes-cluster-bomb-toy/story?id=42596933.

McKim, Robert. 2012. *On Religious Diversity*. New York: Oxford University Press.

Mettrie, Julien Offray de la. 1912. *Man-a Machine*, trans. M. W. Calkins and others. La Salle, IL: Open Court.

Mill, John Stuart. 1957. *Utilitarianism*, ed. Oskar Piest. Indianapolis, IN: Bobbs-Merrill.

Moore, George Edward. 1971. *Principia Ethica*. Cambridge, UK: Cambridge University Press.

Mothersill, Mary. 1965. *Ethics*. New York: Macmillan.

Nicholson, R. A., ed. 1922. *Eastern Poetry and Prose*. Cambridge, UK: Cambridge University Press.

Oxford Annotated Bible, The. 1962. *Revised Standard Version Containing the Old and New Testaments*, ed. Herbert G. May and Bruce M. Metzger. New York: Oxford University Press.

Palmer, Monte. 2007. *Egypt and the Game of Terror*. Lincoln, NE: iUniverse.

Piketty, Thomas. 2014. *Capital in the Twenty-First Century*, trans. Arthur Goldhammer. Cambridge, MA: Belknap Press of Harvard University.

Rawls, John. 1971. *A Theory of Justice*. Cambridge, MA: Harvard University Press.

Sartre, Jean Paul. 1964. *Nausea*. New York: New Directions.

Scarfe, Adam C. 2012. "Skepticism Concerning Causality: An Evolutionary Epistemological Perspective," *Cosmos and History: The Journal of Natural and Social Philosophy*, 8/1, 227–88.

———. 2016. "The Question of the Objective Basis of Whitehead's Theory of the Rhythm of Education: Homeostasis Research and Chronobiology," in *Interchange: A Quarterly Review of Education*, 47/3 (June).

Schelling, Friedrich. 1946. *Die Weltalter in den Urfassungen von 1811 und 1813* (Nachlassband), Manfred Schröter. Munich: Beck.

"She's Just 7." http://www.awf.org/campaigns/countingelephants/?utm_campai gn=fy17fall&ms=B17A08E03M&utm_source

Smart, Ninian, and Richard D. Hecht, eds. 1982. *Sacred Texts of the World: A Universal Anthology.* New York: Crossroads.

Spinoza, Benedict de. 1951. *Ethics in the Geometrical Order*, in *The Chief Works of Benedict de Spinoza*, trans. R. H. M. Elwes, vol. II. New York: Dover.

Strawson, Galen. 2016. "Consciousness Isn't a Mystery. It's Matter." In *The Stone, New York Times*, May 16, 2016. http://www.nytimes.com/2016/05/ 16/opinion/consciousness-isnt-a-mystery-its-matter.html?mwrsm=Email& _r=0.

Stiglitz, Joseph. 2013. *The Price of Inequality: How Today's Divided Society Endangers our Future.* New York: W. W. Norton.

Suchocki, Marjorie. 1994. *Divinity and Diversity.* Nashville, TN: Abingdon Press.

"Super Physics Smackdown: Relativity v Quantum Mechanics . . . In Space." 2012. *MIT Technology Review.* https://physicsforme.com/2012/06/25/ super-physics-smackdown-relativity-v-quantum-mechanics-in-space/.

Tegmark, Max. 2014. *Our Mathematical Universe: My Quest for the Ultimate Nature of Reality.* New York: Alfred A. Knopf.

Thorbecke, Catherine. "House Oks Ongoing Cluster Bomb Sales to Saudi Arabia, Saying a Ban Would 'Stigmatize' the Weapon." http://abc news.go.com/US/house-oks-ongoing-cluster-bomb-sales-saudi-arabia/ story?id=39931315.

Tillich, Paul. 1951. *Systematic Theology*, vol. I. 1951. Chicago, IL: University of Chicago Press.

———. 1952. *The Courage to Be.* New Haven, CT: Yale University Press.

Whitehead, Alfred North. 1978. *Process and Reality: Corrected Edition*, ed. David Ray Griffin and Donald W. Sherburne. New York: The Free Press.

Williams, Terry Tempest. 2016. "America's Evolving Idea," *Sierra*, July/August, 32–35 and 63.

Wirth, Jason M. 2015. *Schelling's Practice of the Wild: Time, Art, Imagination.* Albany, NY: State University of New York Press.

Index

Peirce, Charles Sanders, 33, 175n2
Philosophy, xv–xvi; task of,
xi; and critical analysis of
assumptional background of
science, 31–32; no complete
certitude or closure possible in,
92; critical dependence of on
scientific developments, 32–33; as
endless dialogical searching, 153;
experience as its final appeal,
92; process version of influenced
by science, 32–33; of science,
33; partial truths of should be
welcomed, 91; as beginning and
continuing in wonder, 152
Piketty, Thomas, 127
Planck, Max, 36
Plato, 153
Pluralism, xiii
Popper, Karl, 33
Positivism, Logical, 33
Psychology, behaviorist, 25–26

Quantum theory, 24, 32

Rationalism and Empiricism, 101–
105; René Descartes' rationalism,
101–103; Gottfried Leibniz's
criticism of the dichotomy of,
102–103; David Hume's exposure
of the deep skepticism in extreme
empiricism, 103; Immanuel Kant's
attempted but failed synthesis of,
104; and evolutionarily acquired
innate capacities or predilections
of the mind, 104–105; John
Locke's empiricism, 101–103;
partial truth in each, 103,
105; Baruch Spinoza's extreme
monistic rationalism, 103–104
Rawls, John, xii
Realism, absolute objectivist,
xix, 154–155; perspectival,

xix–xx, 154–158; subjectivist-
constructivist denial of, xix,
xxi, 154–155. See also Truths,
partial
Reformation, Protestant, 128, 137
Relativity, General Theory of, 24
Religion, ix–x; constructive
contributions of, 138–139;
dogmatism (or authoritarianism)
in, 1, 5, 8, 10; cruelties and
disruptions of, 129–131;
importance of critical thought
in, 5–6, 9–10; and the Middle
East, 128–131, 138–139; nature
of, 20; paradox of the speakable
and the unspeakable in, 2–6;
radical transcendence of religious
ultimates in, 1–2, 5–6, 10,
22; Scriptural teachings of as
resources for good, 139; as a two-
edged sword, 139; inexhaustible
wonder in, 1
Religion of Nature, demand,
assurance, and empowerment
aspects of, 13; and fact-value
distinction, 94; metaphysics and,
167–168n8; nature as exhibiting
novelty as well as continuity in,
12–13; nature as power of being-
itself in, 19; nature as shrouded
in mystery in, 13–16; nature,
transcendence and immanence
in, 10–16; nature as transcending
itself over endless time in, 11–12;
nature, religious ultimacy of in,
20; nature, wonders and miracles
of in, 15
Revelation, in the Abrahamic
traditions, 7
Robber Baron period in the United
States, 83–84
Rorty, Richard, 29
Russell, Bertrand, 104